Youth: Transition to Adulthood

PANEL ON YOUTH (1972)

JAMES S. COLEMAN (*Chairman*)

ROBERT H. BREMNER

BURTON R. CLARK

JOHN B. DAVIS

DOROTHY H. EICHORN

ZVI GRILICHES

JOSEPH F. KETT

NORMAN B. RYDER

ZAHAVA BLUM DOERING (*Research Staff*)

JOHN M. MAYS

youth
Transition to Adulthood

**Report of the Panel
on Youth of the President's Science
Advisory Committee**

The University of Chicago Press
Chicago and London

This study grew out of concern by the President's Science Advisory Committee about the ways in which young people are brought into adulthood in the United States at this time in our history. It presents the views of a group of social scientists and educators who met regularly over a period of over a year for discussions which often included other persons. It incorporates responses to questions and comments by the members of the President's Science Advisory Committee.

The report is not a statement of Federal policy. It is published with the objective of encouraging further discussion, research and experimentation in this area.

Office of Science and Technology
Executive Office of the President

The University of Chicago Press, Chicago 60637
The University of Chicago Press, Ltd., London

International Standard Book Number: 0–226–11341–8 (clothbound)
Library of Congress Catalog Card Number: 73–92757

Contents

Preface

As the labor of children has become unnecessary to society, school has been extended for them. With every decade, the length of schooling has increased, until a thoughtful person must ask whether society can conceive of no other way for youth to come into adulthood. If schooling were a complete environment, the answer would properly be that no amount of school is too much, and increased schooling for the young is the best way for the young to spend their increased leisure, and society its increased wealth.

But schooling, as we know it, is not a complete environment giving all the necessary opportunities for becoming adult. School is a certain kind of environment: individualistic, oriented toward cognitive achievement, imposing dependency on and withholding authority and responsibility from those in the role of students. So long as school was short, and merely a supplement to the main activities of growing up, this mattered little. But school has expanded to fill the time that other activities once occupied, without substituting for them. These activities of young persons included the opportunities for responsible action, situations in which he came to have authority over matters that affected other persons, occasions in which he experienced the consequences of his own actions, and was strengthened by facing them—in short, all that is implied by "becoming adult" in matters other than gaining cognitive skills.

Nevertheless, as these activities outside the school dwindled, society's prescription for youth has been merely more of what was prescribed for them as children: more school. It appears reasonable now, however, to look a little more carefully at the task of becoming adult, to ask not the quantitative question, "How much more schooling?", but the qualitative one: "What are appropriate environments in which youth can best grow into adults?". It appears reasonable now, not merely to design new high schools and colleges, but to design environments that allow youth to be more than students. That these environments will include some schooling does not lessen the difference of this task from that of creating more schooling. It is the task, no more, no less, of creating the opportunities for youth to become adults in all ways, not merely intellective ones.

This Panel has attempted to open the discourse which can inform such attempts. It asks both what attributes are necessary to become an adult, and what institutions can fill these needs. It cannot provide final answers, but it asks urgently that we get started with better answers than increased schooling has so far provided.

Parts 1, 3, and 4 of the Report are the responsibility of the Panel as a whole, while Part 2 is composed of sections for which individual Panel members are primarily responsible, as follows:

2–1: History of Age Grouping in America (Joseph Kett)
2–2: Rights of Children and Youth (Robert Bremner)
2–3: The Demography of Youth (Norman Ryder)
2–4: Economic Problems of Youth (Zvi Griliches)
2–5: Current Educational Institutions (Burton Clark)
2–6: Biological, Psychological and Socio-Cultural Aspects of Adolescence and Youth (Dorothy Eichorn)
2–7: Youth Culture (James Coleman)

In preparing this report, we have depended upon aid from a number of persons and organizations outside the Federal Government, listed below, and to a number of Federal agencies. We are deeply grateful for the time they gave generously to help in this examination. Our thanks also go to the people who are not listed who answered our many inquiries, both prior to the establishment of the Panel and during its work.

The following persons presented material to the Panel at our meetings: John Barnard, John Bremer, Urie Bronfenbrenner, David Elkind, Margaret Fallers, Richard Freeman, Torsten Husén, Charity James, Jacob Mincer, David Riesman, Dorothy Ross, Brewster Smith, Beatrice Whiting.

In addition, we thank the following persons for aid in one or another manner: Eli Cohen, Orville Brim, Vernon Eagle, Phillip Jackson, Jeremiah Kaplan, Judge Mary Conway Kohler, Gisela Konopka, Debora Krammer, Charles Kujawa, John Henry Martin, Daniel Patrick Moynihan, Alan Pifer, Dorothy Savage, Eugene Seifrit, Charles Silberman, Paul Swift, Ernst Volinn, K. A. Wells, Frank Westheimer, John Whiting.

JAMES S. COLEMAN
Chairman
Panel on Youth

PART 1: INTRODUCTION

Every society must somehow solve the problem of transforming children into adults, for its very survival depends on that solution. In every society there is established some kind of institutional setting within which the process of transition is to occur, in directions predicated by societal goals and values. In our view, the institutional framework for maturation in the United States is now in need of serious examination.

The purposes of this report are to examine the contexts that now exist for youth, within which they come to adulthood, and assess the fitness of those contexts for the accomplishment of the developments necessary to full maturity, and then to propose alternative settings that seem to be preferable ways of accomplishing that assignment.

Although we recognize that the process of maturation begins in infancy, and in some senses never ends, we have chosen to confine our attention to the age span 14–24. The justification for that arbitrary choice is that essentially none can be classified as adults prior to their fourteenth birthday, and essentially none can be classified as children subsequent to their twenty-fifth birthday, whatever the operational definition of the transition.

When ours was still an agrarian society, the needs of youth were necessarily subordinate to the economic struggle, and the rudimentary occupational requisites permitted them to be brought quickly into adult productivity. The dominant institutional settings within which they grew up were the home and workplace. Choices in the occupational sphere were few: the future roles of the children were generally well-exemplified by those of parents. In short, the task of socialization was resolved by early and continual interaction with the parents and nearby adults.

But as our society moved into the modern era, the occupational structure became progressively more a matter of movement into activities different from those of the parents. A long period of formal training, under specialized instructors, was initiated to provide the cognitive skills seen as necessary for satisfactory performance as an adult, and equality of opportunity itself required postponement of decision. To accomplish these tasks, institutions to provide the instruction were designed, and rules were formulated with respect to

1

school and work. Specifically, schooling to an advanced age became compulsory, and automated promotion, age by age, became the norm. Laws were established against child labor, and minimum wages were specified. These latter not only served their prime function of protecting the economic security of the breadwinner, but also delayed the entry of the young person into the labor force.

In consequence, the schools and colleges have come to provide the general social environment for youth. The world of the maturing child, formerly dominated by the home, is now monopolized on the formal level by the school and on the informal level by the age group. The typical young person has a long preparation for his occupational future, within a highly structured school system, interrupted only by some work at marginal tasks (either part-time after school, or during the summers) and terminated by entry into the labor force or motherhood.

Our basic premise is that the school system, as now constituted, offers an incomplete context for the accomplishment of many important facets of maturation. The school has been well designed to provide some kinds of training but, by virtue of that fact, is inherently ill-suited to fulfill other tasks essential to the creation of adults. Indeed, it would be unreasonable to expect any institution to suffice as the exclusive environment for youth. Signs of dissatisfaction abound, from parents and taxpayers who have an inarticulate sense that something is amiss, from school administrators and teachers who are experimenting with methods and objectives and forms that differ from those of the established system, and from youth themselves, many of whom are showing individual initiative in the search for extra-curricular experiences.

The school now shares the socialization task with the family and the peer group. Because the family has become limited in its effectiveness with respect to the age group of our concern, it is a minor part of the social environment of many youth beyond early adolescence. And the peer group is not only an unsuitable source for development toward adult goals, it also attenuates the invaluable lines of communication and culture transmission across the generations. The way of life we have institutionalized for our young consists almost entirely of social interaction with others of the same age and formal relationships with authority figures.

To summarize, society has passed through two phases in its treatment of youth. In the first, which may be characterized as the work phase, young persons were brought as quickly as physical maturity would allow into economic productivity, to aid the economy of the family. In the second phase, which may be described as the schooling phase, young persons are being kept as long as possible in the school and out of the labor force, to increase their potential for productivity.

We think it is now time for a third phase in society's treatment of its young, including school but neither defined by nor limited to it. We think it is time to reappraise the contexts of youth, to question even the most accepted and ordinary aspects of their current institutional settings, and to consider the reformation of existing structures and if necessary the creation of new ones. We are proposing the establishment of alternative environments for the transition to adulthood, environments explicitly designed to develop not only cognitive learning but other aspects of maturation as well.

The discussion of environments for youth appropriately begins with a discussion of the kind of objectives toward which they should be directed. These objectives represent the criteria by which to assess the present system and the proposed alternatives.

The objectives to which environments for youth should be addressed consist of two broad classes. One is essentially self-centered. It concerns the acquisition of skills that expand the personal resources, and thus the opportunity of a young person. Schools have traditionally focused upon this class of objectives, and often narrowly so within this class. But a second class of objectives is important as well, in which youth is centered on others rather than self. This class concerns the opportunity for responsibilities affecting other persons. Only with the experience of such responsibilities can youth move toward the mutually responsible and mutually rewarding involvement with others that constitutes social maturity. Whatever the set of specific objectives within each of these classes (and those we shall list are certainly not exhaustive), we believe it important that environments for youth address directly both of these classes, not merely the former, as schools have traditionally done.

First among the self-centered class of objectives are those *cognitive and non-cognitive skills necessary for economic independence and for occupational opportunities*. Although survival in the modern world requires as a minimum a considerable capability in the use of words and numbers, the range of necessary skills beyond that minimum varies as widely as the distribution of occupations within the labor force.

Beyond the acquisition of marketable skills, a second objective consists of developing the *capability of effective management of one's own affairs*. The emergent adult faces an increasingly complex world, in which self-direction and self-management are prerequisites to success. The current environments imposed on youth by society, in the form of schools, provide little experience with self-management, in large part because, where there is little freedom of choice, there is little self-responsibility. The need for such experience is manifested in the frequency with which the freshmen entering college, and seniors leaving college, experience shock as a consequence of the enlargement of choice. Environments for youth should provide experiences which develop one's capability for managing one's affairs in an organizationally complex world.

A third objective within the self-centered class is to develop *capabilities as a consumer, not only of goods, but more significantly, of the cultural riches of civilization.* The store of cultural achievements, whether art or literature or music or science, and whether experienced from the standpoint of creator or performer or simply appreciator, enrich the experience of one's life. Some people continue to assimilate these throughout their lives, in a continual expansion of their horizons, but only if they have acquired in youth a sufficient basis of taste and motivation. Environments should provide youth with the kind of experience with cultural achievements that will enable them, as adults, to pursue their tastes in those directions.

As a final objective in this class, environments for youth should also develop in youth the *capabilities for engaging in intense concentrated involvement in an activity.* The most personally satisfying experiences, as well as the greatest achievements of man, arise from such concentration, not because of external pressure, but from an inner motivation which propels the person and focuses his or her attention. Whether the activity be scholarship, or performance (as in dramatics or athletics), or the creation of physical objects, or still another activity, it is the concentrated involvement itself, rather than the specific content, that is important.

The objectives of the second class, with activities directed toward other persons are equally important. Adulthood cannot be accomplished merely by the acquisition of self-serving capabilities. These must be augmented by capabilities for mutually rewarding involvement with others.

First, it is important for each person's horizons to be enlarged by *experience with persons differing in social class, subculture, and in age.* For some young persons this has been accomplished by national service in the armed forces or in activities like the Peace Corps. But for most, the opportunities for a broad range of experiences with persons from backgrounds other than their own are simply unavailable.

A second facet of social maturation concerns *the experience of having others dependent on one's actions.* All persons throughout most of their youth are cast in the role of a dependent on others, while only a few, largely because of family circumstances, have others who are dependent on them. Although a few current school situations do provide appropriate experience of this kind by giving older children some responsibility for the teaching of younger children, this opportunity is atypical. It is important that environments for youth provide opportunities in caring for others who are younger, sick, old, or otherwise dependent, and to engage in activities that are responsible in the sense that they have significant consequences for others. This is a most important apprenticeship for prospective obligations as spouse, parent and citizen.

Social maturity also develops in the context of involvement in *interdependent activities directed toward collective goals,* where the outcome for all depends on the coordinated efforts of each. A cognate advantage of such joint enterprises is that it provides the individual with the opportunity of serving in the capacity of leader as well as follower. All young people are presently subject to the authority and the directives of others, but only a few gain the experience of guiding and leading. Yet those capabilities are necessary for the management of their future families, as well as in their work and their community activities.

These kinds of social maturation are now accomplished haphazardly if at all. A prime criterion for assessment of present and prospective environments for youth is their efficacy for filling this void.

It is important to develop in youth an additional set of attributes that arise from both classes of objectives, a sense of identity and self-esteem. These are attributes toward which environments for youth should be directed, for such identity and self-esteem form the foundation on which an adult life is built. Further, environments for youth can be assessed by these criteria just as well as by the objectives discussed earlier.

In this report we hope to initiate discussion and debate concerning the capabilities that constitute adulthood, as sketched in the foregoing account, and also concerning the institutional forms that are best designed to achieve the various components of adulthood. The times may seem unpropitious for the announcement of far-reaching goals. In recent years our educational institutions have been in continual crisis, and our efforts at improvement have been frustrated by an inordinate increase in the numbers of youth. Yet times of trouble offer the opportunity for major restructuring that would be resisted were the times tranquil. Also, we are now on the brink of a demographic moratorium in which the number of youth will remain approximately constant, permitting us to seize the opportunity for reformation without the apprehension of being numerically engulfed.

The fundamental aims of this report are obviously too ambitious to be accomplished through any single document. The process of social change requires that discussion and debate begin, that nuclei for social inventions be tentatively formed, that experiments be designed with meticulous attention to comprehensive recording of their consequences for all those whose lives they touch, and that forthright decisions then be made when the evidence is in.

The audience for such discussion is obviously broader than the federal governmental structure. Indeed it may be that the joint responsibility, first of assuring that young people acquire a set of capabilities to serve them well in adulthood, and second of assuring that they retain the freedom and opportunity to move in diverse directions, is best shared between different levels of action, the first at the federal and state levels, and the second through local community and private channels. A central emphasis of this report is the importance of encouraging as wide a variety of environments for youth as are compatible with the enforcement of criteria to safeguard their development.

In the next part of this report are a series of background papers describing the social, psychological and physiological conditions relevant to any discussion of youth, the history of the social position of this age group in the United States, and the current educational, economic and demographic situation of youth. The third section abstracts from these papers some of the important issues that must be addressed if the environments within which youth grow into adulthood are to be effective. In the fourth and final section, we suggest some initial changes which may move our society from its present schooling phase of youth institutions into a new phase of an array of environments explicitly designed for the various facets of maturation.

Because our central concern is with the future shape of institutions within which youth grow up in America, we exclude from examination many important and problematic aspects of modern life often associated with youth, for example, drug use and freer attitudes toward sexual behavior. Nor do we make a special point of the grave problems of differential educational opportunity by ethnic group and social class, unless one or another of our specific proposals directly implicates that issue. Furthermore, despite the continuing, albeit attenuated, role of parents and siblings in socialization, we have chosen to concentrate our attention on extra-familial life. Finally, our emphasis has been somewhat unbalanced with respect to the two sexes. Although young women as well as young men participate in much the same school experiences and movements into the labor force, they also experience special problems associated with their incipient roles as wives and mothers. We have not given those problems special attention.

We are concerned about these limitations on the scope of our report, but that concern is lightened somewhat by the awareness that each of them has elsewhere been the subject of specialized scrutiny, whereas the topic on which we focus is ordinarily neglected.

Altogether, the aim of this report is to stimulate the search for institutional inventions which will ensure that youth acquire the capabilities for fulfilling the demands and opportunities they will confront as adults, and thereby gain the self-esteem and self-fulfillment all persons need.

PART 2: BACKGROUND

1. *History of Age Grouping in America*

If the success of revolutions is measured entirely by their completeness, certainly the social revolution which has transformed the role of young people in society during the last century has been among the most successful. The elements of the revolution have been manifold, affecting family relations, educational opportunities, job opportunities, and peer relations. Just as no single cause explains the change, no single factor characterizes it, but some broad trends might be noted. First, young people now spend far more time in formal educational institutions than ever before: as a corollary, they spend less time in employment. Such jobs as they do hold, moreover, tend to be short-term, sought out for immediate spending money rather than as life's work. Whether the school prepares the young for careers or not, the social expectation increasingly has been that it should and will. Hence the length of formal education has been stretched out from the early through the middle teens to the late teens and early twenties. Secondly, in schools young people are not only segregated from the job market, but they are usually segregated with age peers—with exact age peers, in fact. Thirdly, the prolongation of education and the decline of working opportunities for the young has affected the family relationship. Not only are young people economically burdensome within the family, but the family itself is often a burden on the child, for while the family provides the young with many psychological and moral supports, it increasingly is unable to provide them with firm direction toward entry into the job market. Given the highly specialized nature of many occupations in our society, fathers often have only a narrow range of skills to pass on to their sons. Further, even if the son (or daughter) desired to follow the occupation of his parents, it would still be necessary to obtain formal certification through a school diploma or college degree or licensing certificate. At times older siblings can compensate for the defects of parental wisdom, providing for their younger brothers and sisters advice and support as the latter enter the job market. But even this form of counsel is

9

limited by the fact that siblings today are separated in age by fewer years than was true in the past.[1]

If the range of socializing agencies in our society is narrow and specialized, in the past it has been broad and relatively unspecialized. We might begin by noting certain characteristics of the American family in the period before 1860. Although fertility was much higher than it is now, families in 1790 were only somewhat larger. The average American family in 1790 contained 5 to 6 persons; by 1900 it contained 4 to 5 persons.[2] Multigenerational households were slightly more common in 1790 than today, but even nuclear families were probably likely to have relatives in the near vicinity, so that young people were probably exposed to a wider range of generational contacts than simple statistics on family size suggest. (Demos, 1970) Further, the range of ages of family members was likely to approximate the range of ages in society at large much more closely than now. Infant mortality checked some of the tendencies of high fertility, and the combination of the two guaranteed a broad spread in the age range of a family. It was not uncommon for 15-year-old boys or girls to have 10- and 20-year-old siblings; it was quite conceivable to have a 25-year-old brother or sister. Sibling migration in fact provided one of the principal forms of family continuity during the great migrations of the early nineteenth century, as groups of brothers would leave the family either collectively or individually for new parts. Similarly, it was not unusual for young brothers coming of age to be sent to live with married sisters, and to learn the trade of a brother-in-law. Thus even where fathers were not directly passing on skills to sons, the family still functioned, laterally and horizontally so to speak, as a cushion for the start in life.

The age mixture which characterized families tended also to mark educational experiences. While formal educational institutions played a much smaller role in the lives of young people in 1830 than now, a variety of institutions and arrangements existed to serve the needs of young people. Of these the college, while perhaps the best known, was the least typical. The proportion of young people in college had always been small, and it declined even more in the first half of the nineteenth century (Rudolph, 1962:21–34). Much more common were the academies, the distinctive educational innovation of

---

[1] For a discussion of the educational aspects of these patterns, see Coleman (1961); Douvan and Adelson (1966).

[2] The major change between 1790 and 1900 has come in the decline (by nearly 100%) in the proportion of families of seven or more members. (See U.S. Bureau of the Census, 1970:98.)

the early nineteenth century. Academies existed in all sizes and shapes. Many were private "family schools," where the students lived in the household of a single professor. At the other extreme were the incorporated academies such as Phillips Andover and Phillips Exeter, which provided facilities and curricula as demanding as those of many small colleges. Somewhere in between were modestly endowed coeducational academies in towns like New Lebanon, New Hampshire, or Wilbraham, Massachusetts. Whatever the particular form an academy might take, however, the students who attended were likely to be anywhere from 7 or 8 to 25 years old. Further, to the extent to which academies sought to regulate the entrance age, they concerned themselves with floors rather than with ceilings, with keeping out students under 12 rather than young people in their twenties.[3]

In fact, few educators found the association of boys of 12 with young men of 20 in academies or colleges anomalous, perhaps because age heterogeneity in schools reflected the more fundamental age heterogeneity of the family and the peer group. Despite the association of children and adults in the work force, settled agricultural society in early nineteenth-century America was familiar with peer groupings of young people. What characterized these associations of young people, in contrast with twentieth-century peer groups, was the broad range of ages involved. Contemporaries who referred to the "young people" of a town or village had in mind those from 12 or 13 to the early or middle twenties.[4] By all accounts, young people seem to have enjoyed a significant measure of social freedom (Prince,

---

[3] No authoritative study of the academies exists, but see Sizer (1964:12–40) on the range of students, see Phillips Exeter Academy (1883). Several academies are the subject of published histories (e.g., Sherman, 1893).

[4] Prior to the emergence of a formal, official social concern with adolescence, in other words prior to the 1890's, references to age groupings were casual and offhand in character. "Youth," for example, connoted the entire "rising generation," or all the minors, but it was often used more precisely to denote those from 15 to 25 (with slight variations). "Young people" were often distinguished from "children" (although not always) and embraced the broad range of ages suggested in the text. In general, "young people" had more of a corporate connotation than "youth"; that is, it referred to minors in the context of village life, while "youth" (often used interchangeably with "young men") suggested a measure of independence from parental or village supervision. Two other terms, "lads" and "large boys," were common in the literature of the period; "lads" described those from around 10 to around 16, while "large boys" embraced the narrower age range 14 to 16 or 17, or what the twentieth century has called the adolescent. (This term practically never appeared outside of medical literature.) Obviously, there was a measure of overlap between the categories, with distinctions often based more on status than on age. A 15-year-old who had left home was a "young man," but a 17-year-old still following the plow was likely to be a "large boy." For a discussion of some of these distinctions, see Kett (1971a).

1965:49 and *passim;* Kendall, 1872:3; Vassar, 1959:127; Alcott, 1839: 69). Unchaperoned social visiting between the sexes, dances, sleigh rides, and idle chitchat in the evening were the common forms of recreation for young people. Indeed, the two aspects of peer groups in early nineteenth-century agricultural communities, a broad range of ages and freedom from direct adult supervision, were probably related, for the assumption was that the older members of the peer group would take care of the younger ones, that the young men of 18 or 20 would look out for the boys of 14 or 15—an assumption which long survived in the practice of placing young college students of 14 under the supervision of those of 18 or 19. This is not to say that society in the early national period of our history was permissive about sexual indulgence by young people; its official literature was anything but permissive. Nor is it to suggest that young people of the early nineteenth century bore much resemblance to the "flaming youth" of the Jazz Age, for the former were altogether less self-conscious about their social life. Nor is it to suggest, finally, that society sanctioned socialization by the peer group as we understand the latter concept, for the idea of 14-year-olds passing most of their time with other 14-year-olds would have run decidedly against the grain in 1830. But as long as peer groups contained the kind of promiscuous assemblage of ages which characterized schools and families, practical tolerance of their activities was the rule.

Finally, a promiscuous assemblage of the ages affected the work force as well as educational institutions and peer groups. From the age of 7 or 8 onward young males in farming communities, which is to say in most communities, were expected to work alongside their elders. The kind of work performed during these early years varied little from one boy to the next. During the peak work seasons of spring, summer, and early fall they were expected to assist in the tasks of planting, haying, and harvesting. After the age of 7 or 8 boys usually attended school only for a few months, or sometimes just a few weeks each winter. After the age of 12 or 14, many boys stopped attending school altoghether. Sons of farmers were often placed out in service on neighboring farms; those of craftsmen and artisans (as well as many sons of farmers) were apprenticed in trades (Kett,1971b; Farber, 1972:96–108 and *passim;* Demos, 1970: 70–72). Either way, they would leave home to live elsewhere, although the social disposition was to discourage those in their early teens from breaking too far from parental restraint. Apprenticeships were often arranged with relatives; failing that, within the neighborhood wherever possible (Farber, 1972:96–108). No matter where they lived or what they did, however, teen-agers would spend their working hours around those older than themselves, and acquire such competency as they might attain by on-the-job-training. It is worth noting that in this period, learning on the job affected even the professions, which, the ministry expected, still put primary emphasis on the apprenticeships mode of instruction. Professional schools were essentially ancillary to, rather than substitute for, apprenticeship (Calhoun, 1965).

Age mixture was one characteristic of the social experience of youth during the first half of the nineteenth century. Another and no less important facet of youthful experience was seasonal quality of both labor and most types of education. Today we assume that education precedes entrance into the labor market, but in 1830 the relationship was more complex. Boys who attended school at all usually attended for only part of the year, working in the intervals. Farm boys, for example, often attended district schools each winter until their late teens or even early twenties. Similarly, students in academies normally attended after harvest or before planting. Attendance at academies often dropped off during the winter session, when many students sought positions in district schools, and again in the summer when strong males could command wages for farm labor (Kett, 1971lb:8–9). It would be fanciful to suppose that young people who shifted from school to work to school again in the course of a single year were being given an opportunity to utilize what they were learning in practical situations, for the curricula of academies were heavily weighted toward the classics, mathematics, and composition. The seasonal quality of education and labor did mean, however, that upwardly mobile young men did not have to pass prolonged periods in the setting of formal education. Thus the presence of sizeable numbers of 20- and 25-year-old students in academies and colleges does not mean that large numbers of youth were undergoing prolonged education; most of the older students were merely late starters, young men who had not begun their serious education until 18 or 20.[5]

Patterns of seasonal migration during the teen years affected the nature of family relationships as well as the quality of educational experience, for just as young people often stayed in school until their late teens or beyond, so too they often were to be found still resident in the parental home until past their majority. But in each case the experience was more extensive than intensive; both attendance at school and residence in the home were broken up by long periods spent doing something else. Even young people who stopped

---

[5] On the broad age range of colleges in this period, see Thomas (1903).

attending school at 12 or 14, or who never attended school at all, often left home for shorter or longer periods to seek work on a seasonal basis, whether as farm servants in the summer or in construction or trade at almost any time of the year. This sort of frenetic home-leaving was one of the most basic qualities of youthful life experience and it serves to qualify any easy generalizations to the effect that family authority over the young was once very severe. It could be severe, as long as young people were living at home, but in practice the door of many homes was a revolving one (Kett, 1971b, 13–14).

Differences between social class and between the sexes existed, naturally, in the experience of coming of age. The rich had advantages denied the poor; poor young men had a wider range of options than young women. Yet there were elements of similarity between the experiences of young people of different classes and different sexes. Sons of wealthy parents were certainly more likely to enjoy the privileges of advanced "literary" education (i.e., in a college or academy) than sons of poor farmers or artisans. But wealthy parents appear to have had few scruples against allowing their children to work on a seasonal basis at fairly early ages. Wealthy parents, moreover, do not appear to have placed great value on prolonged education for their children. Intensified private schooling up to the age of 15 or 16 followed by entrance into merchant houses or professional apprenticeships was more characteristic of the wealthy and upper middle classes than a prolongation of formal education to 21 or beyond.[6] Sex differences were perhaps more pronounced, since women were effectively barred from the professions (schoolteaching was not considered a profession) and from many occupations. But young girls were often placed out in service, just like their brothers. Further, while male labor was preferred in agriculture, construction, and trade, female labor was sought in industry. Prior to 1860 the factory labor force was primarily composed neither of children under 12 (in contrast to Britain) nor of men, but of young women in their teens or twenties (Lebergott, 1964:125–30; 56–59).

Regardless of class considerations, moreover, some basic features of society promoted early independence. The absence of guilds, the nonexistence or feebleness of certification procedures in most professions and occupations, and the loose and informal character of apprenticeship requirements facilitated various kinds of mobility. By the 1840s, for example, "voluntary" apprenticeship, terminable at

---

[6] In fact, a very high proportion of the antebellum college students were indigent. See Allmendinger (1968).

the request of either party, was the prevailing custom in many parts of America.[7] Still another factor contributing to mobility among young people was the age structure of society. Young people aged 15 to 19 or 15 to 29 formed a significantly higher proportion of the total population over 15 than is true now.[8] Young people were forever pushing out and up; the age structure of society was more triangular than rectangular. None of this should be taken to mean that young men were accorded full adult economic status at age 14 or 15. Rather, the early and middle teens were usually taken up with the drudgery of farm service, a pattern which extended in many cases upward to the early and middle twenties. The point is simply that upwardly mobile young men who left home at 18 or 20 to "start in life" faced relatively few institutional barriers to achievement. Naturally, this could also work the other way around; society presented few institutional props against failure. But the records of the antebellum period abound with instances of 24- or 25-year-old college presidents, 25-year-old Congressmen, and 30-year-old Senators.

Although various social conditions facilitated early independence, concepts of dependency have traditionally been conservative. Legally, the child did not become a man until 21. Nor was this merely a ritual devoid of practical significance. Prior to 21, a child was expected to work for his family, not for himself. If a son earned money outside the family farm, he was expected to hand it over to his father. Variations existed, but always within the broad context of dependency. A son desiring independence at 17 or 18 might make a cash payment to his father in lieu of service, or he might hire a substitute to take his place in the farm work force, or, if the father did not need the son's labor even on a seasonal basis, he might make a voluntary gift of time to his son, thus exempting the latter from labor obligations (Kett, 1971b:10; Frothingham, 1874:25).

Not only were concepts of dependency broad, but even after a young man had achieved independence from parental restraints he was still likely to be officially categorized as immature. Authors of conduct-of-life literature aimed at young men in the 18–30 age bracket routinely described their audience as giddy, romantic, almost harebrained. So too, school discipline (including discipline in academies and colleges) continued to rely on humiliation. In general, the social experience of coming of age and the social training of young

---

[7] Frank Musgrove (1965:77–80) has argued that the period from 1790 to 1860 was also one of great freedom for young people in Britain. See also Handlin (1971: 85–86) and Burn (1865:22).

[8] Between 1830 and 1900 the proportion of young people of 15 to 29 to the total white population over 51 declined from over 52% to under 45% (U.S. Bureau of the Census, 1960).

people were often antagonistic, with the one promoting independence and the other seeking to impress subordination. We might remind ourselves that in a society where everyone worked, a society without protected childhood, institutionalized adolescence, or forced retirement, the performance of work was less a mark of maturity than it is on our own society, where the labor force forms so much smaller a proportion of the total population. Beyond this, we might remind ourselves that there were very few tasks in antebellum society which could not be as well performed by an 18-year-old as by a 40-year-old, very few tasks, in other words, which demanded a high degree of technical skill or education. Young people thus stood in a much more proximate and even menacing relationship to adults than they do now. Thus, even though young people were fully incorporated into the labor force, they were not described as full adults. The usual definition of "youth" was actually very broad, from 15 to 25 (with slight variations), and youth was described not merely as the opposite of age but as a prolonged period of immaturity and lamentable irresponsibility (Hawes, 1828:16; Eddy, 1855; Clark, 1863).

This is not to postulate the existence of some kind of pitched generational warfare in American society of 1830 or 1840. Although adults often referred to youth as a class, youth lacked an image of itself as a cohesive group with distinctive rights and needs. Young people who felt aggrieved or harassed could not fall back on any ideology which justified their rights as youth. Yet the very proximity, physically and economically, of age groups in a society which recognized age groups promoted a certain stiffness in relations between young and old. An example can be found in the history of colleges. Between 1790 and 1850 college life was characterized by frequent eruptions; the degree of disorder was probably greater than anything which has occured since. Student rebellions took place at Harvard, Yale, Brown, Williams, Princeton, Amherst, Virginia, North Carolina, South Carolina, and elsewhere (Morison, 1965: 118, 133, 211–12, 208–10, 252? 54; Bronson, 1914; 188–9; Wertenbaker, 1946: 138–40; Tyler, 1895: 264–66; Battle, 1907, vol.1:*passim*; Tucker, 1962: 232–61; Bruce, 1919, vol. 2:306–11, 267–93). At Virginia the murder of a professor by a student in 1840 was simply the culmination of a series of public beatings and whippings of professors. During a rebellion at Princeton the faculty had to call in townspeople for help in putting down the students, a nice twist on the town and gown theme. At pious Brown, President Asa Messer's house was repeatedly stoned by students in the 1820s. Multiple instances could be cited. These, then, were not student pranks but serious challenges to the application of college authority. Commenting on the situation, a college president observed (Lindsley: 1825:41)

> They [students] form a party by themselves—a distinct interest of their own—view with suspicion every measure of the faculty— and resolve to contravene and thwart their plans as far as it may be in their power.

Antebellum students were less ideological than twentieth-century dissidents. Political issues rarely occasioned student rebellions; rather, the latter usually were touched off by discontent with college ordinances. Even then, students rarely challenged the concept of authority as such, just its application. Yet antebellum students probably posed a greater threat to persons and property than students in the twentieth century (with the possible exception of the last few years). Further, the authority of college officials, theoretically great, was actually very limited. It was a buyer's market in the 1830s; colleges needed students and even well-established ones like Harvard found themselves on the brink of financial disaster when they resorted to mass expulsions to deal with dissidence (Morison: 1965:253–54). Again, the very fact that authority was so tenuous helps to account for the stiff and over-bearing manner most college officials assumed vis-à-vis the students. Or, to put it another way, adults find it easy to "understand" youth, to adopt a familiar and chummy tone, when youth is safely domesti-cated, when young people are in their place, a threat to themselves perhaps but no immediate threat to authority.

We should be wary, then, of postulating the existence of a kind of Golden Age in intergenerational relationships, an age of frankness and honesty unsullied by suspicion and misunderstanding, just as we should guard against exaggerating the degree of misunderstanding which prevails in our own society. It is conceivable that such a Golden Age existed in the primitive agricultural society of seventeenth-century New England, when the range of options available to sons was so narrow as to preclude arguments with elders. Yet is seems more reason-able to suppose that a certain amount of friction has always existed, and that where young people are incorporated more or less fully into the economic life of society adults will not draw the conclusion that young people are to be accorded the full measure of manhood but that young people should have their subordination impressed upon them by one means or another. It also seems likely that the more fully young people approximate equality in their economic relation-ship to adults, the more occasions for friction will arise.

During the last half of the nineteenth centrry and the first two decades of the twentieth century the institutions which affected young people, whether economic or educational, underwent notable changes. Because of radical regional differences, especially in the early part of the period, generalizations about the exact timing of the changes are difficult to make. Industrialization, the systematization and bureaucratization of education, and the dissemination of certification procedures affected different parts of the nation at very different times; what was true of the school system of Massachusetts in the 1850s, for example, was not true of the school system of Iowa until the 1890s. But for present purposes, it is perhaps wiser to take these regional differences for granted and to concentrate on describing the process, nature, and implications of change.

A good place to begin is with the age-grading of the schools, for while it reflected tendencies outside of education, its effect on the young was visible and direct. While complaints about the jagged age distribution of students had long abounded, age-classification was essentially a by-product of the great movement to reform the common schools which began in the 1830–50 period under the leadership of Horace Mann, Henry Barnard, and others. While school reformers sought free public education as a major goal, they were no less interested in systematizing education through classifying schools by age and level of achievement (Barney, 1851). Under the influence of enlightened ideas about childhood which were widely disseminated in America after 1820, moreover, reformers increasingly were disposed to a view of the ideal school as a controlled environment for the child. The school, ideally, was not merely to be a casual, unstructured institution which the child encountered from time to time; it was to be as coextensive with childhood as conditions would permit. In the eighteenth century, for example, schools were often "kept" in barns or private houses; in the nineteenth century they were increasingly located apart from the hurly-burly of business and commerce. The assumption of many school reformers was that the proper "culture" of childhood demanded a segregation of children from adults in asylumlike institutions called schools.[9]

During the middle of the nineteenth century these ideas can be encountered in the school reports of a few of the larger states such as Massachusetts. Yet they were certainly not universally accepted, and the gap between theory and practice long remained a broad one. True, social conditions increasingly favored their spread. Population concentration made age-gradation more feasible. Town and city schools were more sharply age-graded than rural schools. But the process of age-gradation was not altogether smooth; in the 1880s the Boston school

---

[9] On public school reform, see Cremin (1961); on concepts of childhood, see Wishy (1969).

superintendent still found it necessary to complain about the large numbers of 16- and 17-year-olds still in grammar school. But by then their presence was recognized as anomalous (Boston School Committee, 1882:25).

The idea of age-grading was not confined to the lower elementary schools. Inevitably, it affected secondary and college education. The age range in public high schools varied from place to place, but, to a greater extent than had been true of the old academies, the constituency of the high schools by the 1960s was composed of teen-agers.[10] The same development affected private education, both in the academies and the colleges.[11] Again the process was often jerky, but by the latter part of the nineteenth century clear distinctions could be drawn between secondary and higher education both on the basis of the curriculum and the age range of the students. With fewer and fewer exceptions, academies, boarding schools, and public high schools embraced those from around 13 to 19, while the clientele of the colleges typically ranged in age from 17 or 18 to 22 or 23. Such exceptions as existed tended to be at the upper rather than lower limits of each type of school; the 10-year-olds disappeared from academies before the 25-year-olds, just as the boys of 13 or 14 were pruned from college ranks before the young men of 25 or 26. But the direction was clear.

It is impossible to separate age-grading from industrialization. The old system, or nonsystem, of seasonal education in district schools or academies had depended on the seasonal pattern of labor in an essentially preindustrial society. The newer idea of reaching a certain level by a certain age was more likely of achievement in an industrial society, where job demands took up the better part of the year and, hence, where education, if it was to be had at all, had to be obtained before entrance into the labor market. Interestingly, the early humanitarian opposition to child labor in factories (in the 1830s and 1840s in industrializing states, later elsewhere) was aimed less against the fact of child labor than against the inconsistency of factory labor with education (Ensign, 1921: Chap. 3). Thus, early child labor opponents sought not the abolition of child labor but compulsory education for

---

[10] The age range in the Concord High School was 14 to 18; elsewhere, variations existed (13 to 17, 15 to 19) with a scattering over 21 (although the public character of the high school made the legal status of those 21 and over dubious). Basically, this tendency toward concentration in the teens reflected grading at a lower level; in Concord, primary students ranged from 5 to 10, intermediate students from 10 to 14. One notable exception in Concord was the condition of schools in the outlying districts, where pupils between 8 and 22 were still mixed together in 1860. See Alcott (1960: 199, 251–54).

[11] On academies, see Phillips Exeter Academy (1883); on colleges, see Thomas (1903).

part of each year, in effect attempting to restore some elements of the old seasonal work-study pattern.

In addition to population concentration and industrialization, immigration also contributed to the systematization of education. In the course of the nineteenth century the mission of the schools to socialize and Americanize the immigrant in a controlled and comprehensive environment was stated with growing explicitness. School reformers and officials alike increasingly complained about the polygot and disorderly character of American society and defended the school as an agency which would at once bring the children of immigrants under social control and improve their chances for survival in the competitive economic life of America. To accomplish goals of such importance, schools could not be conducted on a random and casual basis, but, to return to a theme mentioned earlier, had to embrace significant portions of the child's experience.[12] These themes can be traced as far back as the school reports of Horace Mann, but they acquired a new stridency in the late nineteenth and early twentieth century as the source of immigration shifted from northern and western Europe to southern and eastern Europe. The presence of massive numbers of immigrants with strange tongues and still stranger customs stimulated in the schools the imposition of an often monolithic "Americanism."

The children primarily affected by the standardization and bureaucratization of American education in the middle to late nineteenth century were those in the age group of, roughly, 7 to 13 or 14. Although reformers promoted public high schools as capstones of the system, the proportion of young people educated beyond the primary level was exceedingly small. Most high schools, although free, had entrance examinations. Prior to the 1890s, very few educators thought of the high school as even potentially a mass institution. Most high school students, and a high proportion of high school graduates, moreover, were female. Boys who attended high school at all were usually withdrawn after a year or two and placed in trades. Prior to the 1890s, expressions of regret about this were rare. Although educators strongly desired the inculcation of literacy and morality in the schools, they assumed that these goals could be sufficiently accomplished with the span of six or seven years of formal education. Many reformers in fact desired the removal of the "large boys" (i.e., ages 15–17) from the education system, for they had long been a disorderly element in the lower schools. Indeed, it is quite possible that in the latter part of the nineteenth century educational opportunities for young people beyond age 14 were actually drying up, for the high schools demanded prolonged

---

[12] On Americanization as applied to the high school, see Krug (1964:417–18).

attendance (9- or 10-month terms) each year, unlike the old academies, and hence were within reach of only those families who could afford to forego the labor of their children during early adolescence, a fact which explains why so few boys, who could command better wages than girls, were to be found in high school (Sizer, 1964).

In the latter part of the nineteenth century boys who left elementary schools at 14 or earlier to enter the job market encountered conditions very different from those met by earlier generations. Industrialization rendered occupations more specialized than ever before, a fact which was distinctly reflected in two themes of contemporary literature. In the 1880s an increasingly large number of tracts on vocational guidance began to appear. In contrast to earlier books on the conduct of life, the newer tracts were written by laymen rather than ministers, were often aimed primarily at teen-agers rather than at young men in their twenties, and substituted job information for moral precepts.[13] The basic assumption of the authors, probably a valid one, was that families could no longer provide young people with hard information about careers or occupations because occupations had grown so specialized. Choices made on the basis of parental wisdom, the authors assumed, were likely to be the wrong choices. In the 1880s another theme appeared: reformers increasingly began to complain that many boys were being locked into "dead end" jobs from which there was no exit, that movement from one type of employment to another was becoming much more difficult (Massachusetts Commission, 1906). All of these assumptions contained elements of truth. While vocational counselors of the late nineteenth century probably underestimated the degree to which older and more informal ways of entering the job market had survived, and while they tended to romanticize the past when a jack-of-all-trades could presumably do whatever he felt like, they did accurately identify some of the most fundamental forces in their society. While work in factories was probably no more dismal than work on farms, the appearance of freedom and some of the reality as well were undergoing contractions.

---

[13] See, for example, Wingate (1898) and Fowler (1910). The traditional doctrine was that of calling. As a writer in 1832 put it, when choosing a profession "disregard altogether the opinions of others. Study into the wants of the community and the wants of your own soul (New England Magazine, 1832: 138). This older emphasis did not die quickly; in fact, it continued to permeate much of the late nineteenth-century literature on vocations. But, significantly, even the most conservative examples of the later literature were often in the form of collections of articles written by specialists from the world of affairs, describing in detail the opportunities available in each field. During the Progressive Era a formal vocational guidance movement emerged under the leadership of Frank Parsons and others. With it came a gradual shift of emphasis away from the concept of calling toward the scientific measurement of interests. For a review of the latter theme, see Fryer (1931:157–75).

Specialization in the late nineteenth century affected professions as well as occupations, for between 1880 and 1920 a succession of strokes were dealt to the old, informal methods of licensing and certification in professions. Prior to 1860 the only profession which demanded prolonged education as preparation was the ministry, specifically the ministry of orthodox denominations. By 1900 formal education was replacing apprenticeship in the legal profession and had completely displaced it in the medical profession (U.S. Commissioner of Education, 1897; vol 2, Chap. 36; Parsons, 1900). Further, many new lines of work, engineering and teaching for example, were rising from occupational to professional status, and demanding formal certification via standardized education. The primary cause of these changes was the combination of expanding knowledge, intense demand for specialists, and a higher sense of professional obligation. At times, however, a simple desire to increase the status of a particular profession lay behind calls for prolonged education. The insistence of some professions on attainment of the bachelor's degree as a prerequisite to professional education, for example, probably had less to do with strictly intellectual considerations than with a realization that higher educational attainments would contribute to a raising of professions in the public estimation. Whatever the sequence of causation, however, the drift of things was clear.[14]

While the social changes which were transforming the social condition and role of young people were in motion long before 1890, it was not until the 1890s and early 1900s that a major social response to these changes took form. We might describe this response as a "discovery" of adolescence, although like most discoveries this one was less an act of pure discovery than a twisting and redefinition of familiar materials. Broadly speaking, one can identify two major constituents of the heightened social interest in adolescence. The first was the exploration of the psychodynamics of adolescence, pioneered by G. Stanley Hall and his students at Clark University in the 1890s, launched fully with the publication of Hall's two-volume *Adolescence* (1904) and disseminated during the first few decades of the twentieth century in innumerable books and articles aimed at helping parents and teachers to understand their adolescent children.[15] Some of the points made in early twentieth-century literature on the psychology of adolescence were merely rephrasings of longstanding ideas. It had long been argued

---

[14] For a discussion of legal education, see Stevens (1971). While the idea that the A. B. degree should be a prerequisite to legal education was present in the 1890's, it was not widely disseminated until the 1920's and 1930's (Stevens, 1971:493–504).

[15] For a representative sample of Hall's impact, see O'Shea (1909); Scott (1908); King (1914). On Hall, see Ross (1972: Chap. 16). On the novelty of Hall's ideas, see Kett (1971a).

that adolescence was a potentially dangerous, critical, and threatening stage of life. Yet the new literature on adolescence was distinctive in several ways. First of all, its primary focus was on teen-agers, especially on those from 14 to 18.[16] Secondly, within the teen-age category the major emphasis was on early adolescence, on the years around puberty. Each of these features reflected social developments. In effect, a stage of life was being defined in terms of a stage of schooling, for the 14–18 range also happened to be the modal age range for high school students at the turn of the century. The emphasis on early adolescence underscored the critical importance the years from 13 or 14 to 16 were coming to have as economic determinants. That is, at the particular stage of industrialization which America had reached by 1890, critical and often irreversible decisions were being made for and by young people during the years of early adolescence (Massachusetts Commission, 1906).

Perhaps the most distinctive aspect of the psychological literature on adolescence in the early twentieth century, however, was its normative character. Adolescence was not portrayed, as it long had been, as a dangerous state of life to be passed through as quickly as possible, but as a season of development which had to be allowed full scope to play itself out. This was the central point of Hall's doctrine of recapitulation, the idea, that is, that the child passed through the various stages of development from savagery to civilization already traversed by the race. Any effort to speed up the process, to short-circuit adolescence by forcing premature commitment or adulthood on the juvenile was self-defeating, since it would only lead to dangerous recrudescences of "savage" propensities in maturity. Instead of portraying youth, in the fashion of Victorian commentators, as a dangerous, harebrained stage of life, Hall insisted on the value of a catharsis to all the instinctive drives of adolescence before safe passage to the next stage could be guaranteed (Hall, 1904: Vol. 1, Chap. 5; Ross, 1972: Chap. 16).

A second constituent of the heightened social interest in adolescence in the 1890–1920 period was the emergence of innumerable adult-sponsored youth organizations. These bore little resemblance to older associations of young men aged 16–30 which dated back to the seventeenth century. Where the latter had been voluntary organizations, started by young people for self-culture, the former were controlled by middle-aged adults, men who were usually morally conservative and tinged by a mixture of authoritarianism, evidenced by their use of military regimen, and rural nostalgia, suggested by their preference for hiking. Organizations like the Boy Scouts and boy's department

---

[16] The older advice-to-youth literature (1820–1960) had been aimed primarily at those in the 18 to 30 age category (Kett, 1971a:passim).

of the YMCA sought to bring spare time activities of young people under rigid adult direction. (Hall, 1904: Vol. 2, Chap. 15; Murray, 1937:39–40 and *passim*). Adult-sponsored youth organizations owed a little to the new literature on adolescent psychology, but more basically reflected antecedent social changes which had stripped young people of many of their roles. To take one example, the emergence of youth organizations succeeded by a decade the professionalization of urban volunteer fire companies which had traditionally, but now no longer, provided teen-agers with opportunities for public service and with abundant personal contacts with young men in the 18–30 age group. Finally, the new youth organizations were pervaded by an incongruous tolerance of socialization by the peer group, by the idea that loyalty to age peers in youth could be sublimated into civic service in adulthood, a concept which conflicted with the rigid adult direction of youth organizations, but which was present all the same.

The institutionalization of adolescence during the Progressive Era embraced juvenile courts, "junior republics," and the like, but its most enduring effects were in the field of education (Holl, 1971). Between 1870 and 1920 many states restricted the use of child labor and established compulsory education (Ensign, 1921: Chap. 4–8); in 1916 the federal Keating-Owen Act prohibited the employment of children under 14 in factories and canneries and under 16 in mines and quarries, and prohibited the employment of all children under 16 more than eight hours a day (Trattner, 1970: Chap. 7). The gap between ideal and real long remained broad. The Keating-Owen Act was declared unconstitutional in 1917; while thirty-eight states by 1917 had provided for compulsory education beyond age 14, all but five of them allowed the granting of work permits at 15 (Krug, 1972: Chap. 8). Despite such limitations, the idea of prolonging education and substantially removing young people from the labor market was explicit in reform literature of the early 1900s (Krug, 1972:4).

The crusade against child labor and the expansion of compulsory education grew out of a variety of forces, including humanitarian opposition to the crass exploitation of juveniles for profit and labor opposition to the displacement of adults by juveniles in the job market. Yet these factors do not really account for the substantial expansion of the high school population after 1890, an expansion which lay behind the prolonged debate between 1890 and 1917 about the high school curriculum. Reformers kept insisting that if the curriculum was made more practical, high schools would attract more students. In fact, they were attracting more students regardless of curriculum content.[17] The same can be said of the colleges; they too experienced a rise in population after 1890 altogether out of proportion to rises in the population as a whole (Veysey, 1965:264). Several explanations, some doubtless better than others, can be advanced to account for these changes. It is possible that greater affluence made it possible for more parents to forego the wages of children and allow them further education. It is also likely that parents with any thoughts of providing upward mobility for their children did not see early entrance into occupations as an avenue of mobility. In the earlier part of the century family connections and kin patronage could more than compensate for the lack of advanced education, but in the more formal and impersonal economic world of the early 1900s they counted for less. In effect, the school was emerging as a certifying agency to replace older and more personal techniques of introducing young people to the market place. The school diploma was coming to have undeniable economic value. A Massachusetts commission in 1906 produced abundant evidence to indicate that students who stayed in school until 16 entered the job market on more favorable terms than those who persisted in school only until age 14. The commission concluded (perhaps a little too quickly) that the extra two years education accounted for the difference in employment prospects (Massachusetts Commission, 1906:70–93). Yet it is also possible that children of middle-income parents were the ones who could forego wages for the extra two years, hence were more likely to stay on in school, and entered the job market favorably not because of their extra schooling but because of their family status. Whatever the priority, it is clear that contemporaries drew as a conclusion that education paid and that more education paid more. What people think is happening, in other words, is often as important as what is happening. Whether contemporaries rightly or wrongly interpreted the signs is less important than the fact that they concluded that education pushed into the teen years as far as possible had cash value (Greer, 1972).

By 1920 the basic forms of the twentieth century's intellectual and institutional response to young people had taken shape. What took place in the next forty to fifty years involved refinement and elaboration more than innovation. Hall's concept of adolescence, for example, came under fire from numerous critics in the 1920s. But the attack was directed more against the absolutistic and pseudo-scientific character of his ideas than at the normative concept of adolescence. Hall had implied that adolescence was invariably a period of "storm and stress" although anthropological studies like Margaret Mead's *Coming of Age in Samoa* (1928) strongly suggested that in some societies the experience of adolescence was natural and without turbulence. Similarly,

---

[17] The high school population rose from 202,963 in 1890 to 519,251 in 1900 (Krug, 1972:169–71).

while Hall had clothed the concept of adolescence in the terminology of the law of recapitulation, more sophisticated studies in the 1920s and 1930s insisted that the study of adolescence must focus on cultural milieu rather than on inevitable biological and historical determinants of behavior (Thomas, 1923; Van Waters, 1925). By the 1940s, moreover, some were questioning the whole idea that adolescence, even in American Society, was inevitably or routinely characterized by "storm and stress" (Hollingshead, 1949:5–7). Yet, despite all these qualifications, the normative character of the concept has endured for psychologists with few exceptions have continued to hold that in our society some sort of prolongation of adolescence is desirable, that youth needs a kind of moratorium to establish identity and autonomy.

In other ways, too, the period since 1920 has primarily been characterized by an extension and elaboration of ideals created earlier. A quick recounting of some statistics speaks for itself. The percentage of the population 17 years old to graduate from high school rose from 6.4% in 1900 to 50.8% in 1940 to 62.3% in 1956 (U.S. Bureau of the Census, 1960:203). In 1900 students comprised only a tiny fraction of the total 14- to 16-year-old population; by 1930 the proportion was just under half; by 1940 it was a little over two-thirds (Krug, 1972:218). At the same time the proportion of young people in the labor force declined. There were fewer gainfully employed workers aged 10 to 15 in 1930 than in 1870 despite a quadrupling of the gainfully employed labor force in the same period.[18] As for college education, the percentage of the population ages 18 to 21 in institutions of higher education (graduate and undergraduate) rose from a little over 4% in 1900 to 8.9% in 1920, 12.4% in 1930, 15.68% in 1940, and 29.88% in 1950 (U.S. Bureau of the Census, 1960:5.6).

If one decade could be singled out as critical for the teen-age population, it would have to be the 1930s. The depression hit youth aged 16 to 24 especially hard. The plight of unemployed youth was dramatized in works like Kingsley Davis's *Youth in the Depression* (1935) and Maxine Davis's *The Lost Generation* (1936). The federal response to the problem was varied. The National Industrial Recovery Act (1933) and the Fair Labor Standards Act (1938) effectively achieved the goals of the Keating-Owen Act by prohibiting employment of children under 16 in a wide range of occupations. On the other hand, the Civilian Conservation Corps and National Youth Administration sought

---

[18] The category "gainfully employed" indicates merely that a person specified his occupation when asked by the census taker whether he had one and what it was. Thus, the category says little about actual participation in the labor force and is plainly inferior to more sophisticated measures of labor force participation worked out since 1930. Still, it is considered a useful indicator over a long period of time (U.S. Bureau of the Census, 1960:68–72).

to provide a range of training and employment opportunities for these over 16. But perhaps the most important developments of the decade lay less in federal legislation than in education. Boys who could not find work stayed in school longer. Only during the depression did it become routine for boys to finish high school; indeed, the high school was defended in the 1930s more explicitly than ever before as a "cure" for unemployment (Krug, 1972:201–24).

Beginning with the Report of the Committee of Ten in the 1890s, running through the Cardinal Principles of Secondary Education of 1918, and continuing up to the present, a prolonged debate has taken place concerning the purpose and content of high school education. Advocates of education for "social efficiency" have contended with spokesmen for vocational education, intellectual education, and life adjustment education. Behind the debate lies the explosion of the high school population, which put insupportable stress on older and more academic notions of secondary education, and the reality that teen-agers have lost many of their economic functions in our society, so that new goals and roles must be defined for them. Out of the debate has come the comprehensive high school which, with characteristic American ingenuity, has resolved the issues in favor of all parties by providing something for everyone. The justification of the comprehensive high school was stated aptly as early as 1918 (Krug, 1972:205–6):

> In short, the comprehensive high school is the prototype of a democracy in which various groups must have a degree of self-consciousness as groups and yet be federated into a larger whole through the recognition of common interests and ideals.

It is doubtful whether any forging of common interests, except in a very vague way, has taken place in the high school. Hollingshead's study of Elmtown's youth (1949) indicated that both the classroom and extracurriculum of the high school reinforced rather than dissipated class lines. The same phenomenon appears today as formal racial integration often produces little more than an informal resegregation within the walls of the school. As a melting pot, the high school has been a dissappointment.

Yet it is equally clear that the high school has performed an important, although originally unintended and unforeseen, function in promoting socialization by the peer group. A number of studies support this suggestion. In *Middletown* (1929) the Lynds noted that in the period between 1894 and 1924 the town's high school had become the focal point of a distinctly adolescent social life (Lynd and Lynd, 1929:211):

The high school, with its athletics, clubs, sororities and frater-
nities, dances and parties, and other 'extracurrucular activities,'
is a fairly complete social cosmos in itself, and about this city
within a city the social life of the intermediate generation centers.

Two decades later Hollingshead observed that Elmtown's youth functioned in two quite separate worlds: from adults they learned a formal,
verbalized public code, from peers a different and informal set of
conventions (Hollingshead, 1949:211). In 1961 James S. Coleman
concluded from a survey of ten American high schools selected across
regional and class lines that American adolescents were increasingly
living in a world of their own, with a self-contained system of attitudes
and values (Coleman, 1961).

An interesting aspect of the cultural detachment of adolescents is the
extent to which adults, far from challenging it, have often promoted
it. The Lynds long ago noted that community leaders in Middletown
supported the orientation of the high school toward sports and pep
spirit (Lynd and Lynd, 1929:212–17). Coleman made the same point
in a different way when he observed that to the extent fathers and
sons shared activities, it was around the interests of the son, for
example in the Boy Scouts or the Little League (Coleman, 1961:
312). Hollingshead concluded that, despite the presence of a number
of community institutions which competed for the services and support
of youth, young people in Elmtown were not given the kind of
developmental tasks which would turn them into adults. His judgment
was devastating but accurate (Hollingshead, 1949:149):

> By segregating people into special institutions, such as the
> school, Sunday School, and later into youth organizations such as
> Boy Scouts and Girl Scouts for a few hours each week, adults
> apparently hope that the adolescent will be spared the shock of
> learning the contradictions in the culture. At the same time, they
> believe that these institutions are building a mysterious something
> variously called "citizenship," "leadership," or "character," which
> will keep the boy or girl from being "tempted" by the "pleasures"
> of adult life. Thus the youth-training institutions provided by the
> culture are essentially negative in their objectives, for they seg-
> regate adolescents from the real world that adults know and func-
> tion in. By trying the keep the maturing child ignorant of this
> world of conflict and contradictions, adults think they are keeping
> him "pure."

Behind changes in the social position of youth lies a more basic loss
of economic function on the part of the entire age group. Society no
longer depends on young people for anything in particular (unless it

be as soldiers) and has been forced to create for them a succession of contrived roles and institutions not tightly woven into the community structure. In a gradual way the change has been going on for centuries, but in the twentieth century the revolution in the economic and social position of youth has virtually moved to completion.

2. *Rights of Children and Youth*

Persons below the age of majority are simultaneously the most indulged and oppressed part of the population. Both civil and criminal law accord minors special consideration and shield them from the full legal consequences of their acts. On the other hand, until reaching ages prescribed by law, children [1] and young people are compelled to attend school, excluded from many gainful employments, denied the right to drive automobiles, prohibited from buying alcoholic beverages, firearms, and cigarettes, barred from the most interesting movies, and deprived of countless pleasures and liberties available to adults. Those under 18 do not vote, do not have the resources to maintain lobbies, and as yet have not organized as a pressure group. Boys and girls participate in demonstrations and protest marches, but decisions on educational, labor, and welfare policies, in which they have a vital stake, are reached without their consent or counsel.

Within individual families, through countless stratagems, children can exercise dictatorial control. In society, however, children are officially powerless. They enjoy such rights as the adult community is willing to sanction and suffer the disabilities their elders deem appropriate to their condition. Advance and implementation of children's rights is the task of adult advocates. The history of children's rights is therefore an account of the changing circumstances, capabilities and conscience of the adult world.

From the adult viewpoint, limitations imposed on the young, galling as they may seem to the sufferers, stem not from tyranny but from affection and consideration. Blackstone described the disabilities of children as privileges granted "to secure them from hurting themselves by their own improvident acts." (Blackstone, 1872: I, 463) Common and statute law have erected elaborate defenses to safeguard children from unscrupulous adults who would take advantage of their weakness and immaturity. "The benefit of the infant"—i.e., a person under legal age—"is the great point to be regarded," declared Justice

---

[1] In legal parlance persons under the age of majority are "infants." In this paper I use the word "children" to refer to the younger portion of the age group 14 to 24, especially to persons under 18 years of age.

Samuel S. Wilde of the Supreme Judicial Court of Massachusetts in 1816, "the objects of the law being to protect his imbecility and indiscretion from injury, through his own imprudence, or by the craft of others." (Oliver v. Houdlet, 1816)

Justice Wilde's opinion was rendered in one of a long line of cases in which English and American courts safeguarded the estates and property rights of minors and, because of their "imbecility," exempted them from many of the obligations and penalties to which adults were subject. William Wetmore Story had these precedents in mind when, in his Treatise on Contracts (1847:27), he warned: "Every person deals with an infant at arm's length, at his own risk, and with a party for whom the law has a jealous watchfulness."

In addition to protecting the property rights of minors (and their guardians) the common law recognized the duty of parents to protect, educate, and maintain children. "These duties are all enjoined by positive law," noted James Shouler, historian and legal scholar, in 1870: "yet the law of natural affection is stronger in upholding such fundamental obligations of the parental state." (Schouler, 1895:234) Relying on the strength of parental affection, the common law allowed fathers wide latitude in determining how the responsibility of protecting, educating, and maintaining offspring was to be discharged. The law deemed the natural instinct for protecting one's children so potent as to need (in Blackstone's words) "rather a check than a spur." The obligation of maintenance was assumed to be so well accepted as seldom to require enforcement by "human laws." (Blackstone, 1872:235, 237) Similarly, "the promptings of parental affection and wholesome public opinion" were deemed sufficient to prevent abuse of parental authority in administering correction. (North Carolina v. Jones, 1886)

Despite the assumed efficacy of parental affection, American legislatures and public officials did not hesitate to adopt and apply "human laws" to enforce the duties of protection, maintenance, and education. A typical statute, the Massachusetts law of 1731, authorized overseers of the poor to bind out as apprentices children whose parents were thought to be unable or unfit to maintain them: "Male children until they arrive at the age of twenty one years, and Females to the age of eighteen, unless such females are sooner married . . ." Social self-protection was the justification offered for such legislation. The community put a high value on order, and it was disinclined to bear the burden of supporting and controlling children whose parents allowed them to grow up without training or discipline.

Considerations of this sort loomed large in the thought of nineteenth century American reformers who advocated strenuous exercise of parens patriae (the duty of the state to protect children from all who would harm them) to supplant the authority of parents who neglected their obligations to offspring.[2] In a democracy, so the argument ran, children, as future citizens, were the state's most valuable possessions. The state, for its own security, had to enforce the child's right to the nurture which would equip him for responsible citizenship. Moreover, children were not chattels of their parents but persons whose welfare deserved prime consideration in all cases where their interests were at stake.[3] The *parens patriae* doctrine provided legal justification for an expansion of governmental authority in education, public health, child labor, and treatment of juveniles with behavior problems. In a 1944 opinion of the United States Supreme Court (*Prince* v. *Massachusetts*) which capped a century of state and federal court decisions, Justice Wiley B. Rutledge declared: "The family is not beyond regulation in the public interest. . . . Acting to guard the general interest in the youth's well-being, the state as *parens patriae* may restrict the parents' control by requiring school attendance, regulating or prohibiting the child's labor and in many other ways. . . The state has a wide range of power for limiting parental freedom and authority in things affecting the child's welfare . . ."[4]

During the latter part of the nineteenth century the expanding activity of the state produced significant changes in the legal status of children. Florence Kelley (1882:83, 89) cited advances in the law of custody and guardianship, improvements in provision for pauper, delinquent, and illegitimate children, and enactment of compulsory education and rudimentary child labor laws as evidence of "growing care for the child's welfare, and growing recognition of his individuality with its need of individual care." She hailed "the total emergency of the child from his former legal oblivion" and concluded that in the late nineteenth century the child's position under the law was unique in the extent to which his well-being was considered.[5]

Miss Kelley belonged to the generation of reformers, active from the 1890s to the 1930s, who expanded the idea of the welfare of the individual child into the broader concept of the rights of childhood. Using the data of medicine, physiology, psychology, and pedagogy, progressive reformers viewed childhood as a critically important period of life, during which the child required protection, care, and spe-

---

[2] For a representative statement of this view, see Hale (1855).

[3] See the opinion of Justice Joseph Story in a child custody case (U.S. v. Green, 1824). For interesting comment on the effects of democracy on the status of children see Tocqueville (1945:192–97) and Spencer (1890:198–99).

[4] For an early and vigorous application of *parens patriae* see Ex parte Crouse (1838).

[5] For a summary of laws relating to children in 1880 see U.S. Bureau of Education (1880).

cial treatment, not just in the interests of future citizenship, but in order to develop and realize his potential as a human being. More effective regulation of child labor by the states, creation of juvenile courts, establishment of the federal Children's Bureau, the manifold activities of that bureau, and improvements in the administration of public child welfare services at all levels of government represent the achievements of the "rights of childhood" movement.[6] The most eloquent summary of the objectives of the movement is the Children's Charter adopted by the approximately 3,000 delegates attending the 1930 White House conference on Child Health and Protection. Because of its importance as a historical document the Charter is reprinted here in its entirety (U.S. Children's Bureau, 1967:11–12) :

The Children's Charter

President Hoover's White House conference on Child Health and Protection, recognizing the rights of the child as the first rights of citizenship, pledges itself to these aims for the children of America.

I   For every child spirtual and moral training to help him to stand firm under the pressure of life

II   For every child understanding and the guarding of his personality as his most precious right

III   For every child a home and that love and security which a home provides; and for that child who must receive foster care, the nearest substitute for his own home

IV   For every child full preparation for his birth, his mother receiving prenatal, natal, and postnatal care; and the establishment of such protective measures as will make child-bearing safer

V   For every child health protection from birth though adolescence, including periodical health examinations and, where needed, care of specialists and hospital treatment; regular protective and preventive measures against communicable diseases: the insuring of pure food, pure milk, and pure water

VI   For every child from birth through adolescence, promotion of health, including health instruction and a health program, wholesome physical and mental recreation, with teachers and leaders adequately trained

---

[6] Legislation affecting children during the Progressive Era is summarized in Carigan (1911).

VII   For every child a dwelling-place safe, sanitary, and whole-some, with reasonable provisions for privacy; free from conditions which tend to thwart his development; and a home environment harmonious and enriching

VIII   For every child a school which is safe from hazards, sanitary, properly equipped, lighted, and ventilated. For younger children nursery schools and kindergartens to supplement home care

IX   For every child a community which recognizes and plans for his needs, protects him against physical dangers, moral hazards, and disease; provides him with safe and wholesome places for play and recreation; and makes provision for his cultural and social needs

X   For every child an education which, through the discovery and development of his individual abilities, prepares him for life; and through training and vocational guidance prepares him for a liv-ing which will yield him the maximum of satisfaction.

XI   For every child such teaching and training as will prepare him for successful parenthood, home-making, and the rights of citizenship; and, for parents, supplementary training to fit them to deal wisely with the problems of parenthood

XII   For every child education for safety and protection against accidents to which modern conditions subject him—those to which he is directly exposed and those which, through loss or maiming of his parents, affect him indirectly

XIII   For every child who is blind, deaf, crippled, or otherwise physically handicapped, and for the child who is mentally handi-capped, such measures as will early discover and diagnose his handicap. provide care and treatment, and so train him that he may become an asset to society rather than a liability. Expenses of these services should be borne publicly where they cannot be privately met

XIV   For every child who is in conflict with society the right to be dealt with intelligently as society's charge, not society's out-cast; with the home, the school, the church, the court and the institution when needed, shaped to return him whenever possible to the normal stream of life

XV   For every child the right to grow up in a family with an adequate standard of living and the security of a stable income as the surest safeguard against social handicaps

XVI For every child protection against labor that stunts growth, either physical or mental, that limits education, that deprives children of the right of comradeship, of play, and of joy

XVII For every rural child as satisfactory schooling and health services as for the city child, and an extension to rural families of social, recreational, and cultural facilities

XVIII To supplement the home and the school in the training of youth, and to return to them those interests of which modern life tends to cheat children, every stimulation and encouragement should be given to the extension and development of the voluntary youth organizations

XIX To make everywhere available these minimum protections of the health and welfare of children, there should be a district, county, or community organization for health, education, and welfare, with full-time officials, coordinating with a state-wide program which will be responsive to a nationwide service of general information, statistics, and scientific research. This should include:

> (a) Trained, full-time public health officials, with public health nurses, sanitary inspection, and laboratory workers
> (b) Available hospital beds
> (c) Full-time public welfare service for the relief, aid, and guidance of children in special need due to poverty, misfortune, or behavior difficulties, and for the protection of children from abuse, neglect, exploitation, or moral hazard

for every child these rights, regardless of race, or color, or situation, wherever he may live under the protection of the American flag

*   *   *   *   *   *   *

By 1933 American statute books contained a variety of laws which attempted to safeguard children against premature, excessive, and dangerous labor, to protect them against neglect, immorality, disease, and insanitary surroundings, and to require them to attend school for so many months a year until they reached a given age. The laws were intended to secure better treatment and wider opportunity for all children. They diminished the autonomy of parents and guardians but by no means supplanted the parent's primary responsibility for supervising his children. The principle was well established that except in unusual circumstances the best place for children was in their own homes; as a corollary it was widely recognized that the well-being of most children could be best promoted by strengthening the economic security of the family.

Implementation of these principles was the objective of the major social reforms inaugurated in the New Deal. In certain areas, however, the New Deal adopted legislation and initiated programs which had (and continue to have) an important impact on the rights of children and young people. Two of these, regulation of child labor and promotion of youth employment, have particular relevance to contemporary issues.

Regulation of Child Labor

According to the census of 1930, 2 million children and youth under 18 years of age were gainfully employed. One-third of them were under 16. As the depression deepened and millions of adults suffered unemployment, more stringent regulation of child labor seemed a possible way of opening jobs for adult workers. A spokesman for the National Child Labor Committee declared in 1933: "It is now generally accepted that the exploitation of children, indefensible on humanitarian grounds, has become a genuine economic menace; . . . children should be in school and adults should have whatever worthwhile jobs there are."

The right of the federal government to regulate child labor had been hotly debated for at least twenty years before 1933. A constitutional amendment granting Congress the power "to limit, regulate, and prohibit the labor of persons under eighteen years of age" had been submitted to the states in 1924, but by the end of 1932 only six states had ratified and twenty-four had rejected it. In the first five months of 1933 six more states had ratified the amendment, and in June 1933 it was under consideration in five states. Throughout the New Deal, President Roosevelt, Secretary of Labor Perkins, and the American Federation of Labor continued to advocate ratification.

While the amendment was still before the states, the attack on child labor went forward under the NRA codes of fair employment (the cotton textile code set the pattern by prohibiting the employment of children under 16) and production control contracts of the Agricultural Adjustment Administration (e.g., benefit payments in the sugar beet industry were conditioned on agreements not to employ children under 14 and not to work children under 16 more than 8 hours a day) .

The major New Deal achievement in child labor regulations came with the Fair Labor Standards Act of 1938. Some historians regard it as a very modest achievement indeed. The act defined child labor as the employment of children under 16 or under 18 in hazardous occupations. It prohibited the shipment in interstate commerce of goods produced wherever child labor had been employed within 30 days prior to shipment.

Notice that what was prohibited was not child labor, but "shipment in interstate commerce." This language was occasioned by the uncertainty of whether the Supreme Court would uphold the constitutionality of any federal legislation directly regulating child labor. Consequently businesses, such as telegraph companies, which handled but did not produce goods were not affected by the law. Moreover, the act exempted children who worked in agriculture "while not legally required to attend school." It is estimated that of the approximately 850,000 children under 16 gainfully employed in 1938, only about 50,000 were subject to the act. Children in industrial agriculture, intrastate industries, the street trades, messenger and delivery service, stores, hotels, restaurants, beauty parlors, bowling alleys, filling stations, garages, etc., were outside the law.

Nevertheless, the act is a landmark in the regulation of child labor because it was declared constitutional. In February 1941, in *United States* v. *Darby* (312 U.S. 100) the Supreme Court unanimously and specifically overruled the 1918 decision in *Hammer* v. *Dagenhart* and upheld the right of Congress to regulate child labor in industries engaged in interstate commerce. The *Darby* case made ratification of the child labor amendment unnecessary. Subsequently, although not until 1949, the child labor provisions of the Fair Labor Standards Act were substantially broadened. Coverage was extended to all nonagricultural establishments engaged in interstate commerce, including public utilities, communication, and transportation as well as manufacturing and mining; oppressive child labor itself, rather than shipment of goods produced by child labor, was prohibited; and the employment of children under 16 *during school hours* was prohibited in commercial agriculture. (This was stronger than "while not legally required to attend school.")

This leaves us today with a large number of children under 16 years of age who (as far as federal laws are concerned) may legally be employed in agriculture outside of school hours and many more children, including those 14 years of age and younger, who may be employed during school vacation. Dale B. Kloak, Chief of the Child Labor Branch, Wage and Hour Division, of the Department of Labor has summarized the current coverage and exemptions of the federal law (Kloak, 1972):

A 16-year-old youth may be employed for any number of hours in any occupation, including hazardous occupations in agriculture—other than those nonagricultural occupations declared hazardous by the Secretary of Labor to which an eighteen-year minimum age applies. After a minor becomes 18, there are no Federal child labor standards governing his employment. Minors 14 and 15 years old may be employed outside school hours in a variety of nonmanufacturing and nonhazardous jobs. Hours of work are limited to 3 a day and 18 a week when school is in session, and 8 a day and 40 a week during vacation periods. . . .

The child labor provisions do not apply to: Children under 16 years of age employed by their parents in agriculture or in non-agricultural occupations other than manufacturing or mining occupations, or occupations declared hazardous for minors under 18;

Children under 16 years of age employed by other than their than their parents in agriculture, if the occupation has not been declared hazardous and the employment is outside the hours schools are in session in the district where the minor lives while working;

Children employed as actors or performers . . . ;

Children engaged in the delivery of newspapers to the consumer;

Homeworkers engaged in the making of wreaths . . . (including the harvesting of the evergreens) .

For the purpose of the Act illegal employment of children in agriculture exists only during school sessions. The Wage and Hour Division cannot enforce any child labor standards in non-hazardous agricultural employment during the summer when many children work long hours for low pay harvesting the crops. It is true that the 16-year minimum in the Hazardous Agricultural Occupations Order applies at any time, but this has little bearing on hand harvesting activities.

In order not to curtail job opportunities for young 16- and 17-year-old student-learners enrolled in bona fide cooperative vocational training programs, exemptions are provided in 7 of the 17 nonagricultural hazardous occupations orders which will permit them to work, under specified criteria, in occupations otherwise prohibited for anyone under 18. The same exemption applies to bona fide apprentices. Special exemptions are provided in the Hazardous Agricultural Occupations Order permitting 14- and 15-year-old minors to operate tractors and certain farm machinery, even though these are hazardous occupations, provided they have taken the 4H Club or Vocational Agricultural training programs on these machines.

Enforcement of the child labor and myriad other provisions of the Fair Labor Standards Act rests with approximately 1,000 compliance officers who annually investigate 3% to 4% of the establishments covered by the act. During fiscal 1971 these agents found approximately 20,000 minors under age 18 illegally employed.

Promotion of Youth Employment

Both during and since the 1930s the plight of idle, jobless youth has seemed a more difficult and challenging problem than the protection of children against premature work. For the past forty years (with the possible exception of the era of World War II) concern has been expressed regarding young people over 16 years of age who remain in school more or less against their will because jobs are not available or who are both out of school and out of work.

As early as 1939 an estimated 1 million youth between 15 and 24 years of age were recorded as unemployed: that amounted to 27% of the total unemployment; in 1933 one-third of the estimated 15 million unemployed were in the 15-to-24 age group. In 1937, when total unemployment had dropped to 11 million, approximately 4 million youth aged 15 to 24 were unemployed (36%); and in 1940, even after the start of the defense boom, more than 2½ million young people remained involuntarily idle. Three-quarters of a million of them had never had a full-time job lasting for as long as a month.

It is obvious that the New Deal did not solve the problem of youth unemployment. Nevertheless, the Roosevelt administration recognized the problem, and it took action which served as precedents for such Kennedy-Johnson programs as the Job Corps and Neighborhood Youth Corps. The two most important of these were the Civilian Conservation Corps (CCC) and National Youth Administration (NYA).

CCC was the earliest and most popular of the New Deal relief agencies. CCC placed boys over 16 and young men under 28 who were out of school, unmarried, and unemployed in resident camps under a semimilitary regime. Enrollees performed "socially useful work," usually in conservation and reclamation, and received a small wage ($30 per month), most of which was allotted to their families. By 1941 more than 2½ million youths had been enrolled in CCC; as late as 1940 more boys entered the CCC each year than enrolled as freshmen in colleges and universities.

Like the army, CCC segregated white and black enrollees. On several occasions Roy Wilkins of the NAACP complained that instructors in camps not only held separate classes for white and black enrollees but also restricted certain courses to whites. Instruction in gardening and typing, for example, was offered in segregated classes to both races; but blacks were excluded from classes in forestry, architectural drawing, and surveying.

CCC offered no help to girls and young women or to youth of either sex who wished to remain in school or college. Beginning in December 1933, the Federal Emergency Relief Administration (FERA) allocated relief funds to colleges and universities for the employment of students up to 10% (later 12%) of college enrollment on part-time jobs at the average wage of $15 per month. In 1934 100,000 college students took advantage of the program.

The National Youth Administration, established by executive order in 1935 expanded the student aid program at both ends to include students attending secondary schools and graduate schools. The work programs were developed and supervised by the schools and colleges subject only to the requirements that recipients be selected primarily on the basis of need, that they carry three-quarters of a normal course of study, and that the work performed be genuinely useful, not displace any of the school's regular employees, and promote an allegiance to society.

NYA also supported community (out of school) work projects for young people. These were similar to WPA projects but the average monthly earnings of NYA workers was only one-third that of WPA workers. By the end of the 1930s NYA was operating 500 resident projects at which young people received vocational education and work experience. Eventually these resident projects were converted into defense and war production training centers.

What the New Deal did not do is often as interesting as what it attempted. One measure the administration declined to support was the proposed American Youth Act, sponsored by the American Youth Congress, and submitted to each session of Congress from 1936 to 1940. This measure provided a much more comprehensive program of federal aid to education, vocational training, and youth employment than was available under NYA. Aubrey Williams, administrator of NYA, expressed sympathy for the principles of the youth bill but stated that, as drafted, the bill would be impossible to administer and questioned the advisability of expanding NYA as rapidly as the bill proposed. The position of FDR and Mrs. Roosevelt on the youth bill was stated in 1941 in a letter to the secretary of the American Youth Congress—a letter signed by Roosevelt but drafted by his wife (Roosevelt, 1941) :

I think the American Youth Congress will recognize that the Administration attempts to propose to Congress legislation which will meet, as far as possible, the objections which different groups are apt to raise and which will have the best possible chance of passing, in order to obtain the objectives which are desired.

The American Youth Act has the opposition of the greater part of the Congress. It is probable that to achieve equality of opportunity for youth and others, a gradual approach must be made, taking into account every step of achievement in private industry in the country and moving toward this objective little by little, by increasing public works when needed, by greater appropriation for NYA and CCC as they appear necessary.

There is never only one way to achieve specific objectives. It is natural for youth to be less pliable, and with their enthusiasm they sometimes carry through their objectives, but as a rule the maturer approach, while it may be slower, achieves the objectives in the long run with a better foundation for permanent solution.

The three decades since FDR's letter the "gradual" and "maturer" approach to securing equality of employment opportunity for youth has not solved the problem. Under the Economic Opportunity Act and other programs considerable efforts have been made to equip disadvantaged youth with the training and habits to enter the world of work. As of yet, however, youth's right to work is much farther from realization than the child's right to protection against certain kinds of work at too early an age. As early as 1957 Kenneth Clark accurately predicted the consequences for youth and for society of denial of the right to work (Clark, 1957):

With increased technological industrialization of our society and with promises of accelerated industrialization in the form of automation, the major problem which confronts contemporary youth is not that they will be prematurely exploited by an industrial economy that is insatiable in its demand for manpower, but that they will be excluded from that participation in the economy that is essential for the assumption of independent economic and adult status. The vestibule stage of adolescence may be prolonged to a point where social and psychological stresses on young people may present for them and the society a most severe problem. . . .

Assuming that there will be a prolongation of the period of vestibule adolescence, a second and related threat to young people may be the abstract threat of a sense of exclusion in that period of their lives that could be a most creative period. It is questionable whether this period of restless waiting can be adequately filled for large enough numbers of these young people by merely

increasing the period of compulsory education. A sense of empti-
ness, restlessness, and prolonged dependence for youth may be
seen as a most powerful, even though abstract, contemporary threat
to the development of the creative aspects of their personality.

The development and dominance of mass media of communication and their role in communicating certain types of values,
ideas, and desires which may or may not be appropriate and available to the masses of American youth must be seen as another of
the important contemporary threats to their welfare and future
development. Significant discrepancies between the realities of
the lives of the majority of young people and the values and
aspirations communicated to them by these mass media may well
reflect itself in an intensification of personal problems and in the
extension of social instability.

*   *   *   *   *   *   *

Curiously enough, in the decade and a half since 1957, while many
young people have fretted through "vestibule adolescence" and have
passively or aggressively rejected adult values, the legal status of
children and youth has been greatly elevated. Recent movements to
extend and broaden the rights of youth are closely related to the
revolution for equality being waged by minorities, women, the poor,
prisoners, homosexuals, and other previously deprived segments of
society. Because children and/or young people are to be found in all
the groups seeking "liberation," it is not easy to single out issues which
pertain exclusively to the young. Moreover, many people deeply involved
in and committed to the struggle are neither young nor black, poor
nor revolutionary, but members of dominant elements of American
society.

One way to open up the subject is to examine various official pro-
nouncements on the rights of young people. Granted that such declara-
tions may be little more than statements of good intentions, they may
also serve as indicators of the state of public conscience and the intensity of social concern. It is interesting to contrast the 1930 Children's
Charter—earnest, maternal, comprehensive—with the defiant, assertive
Bill of Rights proclaimed at the White House Conference on Youth
(1971:23) :

> The Right to adequate food, clothing, and a decent home.
> The Right of the individual to do her/his thing, so long as it
> does not interfere with the rights of another.
> The Right to preserve and cultivate ethnic and cultural heri-
> tages.
> The Right to do whatever is necessary to preserve these Rights.

Recent changes in suffrage and majority have literally emancipated many young people from the disabilities and privileges of legal infancy. In 1944 Georgia reduced the voting age to 18 in recognition of services being rendered in the war by youthful draftees. (The draft age had been lowered from 21 to 18 in 1942). Ten years later President Eisenhower, in a message urging statehood for Hawaii and extension of the suffrage to residents of the District of Columbia, asked Congress to propose to the states a constitutional amendment establishing 18 as the voting age (Eisenhower, 1955):

> For years our citizens between the ages of 18 and 21 have, in time of peril, been summoned to fight for America. They should participate in the political process that produces this fateful summons.

The question of voting by 18-year-olds continued to be discussed throughout the 1960s. The 1960 White House Conference on Children and Youth advocated wider and freer participation in political affairs—particularly by clergymen and teachers—but split on the issue of 18-year-old voting. One Conference forum endorsed the proposal; another opposed it. President Kennedy's Commission on Registration and Voting Participation, concerned with low-voter participation in the age group from 21 to 30, concluded that by the time young people had turned 21 many were so removed from the stimulation of the educational process that their interest in public affairs had waned. In 1969 President Nixon advocated lowering the voting age to 18 on the simple grounds that persons of that age were smart enough to vote. "They know," said Nixon, "they are interested and more involved than were the 21-year-olds of only twenty years ago." (Nixon, 1970) In nonjudgmental language, borrowed from the 15th and 19th Amendments, the 26th Amendment, ratified by the states in 1971, declares:

> The right of citizens of the United States, who are eighteen years of age or older, to vote shall not be denied or abridged by the United States or by any State on account of age.

The 26th Amendment does not affect the right of states to determine the age of majority, i.e., the age at which a person is deemed an adult, capable of controlling his person and property without supervision by parent or guardian, free to make a will, marry, and enter into enforceable contracts. In practice, however, voting age and age of majority have so long been identical that the reduction of voting age to 18 has already promoted a number of states to lower the age of majority to 18.

Even before adoption of the 26th Amendment and the movement

toward lowering the age of majority, student pressure forced college and school officials to abdicate some of the dictatorial powers exercised over student conduct *in loco parentis*. Adult organizations such as the American Association of University Professors and the American Civil Liberties Union offered assistance to youth groups in specifying the rights and freedoms of students in the classroom, in the conduct of student affairs, and in off-campus activities as well as in such matters as confidentiality of student records, disciplinary procedures, and codes of dress and personal appearance.[7]

Supreme Court decisions rendered in the 1960s enhanced the legal status of children in notable respects. In a case involving the right of students to wear armbands protesting the Vietnam War in school, the Court ruled that students were "persons" under the Constitution; as such, they possessed rights which the state must respect and were entitled to free expression of opinion, except when such expression materially disrupted classwork or involved substantial disorder or invasion of the rights of others. (*Tinker* v. *Des Moines Independent School District,* 1969) In the *Gault* case (In re Gault, 1967) and others dealing with juvenile court proceedings, the Supreme Court has ruled that the state, as *parens patriae,* must observe the same scruples of due process and equal protection in dealing with minors as with adults. If the *Gault* and *Tinker* cases are followed, the state (*parens patriae*) will have to observe higher standards in its treatment of all children in the public care (see Kleinfeld, 1971).

In view of increasing sensitivity to the rights of children, it is not surprising that state and federal legislation regulating, limiting, or prohibiting children's right to work should come under critical scrutiny. Delegates to the 1970 White House Conference on Children, without specifically referring to child labor laws, asserted that "earlier laws and conventions designed to 'protect' the weak (women and children) are increasingly being viewed as constraints that must be cast aside." (White House Conference on Children (1970), 1971: 345) Opponents of child labor legislation have argued that American children today are no longer "weak" but "brighter, stronger, healthier, bigger than ever before," and hence that protection from responsibility (in the guise of exclusion from the world of work and too-long exposure to the artificial atmosphere of the classroom) constitutes a deprivation of their rights to participate in "meaningful activity." (Hamburger, 1971)

Defenders of child labor laws reply: (1) that the laws are not intended to exclude children from work but to safeguard them from

[7] See "1967 Joint Statement on Rights and Freedoms of Students" in Joughin (1969:66–74). See also American Civil Liberties Union (1968:9–20).

labor at too early an age, for too many hours a day, and in occupations where the chances of accident and injury are high; (2) that millions of children are presently at work either within or outside the law (neither state nor federal governments give high priority to enforcement of child labor laws, especially in commercial agriculture) ; (3) that the principal barriers to youth employment are not child labor laws but lack of skills and experience, employer attitudes, and a suppy of mature applicants with better qualifications; and (4) that the superior physical strength and mental ability of today's children are due in some measure to the protection accorded them (in the words of the Children's Charter) "against labor that stunts growth, either physical or mental, that limits education, that deprives children of the right of comradeship, of play, and of joy."

Reconciliation of these divergent points of view is not impossible. Eli Cohen, executive secretary of the National Committee on the Employment of Youth, advocating both greater participation in work for the young and maintenance of protection against exploitation, offers the following suggestions (Cohen, 1971) :

> Does this mean that we should repeal all child labor and school attendance laws and let virtually all children work who want to do so? That course would be unwise. Premature employment can be as harmful physically and emotionally as prolonged dependence is to self development. What is needed is a selective approach that strengthens the laws to provide protection where it is needed, and that liberalizes them where they actually serve as deterrents to employment opportunity. The protection afforded to youth in non-agricultural jobs must be extended to agricultural employment so that the same fourteen-year minimum age for employment should apply. In addition, the parental exemption from the prohibition against young children operating dangerous farm equipment should be removed. At the same time, school-work programs should be opened up to the fourteen- and fifteen-year-olds on a broader basis, carefully supervised to see that the work experiences are authentically developmental and lead to worthwhile career opportunities. Hazardous occupations need to be reviewed and modernized; jobs dangerous in the past but no longer so because of improved equipment and safety measures should be removed from that category. The process for obtaining work permits needs to be streamlined in many places. Moreover, the Secretary of Labor has a responsibility to enforce the existing laws more vigorously through an expansion of inspections and tougher prosecution of violators.

The panel's proposals for striking a realistic balance between the rights of children and youth to protection and opportunity will be considered in Part 4.

3. The Demography of Youth

Introduction

Society at large is faced perennially with an invasion of barbarians. Somehow they must be civilized and turned into contributors to fulfillment of the various functions requisite to societal survival. In the typical valedictory address, this is saluted as a fresh opportunity for society to renew itself, to adapt to the changing world around it, and to make yet another attempt to bring the actual more closely in line with the ideal. But with equal validity that invasion can be regarded as a threat to the persistence of the system; the challenge must be faced, even if there is no guarantee of success. At the very least, every society is obliged to allocate a substantial proportion of its human and material resources to the task of socialization.

Intrinsic in the history of every society is a process of demographic metabolism, through which older members age and die and their places are taken by younger members. Two generalizations apply to this process: (1) It is always and everywhere painful not only for the new recruits but also for the society which has the job of converting and digesting them; (2) The difficulty of the assignment, from the standpoint of individual and group, varies directly with the pace of social change. Intergenerational conflict, which is probably universal, is exacerbated whenever rapid social change converts the age distance between parent and child into a distance in historical time as well. Particularly acute and stressful contrasts can occur when the background of the father is rural and that of his son is urban, when the formal education of the son is substantially in excess of that of the father (including the quantum gap between illiteracy and literacy) and when the father is foreign-born and the son native-born, but the principle is quite general.

Although societies do find ways of coping with this pervasive problem, their task is exacerbated if there is superimposed on the system an abrupt quantitative discontinuity. In the first section of this chapter, evidence will be presented to show that the increase in the magnitude of the socialization task in the United States during the past decade was completely outside the bounds of previous and prospective experience. Although the pathways of causation by which this gross arithmetical change tends to impinge on the various sectors of the body politic are various and complex, no subtle argument is required to anticipate large and pervasive problems, and the proliferation of investigatory bodies, like the present one, to study them. The current gross disjuncture in the temporal progression of those to be socialized may be the principal explanation for the evident youthful pathologies which are very much in the public eye. This is not to say that now is an unpropitious time to examine institutions of socialization in the United States, and identify ways in which they may be dysfunctional from the standpoint of both the individual and the society. We regard it as intellectually rewarding and probably socially useful to reappraise the conventional wisdom about socialization, and particularly those aspects which have achieved the status of axioms. Nevertheless, we would do well to consider the extent to which current discontent with the process by which children are turned into adults is attributable less to systemic flaws than to engulfment by numbers.

The Size of the Youth Group

Table 1 shows the numbers of males and females in the age group 14–24 during the century 1890–1990, and the relative change per

TABLE 1—Size of population aged 14–24, 1890–1990, and percent change per decade.

Year	Size (in million)	Percent Change
1890	14.2	
1900	16.5	+16
1910	20.0	+21
1920	20.8	+ 4
1930	24.8	+20
1940	26.3	+ 6
1950	24.2	− 8
1960	26.7	+10
1970	40.5	+52
1980	44.8	+11
1990	41.1	− 8

SOURCES: 1890–1960.   U.S. Bureau of the Census, *U.S. Census of Population: 1960. General Population Characteristics, United States Summary.* Final Report PC(1)–1B. U.S. Government Printing Office, Washington, D.C., 1961. Table 47.

1970–1990.   U.S. Bureau of the Census, *Current Population Reports,* Series P–25, No. 470, "Projections of the Population of the United States, by Age and Sex: 1970 to 2020," U.S. Government Printing Office, Washington, D.C., 1971. Table 2, Series D.

decade. The data through 1960 are from the U.S. Census; they have been extended to the year 1990 by employing what appears currently to be the most reasonable of the most recent array of projections produced by the Bureau of the Census. (The only number for which there may be more than trivial error is the last, since the younger members of that age group have not yet been born).

Between 1890 and 1960, the subpopulation aged 14–24 rose slowly and irregularly by a total of 12.5 million; between 1970 and 1990 it is expected to rise a little more. Yet in the one decade of the 1960s, there was 13.8 million increase, more than in the rest of the century altogether. As the second column of Table 1 indicates, the relative rise in the past decade was unparalleled.

The use of absolute numbers for social indices is often misleading because it suggests that nothing else of relevance is changing. To obviate this criticism, consider the population aged 14–24 in relation to the group aged 25–64, those who provide the time and energy and skill required for socialization of youth, and pay the required taxes. In Table 2, we show the ratio of the number 14–24 to the number 25–64, for the same time span as used in Table 1.

Again in Table 2 we have striking evidence of the statistical uniqueness of the decade of the 1960s—the only decade in the century during which the ratio registered an increase. The demographic explanation of this peculiar pattern of change is straightforward. In a population which, like that of the United States, is experiencing declining growth, largely because of a downward secular drift in the birth rate, the ratio of the numbers in younger to the numbers in older age groups will tend to decrease. There has been only one major interruption in that secular drift—a brief reproductive renais-

TABLE 2—Ratio of the population aged 14–24 to the population aged 25–64, 1890–1990, and percent change per decade.

Year	Ratio	Percent change
1890	0.566	
1900	0.519	−8
1910	0.496	−4
1920	0.430	−13
1930	0.431	0
1940	0.400	−7
1950	0.322	−20
1960	0.322	0
1970	0.449	+39
1980	0.423	−6
1990	0.332	−21

SOURCES: See sources for Table 1.

sance between the mid-1940s and the mid-1960s—which produced a gross malformation of the age distribution, the immediate consequence of which has been the recent extraordinary exaggeration of the size of the ordinarily problematic youth group, relative to the numbers of adults available to cope with it. More realism, at the cost of less precision, would have been achieved by taking into account the circumstance that the period of socialization has itself lengthened. In terms of Table 2, the average boundary between the two population segments has not been fixed (at the twenty-fifth or any other birthday) but has been rising throughout the century. Such an allowance would counterbalance the general impression of decline in the ratio reported in Table 2, but would not contradict the general proposition of the demographic uniqueness of the 1960s in this regard.

The data in Tables 1 and 2, which are macrodemographic in orientation, have their microdemographic parallel at the level of the individual family. Throughout the nineteenth century and well into the twentieth, the average number of births per married woman declined, to a local minimum of approximately 2.5 for women born in the first decade of this century. The baby boom was the work of women born during the 1930s; their average number of births rose to approximately 3.5. Currently the mean number of births per married woman is much closer to 2.5 than to 3.5; the details are discussed in a subsequent section. (Ryder, 1969) Thus there has been superimposed on a general trend toward diminution of the average socialization burden per married couple a brief hiatus during which the responsibility increased sharply. While such gross quantitative changes are not necessarily translated one-to-one into the realm of social facts, they do imply an increase of tension within the prevailing normative system and may produce substantial conflict and pressure for modification.

The size of the population aged 14–24, and its ratio to the size of the population aged 25–64, can be projected year by year with high accuracy through 1986 (barring major catastrophe) because the persons involved have already been born, survivorship in the relevant age range is increasing very slowly, and net external migration is of modest proportions. These data are presented in Table 3, which shows that the size of the group increases from 40.5 million in 1970 to 45.4 million in 1978 (a growth rate equivalent to $+15\%$ per decade) and then declines at least to 1986, to essentially the same value as in 1970 (and with a growth rate equivalent to -13% per decade). The ratio of population 14–24 to population 25–64 reached its local peak of 0.460 in 1971, and will decline at first gradually and then rapidly from now on, to 0.347 in 1986, a value comparable to that of the

TABLE 3—Size of population aged 14–24, and ratio of population aged 14–24 to population aged 25–64, 1970–1986.

Year	Size (in millions)	Ratio
1970	40.5	0.449
1971	41.9	0.460
1972	42.5	0.457
1973	43.2	0.458
1974	43.8	0.457
1975	44.5	0.457
1976	44.9	0.454
1977	45.2	0.450
1978	45.4	0.444
1979	45.2	0.435
1980	44.8	0.423
1981	44.2	0.410
1982	43.4	0.395
1983	42.8	0.383
1984	42.1	0.370
1985	41.6	0.360
1986	40.7	0.347

SOURCES: See sources for Table 1.

immediate postwar period. Should the population ultimately become stationary, the ratio will continue declining and stabilize at 0.283. In short, the relative magnitude of the socialization task is likely to become much smaller than at any time in our past history.

It is difficult to speak of the future size of the youth group for any time beyond 1986, because it will depend more and more on the course of the birth rate from now on. Nevertheless, there are several major social developments which seem likely to continue— in particular the increased use at earlier life cycle stages of more effective means of fertility regulation, and the enlargement of the sphere of career choice for young women. These developments will reduce fertility to or below the replacement level. There are various speculative assessments of the consequences of the approach of a stationary population for society at large, and specifically for the economy. (Ryder, 1973a) Of these, the most firmly based seem to be a higher level of productivity than in a growing population, but a lower level of system flexibility because of the lower mobility of older workers, and more sluggish career pace with age for the individual worker. With specific reference to the younger person, on the other hand, the future would seem bright because younger workers will be at a premium, provided they are willing to move from place to place and from job to job. From this perspective, it is strongly in the interests of the young adult, and by inference in the interests of the society as a whole, that he or she postpone the assumption of commitments, like parenthood, which would reduce adaptability to a changing situation. Such a modification seems to be occurring currently, but no long-range prediction can be made with high confidence.

Absorption of the Baby Boom

Table 4 indicates approximately how the society has absorbed the increase in youth during the decade of the 1960s, with respect to major institutional structures. It shows the distribution of the civilian noninstitutional population, ages 16–19 and 20–24, by sex, among three categories of activity: enrolled in school; other employed; and a residual category, which is small for the male and consists principally of unemployed, but is large for the female and consists principally of housewives.

TABLE 4—Numbers of males and females, enrolled, employed, and other, ages 16–19 and 20–24. Civilian noninstitutional population, October 1960 and 1970.

(In thousands)

| | Age 16–19 | | | Age 20–24 | | |
	1960	1970	Change	1960	1970	Change
Male						
Enrolled	3433	5359	+1926	936	2061	+1125
Employed	1189	1320	+ 131	3394	4267	+ 873
Other	404	545	+ 141	380	708	+ 328
Total	5026	7224	+2198	4710	7036	+2326
Female						
Enrolled	2985	4891	+1906	414	1296	+ 882
Employed	1143	1249	+ 106	2254	4004	+1750
Other	1154	1251	+ 97	2952	3258	+ 306
	5282	7391	+2109	5620	8558	+2938

SOURCES U. S. Department of Labor, Bureau of Labor Statistics. *Employment of School-age Youth.* Special Labor Force Report 135, 1971, Table 1.

As Table 4 indicates, the number of males aged 16–19 increased by 2.2 million during the decade, and the considerable majority (88%) of that increase was absorbed by an increase of 1.9 million in the number enrolled. Civilian males in the age group 20–24 increased by 2.3 million during the decade, and almost one-half (48%) of that increase was absorbed by an increase of 1.1 million in the number enrolled. Although the total number of males increased by 44% in the 16–19 age group, the number employed increased by only 11%

during the decade. For the 20–24 age group of males there is a similar, although somewhat less striking, contrast: the total number increased by 49%, but the number employed increased by only 26%. For civilian males, the institutional solution for the baby boom was predominantly an increase in enrollment in school. One further detail must be added concerning the allocation of males by activity. Table 4 applies solely to the civilian population. During the decade, the numbers of males in these age groups who were on active duty increased appreciably. By 1970 some 5% of the males 16–19, and some 20% of the males 20–24, were in the armed forces. (Current Population Reports P–23, No. 40, January 1972, Table 27). The magnitude of this category can be inferred in Table 3 by comparison of the total numbers of males and females in the age groups. According to current survivorship patterns, there should be a small excess of males over females in age 20–24, but the table shows a deficiency of 0.9 million in 1960 and of 1.5 million in 1970. Thus, military service has played an important role, not shown in Table 4, in absorbing the excess of young adult males which occurred during the decade of the 1960s.

The balance sheet for females resembles that for males, in age 16–19, but not in age 20–24. In the younger age group there was an increase in the total number of females by 2.1 million, and 90% of that increase (1.9 million) was absorbed by an increase in enrollment. In other words, the aggregate increased by 40%, but the numbers employed increased by only 9%. In age group 20–24, on the other hand, the total number of females increased by 2.9 million but only 30% of that increase (0.9 million) was absorbed by an increase in enrollment. The aggregate increased in size by 52%, but the numbers and in the number of females in the "other" category, since an emtables is the absence of appreciable increase in the residual category for females, consisting predominantly of housewives. In age group 16–19, the total increased by 40% but the "other" category by only 8%; in age group 20–24, the total increased by 52% but the "other" category by only 10%. As will be shown below, the role of housewife (insofar as it implies motherhood) is an effective barrier to female labor force participation. In effect the increase in the proportion of young women in employment has been permitted by the decrease in the proportion of them in the housewife category.

To summarize the evidence presented in Table 4, the increase in the numbers of male youth during the 1960s was absorbed to a very large degree by increases in school enrollment and military service, rather than by employment. The same was true of the females below age 20, but not in age group 20–24. There is an obvious connection between the small increases in the number of males employed and in the number of females in the "other" category, since an employed husband is an important precondition for motherhood. The educational institutions have so far borne the brunt of the unique demographic expansion in the 1960s. Accordingly the general sense of dissatisfaction with the outcome of the socialization experience needs to be mitigated by a substantial allowance for the magnitude of the task imposed on the socializers. In the next decade the main thrust of numerical expansion will be transferred, by the ineluctable process of aging, from the school to the labor force.

An increase in cohort size of the dimensions we have just experienced has substantial consequences which reveal themselves most vividly at the major transition points in life. On the material side, movement of the large cohorts into the educational system calls for expansion in the number of schools, the number of rooms per school, and the number of pupils per room, together with all the associated paraphernalia of education. If, as is likely, public expenditure in this sector lags behind the demand, and is less than proportional to the need, the process of education becomes materially impoverished. The same is true with respect to the agents of socialization. Accompanying a decline in the ratio of parents to children is a decline in the ratio of teachers to students. Should this occur concurrently with social change, the problem of transmission of the culture is exacerbated. Social change ordinarily implies an increase in the complexity of the culture, indeed in its sheer magnitude, and probably also in the extent of moral ambiguities. If parents and teachers are quantitatively inadequate to meet the dual challenge of social change and increased cohort size, this does not mean that the socialization process halts, but rather that a disproportionate share in the process will be assumed by the contemporaries themselves. The consequence is likely to involve autonomous directions of development, uncontrolled by adults. Some of these directions may be regarded with bemusement and others with dismay, but they will in any event differ from what would be chosen by adults were they adequate in numbers and resources to maintain charge of the situation.

The process of socialization does not cease with departure from school; in the most general sense it continues throughout the whole of life. The next transition to feel the impact of the large cohort is the labor market. New positions in the labor force are only tenuously connected with the numbers of new applicants. In order that productivity not lag, each new worker must be equipped with the equivalent of the prevailing amount of physical capital per head, in the line of work in question. Finally, there is a decline in the ratio of somewhat older to somewhat younger employees, with a comparable crisis concerning the transmission of those aspects of the culture relevant to the occupation. And again, the context in which this transitory disproportion in number of juniors relative to number of seniors occurs is likely to be one of substantial technological change, a challenging problem even when not magnified by a demographic upsurge.

Yet it is important for us not to be so distracted by this immediate problem of absorption of a large cohort—impressive though the dimensions may be—that we ignore the implications of the long-term trend in the opposite direction. The future decline in the ratio of age group 14–24 to age group 25–64 offers an opportunity to expend even more resources per person in the socialization process. One of the reasons we have been able to solve the problem of expansion of cohort size by lengthening the socialization period is that our productivity makes us rich in time. We no longer need the work of youth, any more than we need the work of the old or the work of women. But to say that the society can afford the luxury of adolescence is not to say that the adolescents can afford it, any more than old or the women. In a society in which work gives meaning to life, obligatory idleness may be a curse rather than a privilege.

Enrollment, Employment and Family Status

One common tendency in considering the problems of youth is to focus on the transition from enrollment in school to employment in the labor force. The former is viewed as preparation for the latter, and the movement between them signals the change from child into adult, at least insofar as that is identified with the change from a state of economic dependence to a state of economic independence. But the process of becoming an adult is more complex than that. One dimension in particular deserves separate attention: status as a family member. A typical sequence is that a person is first a member of the junior generation in his or her family of orientation, next an individual living apart from relatives or with a spouse but no children, and finally a member of the senior generation in his or her family of procreation. The intermediate status may be bypassed altogether; it may also be a terminal status. These changes in family status are closely related to but not identical with the achievement of economic independence.

One characteristic of the change in family status of considerable relevance for our present concerns is that it signals the achievement of maturity as measured by the assumption of responsibility for the wellbeing of another. The conventional definition of economic independence requires provision for the wellbeing of oneself. Marriage, on the other hand, signals the acceptance of responsibility and concern for the welfare of the spouse; parenthood obligates one to accept responsibility for the welfare of the child. Since the family institution is predicated on role differentiation by sex, it is not surprising that the transition in activity patterns with respect to family status, in relation to school enrollment and labor force participation, should vary considerably between males and females.

Table 5 shows in detail by age the extent of participation of the two sexes in the activities of school and labor force. For both sexes, the major transition in school enrollment occurs between ages 16–17 and 18–19, but there is no such clarity with respect to labor force participation, in large part because of the prevalence of part-time work for those whose major activity is education. One major difference between male and female activity is evident in the category "proportion in neither." The Bureau of the Census defines these people as housewives, retired workers, seasonal workers in an off season who are not looking for work, or persons who cannot work because of long-term illness or disability. Clealy the major source of differentiation by sex in these ages is the category of housewife.

TABLE 5—Proportion (per thousand) enrolled in school, participating in the labor force, or neither, by age and sex, October 1970.
(Civilian noninstitutional population)

| | Proportion Enrolled | | Proportion in Labor Force | | Proportion in Neither | |
	Male	Female	Male	Female	Male	Female
14–15 ··········	982	980	180	148	011	017
16–17 ··········	913	886	421	343	021	068
18–19 ··········	544	416	619	529	061	212
20–21 ··········	427	236	716	586	042	284
22–24 ··········	212	094	882	586	035	377

SOURCE: See Source for Table 4, Table A.

Table 6 indicates the extent of overlap of the categories of school enrollment and labor force participation. There are several noteworthy points in this table. In the first place, the differences by sex are small. In the second place, the likelihood that a person in the labor force will also be in school decreases even more markedly with age. In our judgment, part-time participation in the labor force, for those enrolled in school, is much more likely than part-time enrollment, for those in the labor force. Accordingly, in the subsequent presentation, we classify by major activity those who are both enrolled and in

TABLE 6—For those enrolled in school, the proportion (per thousand) in the labor force; and for those in the labor force, the proportion (per thousand) enrolled in school.

| | Of those enrolled proportion in labor force | | Of those in labor force proportion enrolled | |
	Male	Female	Male	Female
14–15	176	149	960	983
16–17	389	335	843	864
18–19	412	377	362	297
20–21	433	448	258	180
22–24	609	601	147	097

SOURCE: See Source for Table 5.

the labor force as enrolled in school. Table 6 is a reminder of the arbitrariness of this coding decision.

Table 7 gives a sense of the recent trends in major activity of youth. In the past decade there has been a marked increase in the proportion enrolled, particularly for the male. The proportion in the labor force (other than those who are also enrolled in school) has declined appreciably for the male, but increased appreciably for the female, as indicated in the preceding section. The explanation of the increase in both enrollment and labor force participation for females is implicit in Table 7. The marked decline, during the decade, in the category "proportion in neither" is almost certainly a decline in the housewife category.

Tables 8 and 9 show in more detail the interdependence of marital status and activity. Unfortunately, these data are available in the necessary cross-tabulations only for 1960, at the time of writing, but they suffice to establish the basic outlines of sex differentiation in these respects.

TABLE 7—Distribution by major activity, 1960 and 1970. By age and sex.

| | Proportion Enrolled | | Proportion in Labor Force | | Proportion in Neither | |
Male	1960	1970	1960	1970	1960	1970
16–19	658	742	269	219	073	039
20–21	258	426	679	532	063	042
22–24	152	212	797	752	051	036
Female						
16–19	608	658	193	205	199	137
20–21	166	236	415	480	419	284
22–24	053	094	400	529	547	377

SOURCE: See Source for Table 4.

TABLE 8—Distribution by marital status (per thousand). By age and sex, 1960.

		Male	Female
16–19	Unmarried	964	837
	Married, no children	020	077
	Married, children	016	086
20–21	Unmarried	734	479
	Married, no children	114	166
	Married, children	147	355
22–24	Unmarried	480	284
	Married, no children	161	154
	Married, children	359	562

SOURCE: U.S. Bureau of the Census. *U.S. Census of Population: 1960. Subject Reports. School Enrollment.* Final Report PC(2)–5A. U.S. Government Printing Office, Washington, D.C., 1966. Table 8.

The primary purpose of Table 8 is to provide perspective on the data to be presented in Table 9. Nevertheless, it is abundantly clear that, to the extent that assumption of the role of parent is a definitive test of the achievement of adulthood, the passage of the female into this category occurs much earlier than that of the male.

Table 9 shows the distribution by major activity of the three marital status categories identified in Table 8, following the same format for major activity utilized in Table 7. The movement out of school enrollment coincides with the movement from unmarried to married (no child), for both males and females. For males the movement is predominantly into the labor force; for females the destination is divided in labor force and "neither." Beyond age 20, there is little

TABLE 9—Distribution (per thousand) of marital status categories by major activity. By age and sex, 1960.

	Male			Female		
	Unmarried	Married		Unmarried	Married	
		No child	Children		No child	Children
16–19						
Enrolled	677	160	135	706	128	080
Other labor force	249	821	836	184	351	139
Neither	074	019	029	110	521	781
20–21						
Enrolled	314	132	080	301	072	029
Other labor force	607	854	901	533	559	184
Neither	079	014	019	166	369	787
22–24						
Enrolled	205	159	077	120	049	021
Other labor force	704	828	904	660	638	198
Neither	091	013	019	220	313	781

SOURCE: See Source for Table 8.

difference in labor force participation for the unmarried and married female, provided there are no children; the same is not true for males. The presence of children, on the other hand, increases the probability that the male will be in the labor force, but sharply reduces the probability that the female will be in the labor force. This is merely statistical documentation of the obvious role differentiation by sex in our society.

The proportion of females, unmarried, who are neither enrolled in school nor in the labor force is substantial at every age, and grows from 11% in ages 16–19 to 17% in ages 20–21 and to 22% in ages 22–24. There are two likely explanations for this. In the first place, females are more likely than males to be "employed" in supportive roles with respect to their family orientation, as essentially unpaid family help. In addition, we note that the category "unmarried" should more properly be labeled "not in the category, married with spouse present." A substantial and growing proportion of this group, although currently unmarried, has been married. For age groups 16–19, 20–21, and 22–24, the proportions of the currently unmarried who are ever-married are 4%, 14%, and 26% respectively (Current Population Reports, P–20, No. 159, for March, 1960). The inference is that a substantial proportion of these women (even though without spouse) are also performing a familial role, because of the presence of children. Unfortunately the available data do not permit us to identify this group more precisely.

The point of this demonstration has been the sharp distinction between the sexes occasioned by the interdependence of marital status and major activity, on the one hand, and the differentiation of roles by sex, on the other. No account of the movement into adulthood can be complete without consideration of the implications of parenthood. In considering the requisites for adequate socialization, this has equal importance with the acquisition of marketable skills for participation in the labor force.

The final table to be presented in this section concerns the interdependence of educational level and age at marriage. There are several points of interest in Table 10 with respect to sex differentiation. First is the obvious difference between male and female age at marriage, 1.79 years. (This difference has been attenuated by the truncation of ages at marriage at 25.0, a necessary step because of the interest in focusing on recent nuptiality experience, without introducing demographic bias). Second, the range of differences by educational level is 1.73 years for males but 3.90 for females. In other words, there is a much closer relationship between age of school termination and age of marriage initiation for females than for males.

Third, the sharpest contrasts between male and female education differentials in median age at marriage occur between those who do and those who do not complete each educational level. The difference is small for elementary school (0.28 for males and 0.34 for females) ; it is very large for high school (0.41 for males but 1.47 for females) ; it is also very large for college (0.58 for males and 1.36 for females). The implication of these contrasts is that, for females, the principal reason for not completing the school level in which enrolled is the intervening event of marriage. In short, it appears that for females, marriage intervenes to terminate enrollment, rather than that enrollment is terminated and then marriage follows. For males, on the other hand, the decision to terminate enrollment does not seem to be related significantly to the event of marriage. This, then, is one further piece of evidence that male activity is dominated by the move from school into the labor force, whereas female activity is dominated by entry into motherhood.

TABLE 10—Median age at Marriage for those married by age 25, by school years completed. For those aged 25–34, 1960.

Years completed	Male	Female
7 or less	20.93	18.46
8	21.21	18.80
11 or less	21.27	18.66
12	21.68	20.13
15 or less	22.08	21.00
16 or more	22.66	22.36
TOTAL	21.64	19.85

SOURCE: U.S. Bureau of the Census. *U.S. Census of Population: 1960. Subject Reports. Age at First Marriage.* Final Report PC(2)–4D. Table 9.

Trends in Marriage and Parenthood

There has been much attention to recent fertility decline in the United States. (Ryder, 1973b) The standard measure of annual fertility, in abstraction from the influence of the age distribution, is the so-called period total fertility rate, a measure of the mean number of births per woman in a synthetic cohort experiencing in each age the fertility rate observed for that age in the particular period. The total fertility rate was 3.7 in 1957; by 1972 it had declined to 2.1. Two kinds of behavior change have contributed to that decline. In the first place, it is apparent that there has been a substantial reduction in the eventual number of births to be borne by real cohorts of women; current estimates suggest that the cohort whose childbearing was centered in the late 1950s will end up with an average of about 3.3 births, whereas the cohort whose childbearing is centered in the early 1970s may end up with an average as low as 2.3 births per woman. The rest of the decline in the period total fertility rate has been contributed by a reversal of the direction of change in the time pattern of childbearing. During the late 1950s, successive cohorts were experiencing fertility at progressively earlier ages, inflating the period total fertility rate above its underlying real cohort value; during the early 1970s, fertility was occurring at progressively later ages, depressing the period total fertility rate below its underlying value.

Changes in the overall level of fertility and changes in the time pattern of childbearing are closely interdependent; the matrix for both is the activity pattern of youth. This section will present some data on entry into marriage and parenthood by males and females of less than age 25, with particular attention to the past decade, suggest some explanations for the trends, and some speculations about the future in terms relevant for the passage from childhood to adulthood.

Table 11 shows the median age at first marriage, 1890–1970. There is an pronounced disjuncture in the time series for both sexes, coinciding with the 1940/1950 decade. Prior to that decade, the male age at marriage had not changed appreciably. In consequence the difference between the male and the female ages at marriage had been reduced from more than four years to less than three years. Part of the explanation for that pattern of change was the existence of a surplus of males in the marriageable ages at the beginning of the series, because they were disproportionately represented among immigrants. A surplus of males tends to elevate the male age at marriage above and depress the female age at marriage below what would prevail in the absence

TABLE 11—Median age at first marriage, by sex. 1890–1970.

Year	Male	Female
1890	26.1	22.0
1900	25.9	21.9
1910	25.1	21.6
1920	24.6	21.2
1930	24.3	21.3
1940	24.3	21.5
1950	22.8	20.3
1960	22.8	20.3
1970	23.2	20.8

SOURCE: U.S. Bureau of the Census, *Current Population Reports*, Series P–20, No. 212, "Marital Status and Family Status: March 1970," U.S. Government Printing Office, Washington, D.C., 1971. Table A.

of a male surplus. As the migratory flow declined, so did the male surplus, and the median ages at marriages by sex converged.

The disjuncture between the median ages at marriage for 1940 and those for 1950 is only partly explained by the circumstance that the earlier figure reflected substantial postponement of marriage because of the depression of the 1930s. Social scientists had expected a trend upward rather than downward in the marriage age, primarily because of the increase in years of schooling and the advancement in age at entry into the labor force, together with the impression that the interests of individuals were gradually increasing in importance for decision-making, relative to the interests of families. This compelling logic was obviously contradicted by postwar evidence.

Part of the explanation for the pattern of early marriage age during the 1950s derives from peculiarities of the period. Since the cohorts then coming of age were smaller in number of members and better education than their predecessors, they were sooner able to achieve the economic position considered necessary for assuming marital responsibility, and they were even assisted in marrying before and in anticipation of that time by the increased availability of credit, particularly from the federal government. But there were powerful underlying developments as well, which were probably on balance more important, and deserve special attention because of their continuing relevance. First, there is the well-known trend toward earlier biological maturation, as indexed by the persistent decline in the mean age at menarche. Second, our society has a very strong norm of marriage as virtually an obligatory state for the adult, as soon as it can be afforded. Accordingly, an upward trend in income should lead to a downward trend in marriage age. Third, American society has been populated by diverse subcultures, each of which represented, for a time, a relatively closed marriage system. Progressively with time, this "nation of nations" has been developing a single culture, with declining heterogeneity on the one hand, and declining importance, in the choice of marriage partners, of ascriptive relative to achieved characteristics, on the other hand. This has in effect enlarged the marriage market and increased the probability that any individual will marry. Finally it may be suggested that even the increase in years of schooling has worked in favor of more and earlier marriage. So long as the normal age of leaving school was younger than the age for initiating mating activities, enrollment was largely irrelevant to marriage. But now essentially all boys and girls remain in school until they are 18. Of the many functions performed by the American high school, one of the most significant latent ones may be its role as a marriage market. The high school gathers nubile males and females

in substantial and equal numbers, residentially selected for social homogeneity, and exposes each sex to the other on an age-graded basis for
long periods in a variety of contexts. While it is certainly the
case, cross-sectionally, as shown in Table 10, that more schooling
means later marriage, it is not clear which is cause and which effect,
and it would in any event be invalid to infer a longitudinal relationship from this crosss-sectional evidence.

TABLE 12—Proportion (per thousand) ever-married, by age and sex, 1960 and 1971.

	Male		Female	
	1960	1971	1960	1971
14–17	010	007	054	027
18	054	044	244	167
19	129	115	403	292
20	242	192	540	420
21	366	342	654	534
22	484	414	744	658
23	595	544	806	761
24	666	670	843	784

SOURCE: U.S. Bureau of the Census, *Current Population Reports*, Series P–20,
No. 225, "Marital Status and Living Arrangements: March, 1971," U.S.
Government Printing Office, Washington, D.C., 1971, Table B.

In the past decade there has been a reversal of nuptiality trends,
as shown in Table 12. With one exception (for males age 24), the
decline in nuptiality has characterized every age of males and females,
and that exception is probably attributable to a statistical defect in
the sample data on which the comparison is based. The reduction in
the proportion of persons ever-married has been much more pronounced for females than for males. Some attention has been paid in
the literature to one demographic circumstance which might differentially affect male and female nuptiality; the hypothesis has been
advanced that, when cohort size is increasing rapidly (as has been the
case for these ages during the past decade), the fact that younger
girls (from later cohorts) tend to marry older boys (from earlier cohorts) will disadvantage the former in the marriage market, and advantage the latter. This helps to explain the discrepancy in amount
of decline, male and female, but is insufficient to account for the
general movement. The most important implication of rising cohort
size for nuptiality is probably that the increasing difficulty of assimila-
tion of larger cohorts into adult life is manifested in a delay of their
marriage date. In addition to this, a major role has been played
by the advent of modern contraceptives, specifically the pill and

the intra-uterine device. Since early marriage is frequently provoked by conception, increased use of effective contraception is likely to raise the age at marriage. In the last several years legalized abortion in some states may have been playing a similar role.

As pointed out in the preceding section, the distribution of females by major activity is most strongly influenced not by marriage but by motherhood. This influence is illustrated in Table 13. This table shows the cumulative proportions of young women who had achieved the status of parent by each birthday in the age range of our youth group. The data are shown for four birth cohorts of women, at 15-year intervals, selected to represent four distinct reproductive patterns represented in twentieth-century American fertility. The years corresponding to the respective age spans are: 1916–26 (pre-depression); 1931–41 (depression); 1946–56 (postwar); 1961–71 (current). As a convenient index of the information in this table, we can calculate the mean number of years of motherhood per cohort, prior to the 25th birthday (found simply by adding the proportions for each cohort). The result is 2.8 years for the pre-depression cohort, 2.3 years for the depression cohort, 3.5 years for the postwar cohort, and 3.1 years for the current cohort. This outcome is the combined consequence of the probability of eventually having a first birth (which was approxi-

TABLE 13—Proportion (per thousand) with at least one live birth, by age, for four selected female birth cohorts.

By exact age	Cohort 1902	Cohort 1917	Cohort 1932	Cohort 1947
15	003	003	003	004
16	010	010	014	015
17	031	028	045	042
18	067	066	103	091
19	143	125	184	163
20	242	192	292	258
21	232	260	396	348
22	396	327	494	431
23	466	386	583	513
24	526	443	660	580
25	576	499	721	630

SOURCE: The experience for years 1917–57 inclusive is reported in: Whelpton, Pascal K., and Arthur A. Campbell, "Fertility Tables for Birth Cohorts of American Women, Part I, "National Office of Vital Statistics, *Vital Statistics—Special Reports,* Vol. 51, No. 1, January 29, 1960. An extension of these tables for years 1958–64 inclusive is contained in the 1964 edition of *Vital Statistics of the United States (Natality).* Subsequent data for each of the years 1965–68 are contained in the comparable volumes of vital statistics for the years in question. The writer has estimated data for years 1969–71 on the basis of preliminary reports of crude and age-specific birth rates.

mately 80% for the first two cohorts and approximately 90% for the last two cohorts) and the average age at first birth for those who eventually have a first birth. These are not in fact separate phenomena, but different facets of the same phenomenon, because delay of entry into motherhood is causally related to non-entry, biologically by the accrual of impairments to fecundity and sociopsychologically by the experience with alternatives to parenthood.

What the table tells us then is that young women are having substantially more experience with motherhood, prior to age 25, than was the case a generation ago, even though there has recently been a small decline. This observation is in distinct contrast to our other commonly used indices of entry into adulthood—age of leaving school, and age of entry into the labor force—both of which have risen substantially over the course of the twentieth century. There has simultaneously been a lengthening of the period of preparation for an occupation, and a shortening of the period of preparation for family formation. This raises the question of the relative priorities to be assigned to different measures of maturity, in attempting to answer the question of whether the entry into adulthood is later or earlier than it was formerly. Entry into the labor force can be identified with financial autonomy, i.e., with assumption of the responsibility of providing the wherewithal to meet one's obligations for oneself. Marriage carries with it the connotation of a long-term diffuse commitment to another person of the same generation, and ordinarily the assumption of the joint responsibilities of maintaining a separate household. In our view, the definitive step into adulthood comes with parenthood—the assumption of an essentially irreversible diffuse commitment to the support of another who will remain in a dependency status for a long time. At the very least, the contrast between later entry into economic adulthood and earlier entry into familial adulthood is a vital component in the understanding of the present state of American youth.

Conclusion

The purposes of this essentially descriptive account of the demography of youth have been (1) to identify the uniqueness of the size of the youth group in the past decade, in contrast to both the previous history and the likely future; (2) to examine the interdependence of school enrollment and labor force participation on the one hand with family status on the other; (3) to identify the distinctive characteristics of the passage of the female from childhood into adulthood; and (4) to describe and explain recent changes in the reproductive behavior of the young.

Although there are many sources of data of relevance to the statistical appraisal of youth, there remain serious deficiencies in their useful-ness for analysis. One problem is that each of the interdependent strands of experience receives particular attention by specialists in the activity concerned (such as education, or labor force participation, or nuptiality and fertility) to the hindrance of their joint considera-tion. A second problem is that the behavior patterns change rapidly with age and with time and therefore require, for effective study from a methodological standpoint, data collection on a longitudinal rather than cross-sectional basis. A third problem is that individuals who are experiencing status change (and that is the outstanding characteristic of youth) are by virtue of that fact the most difficult to capture statis-tically by means of conventional sample surveys.

Every society uses the vehicle of the new young adult cohort of males and females to write its future history. Therefore wise policy dictates a systematic program of longitudinal data collection of the status changes of successive cohorts of young men and women.

4. Economic Problems of Youth

Some of the major decisions facing young men and women are how much to study and what, whether to work full or part time and what job and where, whether to get married and to whom, when to leave home, and where to go. All of these decisions are subject to serious constraints imposed on the individual by his family's economic re-sources, his own talents and abilities, the institutional setting of the choices open to him, and the information on alternatives available to him. The decisions he or she will make during this period, and the decisions of his or her family, will have long-range consequences for "success" in later life. Unfortunately, these decisions are usually made in the face of some ignorance about one's own talents, about the accessible range of options, and in the face of significant uncertainty about the future state of the world. The character of the problems facing youth changes significantly with age. With 16 as the currently first acceptable age of leaving school (legally and socially), the economic decisions of the 14- to 16-year-olds have mostly to do with the alloca-tion of time within schools and with the problem of access to consump-tion goods. The 16- to 18-year-olds make a major decision as to whether or not to continue education, what kind to pursue, where to pursue it, and how to finance it. Those who do not continue formal schooling have to find jobs and search for jobs with better future prospects. Beginning with age 16 there is a continuing tug between the question of continuing schooling or starting work and gaining more complete independence from the family. Sex, marriage, and the start of family formation all interact significantly with these choices and affect their outcome.

Figure 1 illustrates this pattern of transition from school to work for young males as of 1971. Almost all (over 97%) of 14- to 16-year-olds were still in school in 1971. About a quarter of those in school were working, mostly part-time, in services, sales, and casual labor. The big transition to work starts around the age of 17 and is largely completed by age 24, with more than 80% of the youths at that age out of school and more than 90% of those out of school working or serving in the Armed Forces.[1] This transition is not abrupt, however: those that do stay longer in the school system participate increasingly in the labor force, the fraction employed (for those in school) rising from about a third at age 16–17 to over half at age 22–24. Graduate education prolongs this transition past the age of 25 for about a tenth of the total cohort, but for the vast majority the transition to full-time work status and more or less economic independence is completed by age 24.

Young women follow a similar pattern except that they terminate schooling at a somewhat faster rate after age 16, moving into marriage earlier, and into out-of-house employment at a slower rate than young men of the same age. For young women, "keeping house" represents an important alternative employment pattern, with about a sixth of the 18- to 19-year-old and a third of the 20- to 24-year-old women engaged in it.[2]

The 14- to 17-year-old youth is dependent on his family for most of his consumption needs. His major activity is schooling and the type and quality of schooling that he or she receives is to a large extent out of his control. Major intrafamily conflicts occur around these two issues—consumption and schooling. The first involves the question of the intrafamily allocation of resources to the consumption of its individual members. To the extent that these resources are limited and the tastes of the younger and older generation diverge, the usual approach of economists—to treat the family as a single decision unit with common tastes—fails to reflect the actual situation adequately.

---

[1] About 1/5 of the recent male youth cohorts served in the Armed Forces, though the influence of the draft on the status of youth and the choices open to them was much more pervasive than this percentage would indicate.

[2] See Part 2-3, The Demography of Youth, for more detail on transition patterns of women.

Some of the consumption issues are solved by the youths finding part-time work and financing themselves the "supernumerary" aspects of consumption (such as clothes, records, and entertainment). About half of the youths of this age engage in part-time work.[3] While there seems to be little data on the topic, it is doubtful whether more than a small fraction of them contribute much of their earnings directly to the total family resource pool.[4]

Work also serves as an important source of acquiring experience and training on the job, provides exposure to the world outside the schoolroom and the neighborhood, and initiates the process which will ultimately lead to the youth's independence. Work opportunities for the young have been limited by a variety of institutional arrangements, child labor laws, and by rising minimum-wage rate levels which make the employment of unexperienced and untrained workers uneconomic to employers. Job opportunities for the young have grown in line with the growth in their numbers but largely in the part-time, non career-ladder type of job. Between 1960 and 1970 all of the increase in the employment of 16 to 19 year olds occurred in the "in school" category, reflecting the continued rise in the school leaving age of the successive cohorts. By staying longer in school, entry into the full-time labor force was being postponed for growing numbers of youths, limiting their work experience to part-time and casual work.

Whether part-time work has any effect (beneficial or otherwise) on performance in school is something we know almost nothing about. This is connected to our lack of a clear notion about which aspects of the schooling experience are important for "success" and what kind of "success" is socially valuable. Considering the fact that an enrolled young person spends about 30 hours or more a week in school and perhaps another 10 hours or so a week at homework, we know very little about the effectiveness with which these hours are utilized by the schooling system or by the individual himself. It is not clear how much "slack" there is in the system and whether the same goals could not be accomplished in less time.

The young person in this age bracket (14 to 16) finds himself in a school chosen for him by society or by his parents. He has little control over curriculum (expect for a selection among a limited list of elective courses), teachers, or other study arrangements. The main variable under his control is the amount of effort he himself actually puts into the whole process. The presumption is that more effort leads to addi-

---

[3] This fraction appears to be remarkably independent of total family income. See U.S. Department of Labor, Career Thresholds, Vol. 1, 1970, Table 3.6.

[4] See U.S. Department of Labor, BLS Bulletin No. 1657, 1970, Tables 7.2 and 7.3, which imply that teen-agers are not an important source of family income.

tional success. The effort is elicited by promises of future returns via success in college, jobs, and social mobility, immediate returns via grades, the intrinsic interest of the subjects studied, and direct pressure from family and teachers. Actual success depends also on the individual's intellectual ability, the home circumstances under which he has to study, and the quality of instruction that he receives. To the extent that he perceives that his additional efforts are bearing little fruit, it may be pointless for him to exert himself, in spite of all the exhortations.

The point is that the major costs of schooling are borne by the youths themselves. They are spending a large and important part of their life within the school system. Moreover, they are not passive "inputs" that are worked over by the system. The success of the education process depends on their active cooperation, which has to be elicited. In earlier periods, there was a more immediate system of rewards and punishments. With enlightenment and the decline in parental and teachers' authority, the whole rewards system has become more indirect and further in the future. It promises better opportunities of economic advancement and social mobility to the successful and threatens economic disaster to the failures. To the extent that the actual educational reality is flawed and little of real substance is learned in some schools, or to the extent that for whole groups of children the promised social mobility appears to be entirely unrealistic, there is little point for them to expend the effort that the system is trying to elicit from them.

To summarize this section, the 14- to 17-year-olds are still almost entirely dependent on their families and are constrained to spend most of their time in school. For them, and for society, the major issue is how to utilize that time more effectively. In addition, we may want to ask whether it is desirable that schools as currently constituted should play such a dominant role in this age bracket. But little is known about alternative arrangements of study and high school completion. The visible conomic choice available to this age group is participation in the part-time labor force. While it does expand the youths' horizons, most of it is casual and does not contain important training components. It serves, however, to augment the consumption budgets of the young and provides them with their first economic independence experiences, letting their consumption decisions diverge from the overall family allocation and consensus.

For the 18- to 20-year-old, the major economic decision is whether to continue with the formal educational process and what kind of education and training to pursue. The main alternatives to schooling are entry into the full-time labor force, service in the Armed Forces, and—for girls—marriage and household work. Currently, only about 4% of a cohort do not reach high school. Of those in high school, about 14% drop out beore graduation. About half of those graduating from high school will go on to college but only about 60% of these will finish it. About half of the college completers will enter postgraduate education. Thus, the years between 17 and 24 are characterized by a more or less continuous decline in the fraction of the cohort remaining with the formal educational system. Throughout this period decisions have to be made as to whether or not to continue. This decision is an investment decision on the part of the individual youth, his family, and society, and economists have found it useful to view it as such.

The decision to continue with formal schooling can be thought of as a decision to continue investing in the production of a particular kind of human capital. Roughly speaking, an individual will continue to invest if the expected returns from this activity exceed his (or his family's) opportunity costs. The returns can be thought of as a product of two components: the expectation of returns from a particular level of achievement and the probability that the particular individual will in fact succeed in attaining this level. The first is largely determined by outside market forces, and individual differences come in only via differences in knowledge about the actual state of the world. The second part is largely a function of individual experience and ability, the student's perception of how efficient he and the schooling system are in using his time, and the extent to which additional time spent within a particular framework will lead to an actual increment in his human capital. Lack of success with the system appears to be the major reason for dropping out at the high school level. Dropouts are concentrated heavily among children from poorer homes, but it appears that the most direct cause for dropping out is their perception of lack of success and the probably correct view that additional time spent on schooling would be wasted. Whether this is the fault of the school system in not finding the right approach to them or a reflection of the lack of ability on their part to pursue a particular line of study is far from clear. But from their point of view, they are probably making the right economic decision.[5]

Since only about half of the high-school graduates go on to college, it is easier to observe the impact of economic factors at this transition. College attendance is strongly related to family income, parental education, and scholastic achievement in high school. From the point of view of the individual, high family income is likely to be associated with a lower real cost of financing his education, both because

[5] See Shea and Wilkins (1971) and Bachman et al, 1971.

his parents are willing and able to spend a larger absolute amount on his education and because they can borrow at an effectively lower rate of interest. He will, therefore, (other things being equal) pursue it longer and further. To the extent that the youth and the family do not have the same valuation of the family's money, and to the extent that family transfers to him are tied to his pursuing an educational career, it may pay him to invest in schooling even if the overall rate of return is very low or even negative, as long as somebody else (the family or the state) is bearing most of the costs. In other words, since some youths are effectively "paid" to go to school, they may do so even though the process itself adds little to their productivity, and they may not spend their time as efficiently as they might have if it were their own decision and they themselves were paying for it.

That something like this may be happening is reflected in the occasional complaints about being "forced to go to school" and in the data on college attendance by social class and scholastic ability. In general, most scholastically successful youths get to college, even the poor ones. (More than two-thirds of the scholastically successful-upper quintile-young males from the lowest socioeconomic quintile go on to college versus 91% from the highest socioeconomic quintile.) What really separates the rich from the poor families is that often even the scholastically unsuccessful children of the rich go to college (about 40% of the scholastically lowest quintile) while almost no such children of the poor do so (about 10%). It appears that the well-to-do families try to buy additional schooling even for their less promising children. (See Wolfle, 1971, p. 105). Of course the big difference between rich and poor families is in the absolute number of scholastically successful children in the first place, but that is a different topic.

An important aspect of the educational process is the difference in incentives facing the various participants in it. The major input from the point of view of the student is his time. From the point of view of the school this is a costless resource, one that it has little incentive in economizing. Similarly, teachers are seldom rewarded in proportion to their success in transmitting knowledge to their students. This makes them less interested in finding new and better ways of teaching. Particularly at the college level, neither the student nor his family is paying all the cost of the student's education, while the college does not collect directly the returns for its successful teaching. Thus the different participants have different views about what they are paying, receiving, or delivering. Given the lack of a good market in such educational services (although there is some competition between colleges, and families do shop around at bit at this level), there is no reason to expect that resources (the school's plant and the time of teachers and students) will be used efficiently in this industry.

A growing body of evidence shows young persons to be responsive to economic incentives in a wide variety of educational and work decisions.[6] For roughly comparable decisions, it suggests a greater responsiveness relative to the rest of the population on the part of the young. There are two reasons for this. First, the young represent "new investment" in human capital while older persons, with initial investment decisions behind them and fewer years to reap benefits from further investments, are a relatively fixed stock of existing human capital. In an important sense, for occupational and training decisions, only the behavior of the young reflects the economic present, providing a mechanism for the "long run" to adjust to existing conditions. Second, for such decisions as participation in the labor force and the allocation of hours to work, the fact that relatively fewer of the young work full time creates a larger buffer population for adjustment, allowing the labor force to expand and contract in response to current economic conditions.

While recent economic studies of career decisions have focused largely on college students, the results are still of value in analyzing the decisions of youths in general. The chief findings of empirical work:

1. Young persons are very responsive to economic opportunities in alternative careers with, for example, the proportion of college freshmen enrolling in engineering closely linked to salaries and job opportunities.

2. In fields with long training ladders, the relative number completing programs also responds to incentives, the frequency of dropping out rising when long term prospects worsen.

3. Scholarships, fellowships and related subsidies influence decisions to the same extent as salaries, when both are measured in discounted dollars.

4. The training requirement for skilled work creates a 'recursive market structure' in which students enter the labor market several years after making their career decision on the basis of market information available then. Such a structure often produces 'cobweb cycles'—ups-and-downs in entrants and salaries—and the potentiality of serious post factum errors in decisions, when market conditions change drastically (vide the United States science market in the past few years).

5. Both at the college and high school levels, students appear to have "reasonably good" information about opportunities and realistic wage expectations, which is consistent with observed responsiveness.

---

[6] This section is based on an unpublished memorandum by R. B. Freeman.

6. Black students, perhaps because of low family income, show especially great responsiveness to changes in job opportunities, moving in recent years rapidly into 'traditionally closed' professions.

All of these findings refer to male students and all but #5 to college students. The career choices of women have yet to be seriously studied.

One disturbing index of conditions in the more general youth labor market throughout the sixties has been the rather high unemployment rate, which has actually risen in the past decade both absolutely and relative to the unemployment rate of the adult population.[7] The fact that the unemployment rate of young people is higher than that of adults is not surprising. Entry into the labor force and job-shopping during the early years of work experience are reflected in high unemployment counts. This is certainly true of the 16–19 age group and somewhat less so of the 20–24 group.

There are several additional factors which contribute to the size and growth of the unemployment rate in the young population groups. First, the number of students working seasonally (in the summer) and otherwise part time has increased greatly. The large turnover—between work and school—is associated with unemployment. As the proportion of students and of student job-searchers grows, this component of unemployment increases in importance. Indeed, about 75% of the unemployment observed in the 16–19 group is associated with entry and reentry into the labor force. Second, the young people in these age group who left school have progressively shorter work experience, since the successive cohorts graduate later. Higher unemployment is typical of less experienced workers, so growing unemployment is the statistical reflection of diminishing experience in (fixed) young age groups.

None of these factors by itself indicates a deterioration in the teenage labor market. A worsening of employment conditions should be reflected in the duration of unemployment. But the duration of youth unemployment is short (most of it is less than six weeks), and has not increased together with the rate (except in recessions).[8] Actually, the absolute amount of teen-age unemployment per year is less than might appear from the teen-age unemployment rate (see Hall, 1972). Since teen-agers spend relatively few weeks in the labor force, their rate of unemployment is high because they spend a large fraction of the time that they are in the labor force looking for work. On the other hand, some of the worsening of teen-age labor market conditions

---

[7] This section is based on an unpublished memorandum by J. Mincer.

[8] The probability of leaving the unemployed status is significantly higher (hence the duration of unemployment lower) for 18-year-olds than for adults. Moreover, a recent study (Perry, 1972) shows that this has changed little over time. Young people find jobs about as fast as they did sixteen years ago, but they look for work up to 60% more often.

may not show up as an increase in the duration of unemployment to the extent that lack of success results in dropping out of the labor force back to school or to other activities not in the labor market.

One factor which adversely affects the condition of young inexperienced workers in the labor market is the upward trend in minimum wages relative to the existing wage distribution. Most 16- to 19-year-olds are employed at or below minimum hourly rates.[9] Each successive hike in the minimum wage and the progressive expansion of coverage reduces employer demand for inexperienced workers.

The particularly bad effect of minimum wage hikes is that they limit the opportunities for training or learning on the job. Apprentices and informal learners must accept initially low-paying jobs—their lower wages reflect not only lower productivity but also the costs of training which the firms provide, formally or informally. The minimum wage blocks this route to advancement and forces a detour via more school learning, at best.

Not all of those prevented from job experience at young ages stay longer at school. According to empirical analysis of minimum wage effects, the labor force participation rate of nonstudents has also been adversely affected. What happens to the double dropouts (out of the school and out of work) may be guessed, but is not well documented.

The increasing tendency of bypassing relatively unskilled work experience via schooling is, of course, strengthened by the growth of public subsidies to universal schooling at progressively higher levels. The minimum wage hikes (and draft policies in the recent past) are additional factors producing a growing number of reluctant students. To some extent the growth of a (largely seasonal) student labor force represents an attempt to overcome the growing confinement of youth to schooling and the growing postponement of economic and personal independence.

Trends, Symptoms, and Projections

The major visible changes in the economic conditions of youth have been the increase in the fraction of youths staying on longer within the schooling system and a rise in the already high teen-age unemployment rate. What is perhaps less well known is the relationship between these changes and the demographic changes of recent years. Between 1960 and 1970 the proportion of the population between 14 and 24

---

[9] In 1969, more than half of employed men between 16 to 19 years of age were earning less than $1.75 per hour and about 40% were earning $1.50 or less an hour. (See U.S. Department of Labor, Special Labor Force Report No. 132, 1971, Table 1.

jumped from 15% to 20% after declining for over 50 years. In absolute numbers the youth population grew by 50% in the sixties (from 27 million in 1960 to 42 million in 1971) .[10]

The cohort size (in the 16-to-19 bracket), which had fluctuated around 2.3 million per single age year between 1929 and 1957, started growing in the late fifties, reaching 3 million in 1963 and hitting the 4 million mark in 1972, at which level it will stabilize for the next 10 years or so. These changes in the youth population, and the associated changes in the supply of youth labor, far dwarf any changes in industrial structure or technology that would alter, *ceteris paribus,* the demand for young workers. Though additional study is needed, it appears that whatever youth labor market problems have been encountered recently resulted largely from the extraordinary shift on the supply side.

While there has been a significant increase in the youth labor force, primarily via an increase in the participation rate of students, the crest of the wave has only now begun to reach the full-time, education-completed labor market and will be inundating it in the years to come. Until now, much of this wave had been deflected and delayed by an increase in the number of youths staying on within the educational system and an increase in the duration of their stay there. For example, while the population of 16- to 19-year-olds increased between 1957 and 1970 by 6 million, the "not enrolled in school" labor force component of this age group increased by only 0.6 million. Similarly, in the 20–24 age group, which increased by 6.5 million between 1960 and 1970, the "not enrolled" labor force increased by only 2 million in the same period.[11]

This process has been and will be accompanied by a significant rise in the absolute number of highly educated young people entering the full-time labor force. In 1950 there were less than a million college graduates in the 25–29 age bracket. Between 1950 and 1960 the number of college graduates in this age category grew by 40% but the absolute numbers remained relatively small (1.2 million in 1960). Between 1960 and 1971 the number of young college graduates doubled (to 2.4 million). It is now projected that their numbers will continue to grow rapidly in the next 15 years, reaching 3.2 million in

---

[10] See Chapter 2–3, The Demography of Youth, for more detail on demographic trends.

[11] Another way of looking at it is to compute the changes in the young labor force in terms of "full-time equivalents," allowing for changes in the number of hours per week and number of weeks per year worked by them. Thus, for example, while the population of young males age 18–19 grew by about 1.1 million between 1960 and 1970, the full-time equivalent labor force grew only by 0.1 million in this age group. (Data from Amacher and Freeman, 1972).

1975, 4.0 in 1980, and 4.9 in 1985.[12] Between 1964 and 1975 the absolute number of college graduates in the 25–29 age group will have grown by 1.8 million (from 1.4 to 3.2) .

Until recently, however, the impact of this growth in higher education on the labor force was delayed because of the large expansion in graduate education. At the B.A. level, the absolute number of new entrants into the labor force did not change significantly between 1952 and 1968, hovering around 110,000 per year, while the total number of new B.A. degrees awarded annually was reaching the 400,000 mark. The difference was largely being siphoned off into graduate education. Since 1968, the number of new entrants with B.A.'s has risen sharply, while the number of new entrants with Ph.D.'s has begun accelerating already in the early 1960s, rising from about 8,000 per year in the mid-1950s, to 11,000 in 1963, 23,000 in 1969, and 32,000 in 1972, and it is projected to reach the rate of 43 thousands per year by 1975.[13] It is not clear where the growth in demand for these highly educated young people will come from.

The trend toward more education started much earlier. It was fed by the rising incomes of parents, which led them to spend more on their children, and the rising opportunity cost of time, which led them to allocate a major share of these increased expenditures on improving the quality of their children's lives rather than the quantity of their children. There are diminishing returns to the intensity of investment in education: it costs more than double in real terms to cram two years of schooling into one. This has led perforce to a prolongation of the time spent in school by children. It is also likely that higher incomes have led parents to the buying of more "dependence" of their children on them, by subsidizing longer periods of their stay in school. These trends have also been fed by the expansion of various public-supported schooling opportunities and subsidies (the G. I. Bill and the expansion of state universities) which reduced or attenuated the rise in the real cost of schooling to these families. In addition, and perhaps most importantly, these decisions and trends were validated by the perceived and actually realized relatively high rates of return to high school completion and college attendance. The importance of additional education both in terms of its economic return and its effect on social mobility was underlined by the use that was made of it for upward social mobility by several visible groups (e.g., the Jews) in the society.

The trend towards more education was reinforced by the persistence of these high rates of return to higher schooling in the face of a con-

---

[12] See Current Population Reports, Series P–25, No. 476, 1972.

[13] See Amacher and Freeman (1972), Table 10, and U.S. Department of Health, Education, and Welfare (1971), p. 43.

tinuing expansion in the number of educated people. What was perhaps not realized at the time is that the persistence of these high rates of return was based on a constellation of events that may prove rather temporary. The higher education boom was sustained by at least three sources:

1. The first round of cohorts to be educated after World War II were relatively small and a stable fraction of the adult population. (Between 1940 and 1960 the 25- to 29-year-old college graduates constituted only about 1% of the total 25- to 64-year-old population.)

2. The demographic wave of the post World War II baby boom came along in the fifties and early sixties and increased greatly the demand for teachers at all levels.

3. At about the same time the government superimposed on all of this a space-defense-R&D boom, resulting in a scramble for young, educated talent.

All of the above combined to sustain the rates of return to education during the 1950s and into the middle 1960s in spite of the rising numbers of educated workers.

Unfortunately, these fortuitous influences have probably run their course. The educational system may have come close to reaching its equilibrium level of primary and secondary teachers for the next 10 years or so. Given that most of the current stock of teachers is quite young, the gross-investment demand from this source may approach zero in the near future. At the college level some expansion is still projected but it may not materialize if the current budget squeeze continues and enrollment rates actually turn down in response to the projected market conditions. At the same time, for the next five years or so, an annual wave of about a million additional highly educated workers will be arriving at the doors of the full-time labor force. If the R&D boom does not get going again and the educational system does not move to some new highly intensive way of dealing with disadvantaged children, the outlook is rather bleak. It is quite probable that the rates of return to education will fall, perhaps even sharply, and they may have already started falling.[14] This will lead to a new problem, a problem with which the United States has had little experience, the existence of a relatively large group of highly educated but underemployed and disappointed young people.

[14] Starting salaries of college graduates have been essentially flat in the 1970–72 period while the wages of production workers have been going up at about 6% per year (Amacher and Freeman, 1972, Table 13). The median usual weekly earnings of 16- to 24-year-old males *fell* by about 12% between 1967 and 1971 relative to the earnings of those aged 25 years and over. (See Special Labor Force Reports, No. 143), Table 2, 1972).

5. *Current Educational Institutions*

All social systems contain incidental occasions for learning. We instruct one another informally and learn something new as we raise a family, earn a living, minister a church, nurse the ill, encounter friends, govern a group, or communicate through a mass medium. The institutions we call educational are those designed to separate instruction from other activities, transforming the incidental into concentrated effort. Teaching becomes specialized work and learning takes the form of systematic participation that is socially separated in a student role and assembled in a particular organizational place. If at one time such deliberate schooling was an option of society, the time has long past when it could be considered an accident of history and waved aside. Modern societies require educational institutions. But then the more important questions still remain: who will participate? what form will the educational institutions take? how will they mix with other institutions of society?

Who will participate has been answered in the modern and modernizing nations around the world in a move toward universal education of which the United States has been the foremost example. The American system has steadily changed its character from elite to mass, first at the elementary level in the nineteenth century, then at the secondary level in the first half of the twentieth century, and now in higher education in the years since World War II. This experience with expansion took place a quarter to a half-century and more ahead of the trend in other industrial societies. The American secondary school enrolled only 15% of the age group 14-to-17 in 1910 but then advanced all the way to 80% in the three decades up to 1940, while at the latter date the share of the age group caught up in secondary education was still a minority in Britain, France, and Germany. In higher education, the American system was elite at the turn of the century in that it enrolled only 4% of the age group 18-to-21, but slowly expanded to about 15% by 1940 and then leaped to over a third by 1960, while the European systems in the middle 1960s were below or just reaching the proportions found in America before World War II.[1] The countries of Western Europe moved seriously toward universal secondary education only in the 1950s and 1960s and to the edge of mass higher education only in the last several years. Thus, American

---

[1] Students enter higher education in European countries at a later age than in the United States, making 20 to 24 the more common age group for comparative statistics than the American bracket of 18 to 21. Enrollments, as percentages of that age group, were in 1965: United States, 41%; Britain, 12%; France, 17%; West Germany, 10% (Organization for Economic Cooperation, 1970: 68).

schooling has been characterized by a relatively high rate of participation that has made it the first national system to establish the secondary school as a universal framework for the experiences of early adolescence and the first several years of college as a formal setting looming evermore inclusive for later adolescence and early adulthood.

The shift to mass involvement in American educational institutions has been accompanied by a trend toward large-scale organization. We did not multiply small systems to handle larger numbers but rather have let the small grow large or have consolidated small units into large systems or have let small ones die while large ones grew larger. The trend has been encouraged by economies of scale and the advantages of specialization. The most important reform document of a decade ago—the Conant Report—pressed hard for the elimination of small high schools on the premise that they could not economically provide the specialized courses appropriate to modern expertise.[2] The trend toward largeness has long been stimulated by the influential models of effective scale provided in other institutions, particularly big business, and the derived ideologies of school administrators that emphasized management and efficiency. (Callahan, 1962) Underlying all planned adjustment has been the social realities of urbanization and population growth. The flow of people out of rural areas has eroded the small districts of the countryside, while their movement into the cities, along with the pre-1924 immigration from Europe and the post-World War II population expansion, has swelled the urban districts that had become fixed as coterminous with city boundaries. The already large became larger. At the extreme we find New York City, where a population growth from 3.5 million to 8 million between 1900 and 1950 has led to a public school system of 1 million students and 50,000 teachers. (Sheldon and Glazier, 1965)

Administrative consolidation and reorganization has reduced greatly the number of school districts in the United States in the last four decades: the exceedingly large number of 120,000 in 1930 was cut to 80,000 in 1950 and then reduced drastically to less than 20,000 in 1970, and the elimination continues. (U. S. Dept. of HEW, 1972:44) An increasing proportion of the young are found in the larger districts: in 1967, just 170 systems that had enrollments of over 25,000 together contained over 12 million students, or nearly 30% of the total. Another 30% of the students were in systems of 6,000 to 25,000

---

[2] "Small high schools can be satisfactory only at exorbitant expense. . . . In many states the number one problem is the elimination of the small high school by district organization. . . . Aside from this important change, I believe no radical alteration in the basic pattern of American education is necessary in order to improve our public high schools." (Conant, 1959: 37, 38, 40).

enrollment. (Dept. of HEW, 1972:45) During all the growth in student numbers and the reduction in number of districts, the number of public secondary *schools* remained about the same (22,000 in 1930, 26,000 in 1970). (Dept. of HEW, 1972:46) The administrative trend is clear: a country that in the past organized its public education in the form of tiny schools in small districts is transforming that structure into one of large schools in huge districts.

Mass involvement in higher education has also been accommodated by large-scale organization. A large college before the Civil War had 500 students, and most were much smaller. A large university at the turn of the century had several thousand students. Large campuses in 1960 had 20,000 or so. Then the major expansion in student numbers of the 1960s—from 3.8 million to 8.5 million—was handled organizationally by increase in size all along the line and especially in massively organized state universities, city universities, state colleges, and community colleges—and multicampus systems thereof. Pennsylvania State University has over 50,000 students; Northeastern University, 40,000; San Diego State College, 35,000; and Chicago City College, a two-year institution, 40,000. More than 50 universities have 20,000 or more students; more than 60 four-year colleges have over 10,000 students; and 120 two-year colleges have over 5,000—and this set of about 230 large institutions encompassed in 1970 some 4 million students or nearly a half of all college enrollment. (U.S. Dept. of HEW, 1972:85) Efforts to coordinate the growing number of university campuses, state colleges, and community colleges have produced increasingly strong statewide systems of control and administration that encompass very large numbers of teachers and students: about half of the states in 1970 had over 100,000 students in the public institutions. (U.S. Dept. of HEW, 1972:66) Again the administrative trend is clear: from small and relatively autonomous units to large campuses in multicampus systems.

As the places where teachers and students assemble have steadily become larger, they have followed the advantages and dictates of large-scale organization in becoming internally more specialized and structurally more complex. They are conditioned increasingly by the concerns of formal administration, especially the need to link the many parts in an hierarchical structure of responsibility and to routinize procedure for uniform application and dependable control. When school superintendents and chancellors of higher education must coordinate the efforts of thousands of instructors and tens of thousands of students in unitary systems, they need large administrative superstructures that in time develop a logic and momentum of their own. The large systems are also conditioned more than the small by the problems of organized professionalism. Professors have long had a powerful claim to individual and group autonomy and formed loose administration in separate colleges congenial to a "community of scholars." But the elaboration of administration around them locally and in larger networks has reduced that autonomy, and professors have reacted by strengthening their bargaining tools in professional associations and unions. Public school teachers have had a weak professional standing and considerable status insecurity; and, as they feel stifled by bureaucracy and vulnerable to lay intervention, they have reasons beyond economic gain to organize themselves as a militant interest group.

The discussion of youth culture in Chapter 7 points out that the young are now different from their counterparts of the past in that they are more shaped by a self-conscious subculture formed around the adolescent stage of life. The instructional settings organized for them by society are also becoming fundamentally different. What is new in the present era as contrasted to pre-1945 America is a long self-conscious stage of adolescence *and* the formal envelopment of that stage within large and complex organizations that operate in a mesh of bureaucratic and professional controls.

High rate of participation and massive organization are characteristics shared by secondary and postsecondary education in the United States. There are additional features that are found at one level and not the other, producing somewhat different institutions of schooling for the 14-to-18 age group and those in the years between 18 and 24.

Distinctive Features of the Secondary Level

Mass secondary education in the United States has been dominated by one type of organization: the public comprehensive high school. The comprehensive school was designed to include all curricula and all social strata, avoiding the assignment of students to different specialized secondary schools characteristic of European systems and thereby providing a democratic melting pot that postponed for a few more years the eventual assignment of students to educational tracks that lead to different careers and life chances. The student intake of the comprehensive school has been established by the catchment area defined for it by school authorities. For most American students, the situation has been one of little consumer choice. Private-school enrollments have long been minor, recently about 10% of the age group, and have been concentrated in the Catholic middle class of Eastern and Midwestern cities. For others, especially the poor, going to school has meant going to the public comprehensive school of neighborhood assignment.

This instrument of democratic inclusion has now become implicated in three forms of segregation: separation of the young from the rest of society; separation of age strata within the ranks of the young; and segregation by culture and race within the general population.

Separation of the Young

A hundred years ago, in 1870, less than 5% of the high school age group could be found in school, with all the rest already out of the system and at work. Now nearly all (90%) stay in the educational sequence through a high school diploma and are to be found in and around the school through age 17 to 18. This change in the social location of the years of youth has been accompanied by an impressive alteration in the day-to-day grasp of the school. A hundred years ago, the school term averaged about 130 days. Today, it is near 180 days or 50 days more a year. But the more fascinating figures are those that tell whether the young actually come to school when they are supposed to. (U. S. Dept. of HEW, 1972:28) :

Public elementary and secondary schools	1870	1920	1968
Length of school term (days)	132	162	179
Days actually attended	78	121	163
Percent of term out of school	41	25	9

The days actually in school have doubled in the century, from less than 80 on the average to over 160. And while students were out of school on "school days" a great deal in 1870, and their nonattendance was still sizeable in 1920 (25% on the average), today in the national picture a scheduled school day is a day in school. Whether we speak of years in school during the time of adolescence, or hours, days, and weeks in school during any one of the years, the forms of escape of the past have been steadily reduced.[3]

This absorption of adolescent time by the school has contributed greatly to the dominance of the student role among the many roles that a young person might have. His family role has been diminished as the family has declined in size and strength. The delaying of work until after the completion of schooling gives the adolescent no place in the work force. The mass media have entered the lives of the young, but the media remain remote from the specific social setting of the young person and largely provide him with the passive role of mass spectator and some activity as consumer. The school is where we find

---

[3] The national averages obscure great differences among types of schools in attendance rates. In some inner-city schools currently, a quarter or a third, or more, of the students may be missing on a given day.

the adolescent: for at least ten years and usually longer the school is the only regular place provided by society. This has become so much the case that one can speak of the family as closing its doors to the young during the day when they are "supposed to be in school."

The comprehensive school has thus been successfully inclusive in sweeping up all the young during the prime work hours of the day. The inclusiveness is fixed firmly in laws that compel attendance, in an administrative system that assigns the young to schools and grades and classes and controls movement from one to another, and in the moral injunction that one should remain in school as long as possible. But with all other roles diminishing and the student role strengthened in scope and depth, the inclusiveness now entails problems of segregation of youth. The young are set apart, and their apartness is characterized by dependency. A longer time in school, by year and day, is a longer time in a dependent state of peculiar qualities. The diffuse dependency found in relation to parents is replaced by the specialized dependency found in the relation of clients to professionals and bureaucrats. At the same time, the dependency is not optional and limited, as client relations commonly are, but is required and involves a repetitive round of movement from one expert to another that is prolonged over many years. The student role has become preeminently one of segmental relation to specialists in a setting of bureaucratic procedures. Growing professional competence on top of increased administrative authority renders teachers more dominant and in control. Perhaps a basic characteristic of the school as a social system nearly everywhere is that the student role is essentially passive. (Boocock, 1972) But the passivity seems to take on new qualities when it is shared among a very large number of young people, prolonged over more years, and involved in relations with specialized teachers who know little about the students as individuals. And the deepening passivity promotes counterforces: a seeking by the young of autonomy and activity in the world of their own—the youth culture—and a highly resentful reaction to what they are asked to do as students.

The special dependence of youth-cum-student is a universal situation, one through which all of the population passes and that holds for a large segment of the population at any one time. Whatever the outcomes, they will be widely distributed.

Separation of Age Groups

A second segregation effect of the American public comprehensive school that has developed increasingly through the years is the differentiation of the young in groups that have a narrow age range but are large in absolute numbers. The most important line of cleavage within the student role is school grade. The grades have become fixed as one-year segments in a twelve-year sequence. They are then secondarily clustered in elementary, junior high, and senior high schools. As schools have grown larger, teachers have specialized more by grade and administrative systems have developed to control the flow of a large number of students within the classrooms of a grade or two. A thousand tenth-graders interact largely with others of the same level, much as any segregated social stratum with well-defined boundaries. The formal system provides little interaction among students up and down the age structure. Then, with automatic promotion from one grade to the next, each grade has a narrow age range. The basic structure then ends up promoting interaction and identification within a narrow age band.

To realize how far we have moved toward age-grade segregation, it is useful to recall the other extreme where grades and ages are mixed across many years. The one-room schoolhouse of old—and a few are still with us in rural areas—consisted of a teacher and a dozen to thirty or more children, aged 6 to 14, distributed across six or more levels of instruction. The teacher moved about the room physically and shifted gears intellectually as the question of the 7-year-old in mathematics was replaced by the problem of the 12-year-old in history. The teacher was bound to use the older students as tutors of the younger ones, to help reduce her multi-ring circus to a manageable task. And the students were always hearing and seeing the experiences of others who were older and younger. The school was, then, extensively "ungraded"; and, in the face of its many weaknesses (minimal equipment, lack of specialists, dependence on the ability of one teacher), it had advantages in relationships that were individualized, personal, and informal. The young also gained experience in tolerating one another's differences and in caring for still younger members. Such schools leaned heavily for advantage not on systematic instruction by specialists but on generating a close community within which group norms call for achievement and induce self-interest in the necessary intellectual struggle.

Grade mixing varies from that extreme of integration to the one now increasingly found in large junior and senior high schools of the country in which the teacher not only specializes in the teaching of one grade, but within the grade, of one subject. Students move, within the boundaries of a single grade, to the room of one specialist and then on to the room of another. Certain modern reform efforts attempt to swing the school back from this narrow age segregation and task specialization, to recapture some of the advantages of the older style of smaller schools. "The ungraded primary" lumps together three or more years of schooling; the open-corridor school replaces whole-class lessons with individual and small-group activity; and some compensatory programs use older youth as teacher-aide models to raise the self-esteem and motivation of younger ones. But the stratifying of the young by grade and age is now strongly institutionalized in the operations of the schools, interlocked with economies of scale, the gain in order provided by bureaucratic structure, and the subject-matter competences and professional rewards offered by specialization.

Segregation by Culture and Race

The most bitter aspect of American educational institutions in the years since World War II has been the enlargement of educational inequality in metropolitan areas. The practices of the housing market together with the personal choices of the advantaged social groups have increased rather than decreased the residential separation of social classes and races. (McEntire, 1960) The middle class has come to live further away from the lower class in separate suburban towns served by separate school districts. The bulk of whites and blacks are also further apart geographically, with the blacks concentrated in the heart of the city and the whites either far out from the center or stubbornly clinging to the white ethnic sections of the central city. With the public comprehensive school zoned by neighborhood and town, the increased segregation in housing has brought increased segregation in the schools. (Havighurst, 1963) Along lines of social class and ethnic-group culture as well as of race, the comprehensive schools have become more socially selective and more unequal in the climate of achievement that is set largely by the social mix of the student body. (Coleman, 1966; Havighurst, 1963)

The impact of residential segregation on school segregation was long not absorbed into official and public consciousness. As the issue of racial integration in the schools came to the fore in the 1950s, attention went first to *de jure* segregation found in the border states and the South. It was only in the early 1960s, a mere decade ago, that the concentration of the "culturally deprived" and "the disadvantaged student" in the city ghetto became perceived as an even more fundamental and tenacious problem.[4] And there has been a natural ideological

---

[4] See, for example, Riessman (1962) and National Education Association (1962). It was after the appearance of such publications that the *New York Times* and other major newspapers began to highlight the educational problems of the big-city ghetto (e.g., Barclay, 1962). This theme began to dominate the earlier concerns with school integration in the South, that centered on the Supreme Court decision of 1954, and with the Rickover-Conant search for excellence, focused on the gifted, that received so much attention in the several years immediately following the launching of Sputnik in 1957.

resistance to the realization that comprehensiveness has become transformed into segregation along social lines, since the concept of the common school has been central to desires to educate for democracy. But reality has gone the other way: educational inequality, always with us in history, has become more structurally fixed in the institutions of public schooling.

We have noted three effects of current institutions in public education: a separation of the life experiences of the school from the community; a separation of age groups from one another within the school; and a separation of the young from one another along the lines of social class, ethnic, and racial clustering—"cultural segregation." Later in the report, we focus further on the first two effects, since we are interested primarily in the features of current institutions that potentially affect all of the young, even if they appear first and most strongly in the upper middle class. Thus our focus is not on cultural differences among the young, nor specifically on the inner-city school. We note, however, that the problems set by youth and age segregation, on which we concentrate, may well be heightened by cultural segregation, and appear sharply in slum schools. The idea that young people should be separated by grade, for example, runs more counter to the social organization of the slum family, "where kinship and the conglomeration of brothers and sisters and relatives are the organizing principles of survival," than to the operation of the upper-middle-class nuclear family. (Janowitz, 1969:104) Similarly for fixed daily time schedules and the yearly schedule of the summer vacation. If in concentrating on youth and youth culture we make little explicit reference to the situation of the poor and the black, the general problems of educational structure that we discuss bear heavily on them.

The Minor Forms of American Secondary Education

We have emphasized the dominance of the public comprehensive school at the secondary level of American education since it clearly towers above all others. But some variety has been provided by private schools, secular and parochial, and specialized public schools. The private sector, although weak nationally, has long offered alternatives for a large part of the population in many cities and towns of New England, the Middle Atlantic states, and the Midwest. The Catholic schools in some cities have a considerable drawing power that leads to a serious loss of support for the public schools; and occasionally the combined drain of Catholic and other private schools have left the public schools as a dumping ground for those who could not escape. The private sector can also have influence beyond its size in providing room for experimentation and the construction of influential models. But overall the nonpublic institutions have become a smaller and smaller part of the whole, declining from about 18% of the secondary school enrollment in 1900 to about 10% in 1970.

Specialized public secondary schools are also still found in the United States, emphasizing academic excellence or vocational education or the arts. They select students from a large area, often citywide or even from a set of adjoining districts, rather than admit routinely all whose homes are in the neighborhood. They too can have influence beyond their size, since their specialization allows them to build a distinctive character and competence and to become known as a place where a particular thing is done well. The Bronx High School of Science has been a noteworthy instance, allowed to draw students from all of New York City on criteria of academic motivation and achievement and to develop programs appropriate for an academic elite. But schools deliberately specializing in academic excellence have continued to disappear, overwhelmed by the accepted philosophy and power of the comprehensive form of organization. Their place has been taken in part by comprehensive schools whose catchment areas are so socially segregated, in the affluent suburbs and well-to-do parts of the cities, that they concentrate on programs for the many able students provided by the neighborhood.

Vocational schools have been the most numerous of the specialized public schools. There have been special federal funds behind vocational training since the Smith-Hughes Act of 1917, which even specified what courses were to be supported and hence pushed vocational education toward a national uniformity. But little has gone well in American vocational education, as through the years the federal funds ended up supporting education for fields of work in decline—agriculture and the industrial crafts of the 1910s and 1920s—or went to classes in homemaking for girls that led away from jobs. (Panel of Consultants on Vocational Education, 1963; Venn, 1964) School districts also did not have to organize such courses in separate vocational and technical schools but could place them, as they increasingly did, within the comprehensive schools, there, as in homemaking, to be adapted to the general curriculum. The separate schools proved vulnerable: they were not able to solve the problems of the low esteem accorded vocational as compared to academic training; in many cities they became a dumping ground for poor students; and comprehensive schools could argue powerfully that their general education was a better preparation for work than the narrow training offered in the vocational school.

Of considerable interest today are the special programs and schools that are being newly organized (or newly revised and emphasized) as attacks on student disaffection. These new ventures are essentially of two types. one that attempts to link the school to outside work and cultural organizations and one that attempts to establish a communal grouping of students and teachers. Most prominent as links to the outside world are work programs, where students are located part of the time in outside jobs or placed in a special school that operates somewhat like a small business, intending to give students who are failing in school or who have lost their motivation a chance to feel the realness of work and to regain some sense of mastery and direction that can be turned back to the normal school setting. The work programs, old and new, have related very little to middle-class disaffection, concentrating instead on the disadvantaged who are failing or are not trying or are rebelling in the regular programs. They immediately run into the problem of low status accorded anything that appears to be vocational rather than academic, and for the poor rather than all the students.

The route of communal grouping has been taken in the "alternative schools" that have attracted so much attention because of their dramatic qualities—and because they relate to the disaffected sons and daughters of the educated. The alternative school moves a small number of students and teachers—all volunteers—out of the regular school building and into a separate location, there to work out a fresh start with all the old rules suspended. Students and teachers attempt to replace the old hierarchy of authority with greater equality of relation, to establish new foci of concentration in courses, and to provide great freedom in the application of effort and the scheduling of activities. The alternative schools have seemed a promising alternative to many, almost a necessity for sophisticated youth in the upper middle class who claim, and act out the claim, that they cannot stand one or another basic feature of the regular school, whether it is the way that history is taught or too much traffic control in the hallway or an emphasis on sports.

Unfortunately, for purposes of experimentation with new forms, the alternative schools, inside and outside the public schools, have averaged such a short life—less than two years—that they have offered little gain. Philosophically antiorganization, they quickly get on the road to failure. The alternative school typically attempts a town-meeting democracy in which all issues are to be decided by all in a body of equals. Two early results are the boredom and frustration that follow upon endless discussion, and the breakdown of organizational routine. In a few months the teachers "discover" that they are more competent in certain matters than the students, and guiltily begin to make decisions. A professional corps then reappears, with some differentiation of power and interest from that of the students, and all can perceive the drift back to the old ways they had hoped to escape. Then, when a school appears to be composed of "corridors of wandering souls," a phrase used critically in the alternative-school movement, some parents and students become disenchanted, some students withdraw, and the moral and financial bases of the enterprise crumble. The alternative schools have taught anew the lesson that no simple solutions work in educational reform. "Grooving" and "self-actualization" will not make a school.

In short, recent efforts to establish a new variety in American secondary education have not gotten very far. Their support has been hesitant and uneven. The new starts that center on work or job training have to solve the dumping-ground problem. The new places for disaffected affluent youth have been deficient in such minimal requirements of organization as a capacity to set goals, divide the labor, and delegate authority.

Distinctive Features of Higher Education

As we move to the structure of American higher education, some of the features we have portrayed as distinctive of the secondary level are still found but with less weight. Segregation by culture and race exists, but it is not tightly linked to neighborhood of residency since colleges and universities have much larger catchment areas than do schools, and students have greater freedom in choosing among places, including leaping across the nearest ones to go farther away from home. Segregation of the young is also found, especially on residential campuses; but college students more than high school students have either begun their own family or anticipate soon doing so and are involved in part-time or full-time work. In the advanced years of college, linkage to basic adult roles is under way. Similarly for age-grade segregation: some exists, but students mix considerably more across the grades and older adults are increasingly found in the classroom. Thus these forms of separation have less weight for the 18-to-24 age group than for the years of early adolescence spent in the secondary school.

The most important structural difference between mass secondary and mass higher education in the United States is that while the first is dominated by one form of organization, the second is uncommonly pluralistic. There is a strong and prestigeful private sector that is exceedingly heterogeneous within itself, with over 900 four-year colleges, secular and religious, ranging enormously in academic quality and style; some technological schools and finishing schools; and dozens of universities that range from the best in the nation to ones able to attract only mediocre students from a few miles away. The public sector, ever more massive and dominant in enrollment, is ever more differentiated into state universities and state colleges of varying student composition, and short-cycle units, the two-year community colleges, that now number over a thousand and absorb over one-half of all college freshmen.

American institutions of higher education are heterogeneous not only in comparison with the American secondary level but also with the higher education structures of other countries. The European systems have been monopolized by the state or public university to the point where they have difficulty in creating viable secondary and tertiary sectors. Private institutions are generally few and under general state supervision. First-tier or short-cycle institutions, similar to the American community college, are especially difficult to create, since they are considered so inferior in status. Differentiation has occurred chiefly through the creation of technological and teacher training institutions that parallel the university in length of training of the first degree. But the European systems are plagued with the problem of a traditional homogeneity of form as they move into an age that requires different kinds of places for a more heterogenous clientele and for the complex requirements of a highly trained labor force.

This is not the American problem. Our varied structure instead poses problems of consumer knowledge and choice and of appropriate matching of students and colleges. There are basic problems of institutional connection and permeability in the large state systems of higher education, centered on the need for large numbers of students to transfer systematically and without great loss from one college to another. With over 500,000 students now transferring annually, half of them from community colleges, transfer has now become for students and institutions alike the number-two access problem. (Willingham, 1972)

The problematic features of American higher education in relation to youth are increasingly located in the community college, which operates more like the American comprehensive secondary school than any other component of higher education. In the manner of a senior high school, the public two-year college is based on a local catchment area, takes all students, is free or low cost, and is nonresidential, with students commuting from home. With its open door, it intends to be comprehensive across social strata and races and comprehensive in curricula, assembling in one place transfer programs, one- and two-year terminal programs, adult or recurrent education, and now an increasing amount of remedial or subcollege work that permits students to repair the damage sustained in earlier years of schooling. A place of option and trial, it has many students hoping to transfer to four-year colleges and universities who will in fact terminate their schooling during these two years. (Clark, 1960a; Clark, 1960b) The community colleges have difficulty in maintaining a balance among their programs, since the general tilt is toward high status for the transfer work, low status for the terminal, and marginality for the adult courses.

For American youth, the hometown or neighborhood community college is increasingly the automatic place, the college that represents the upward extension of the continuous schooling structure of the elementary and secondary years. In a growing number of states, it is as easy to enter and as natural to attend as the high school. The young person leaving high school is automatically promoted to it, qualified to enter, and more of his graduating high school class is proceeding there than to any other single institution of study or work. Its availability promotes a situation in which the decision by a young person to discontinue his education after high school requires more deliberate effort than that of simply remaining on the age-and-grade escalator that moves his peers on from the twelfth to the thirteenth year.

Thus, this short-cycle form of college that is the main means of accommodating mass higher education in the United States is involved in the problems of continuous schooling and youth segregation that are fundamental in the structure of secondary education. The problems are lightened somewhat at this level by a greater degree of choice and a stronger sense of voluntary participation. But they are deepened by the strain of still being "in school" two more years, at the ages of 19 and 20 and later, still in many cases removed from adult responsibilities, and facing points of decision more momentous for one's career.

Institutional Legitimacy, Resilience, and Load

American educational institutions are clearly having systematic troubles in teaching the children of the poor and the offspring of the upper middle class. The bureaucratic and professional organization of modern teaching is not making effective connection with the values and practices of the current urban lower class. The daily routines of educational organizations as now structured are also boring increasing numbers of affluent adolescents in the cities and suburbs whose background and life style generate new demands for variety and flexibility in instruction. These large strata within the young have generated a general adolescent sense of disconnection between self and school that spills over into the more stable lower middle class of the cities and the relatively contented middle class of the countryside. The result is a sizeable loss of confidence in schooling among the young.

In addition, we have come to the point of a serious diminishing of confidence among parents and teachers and finally administrators. Parents among the urban poor give up on current educational institutions when they think they cannot get even the simplest of educational services—decent teachers in decent buildings who can maintain discipline and produce functional literacy in reading, writing, and arithmetic. Intellectual critics in the upper middle class, through two decades of heavy criticism, have convinced increasing numbers of educated parents that there is something basically wrong about the public schools. So much public questioning must sooner or later affect the self-esteem of teachers. Teachers can pull together defensively and back one another, like any other occupation under attack, but there are limits to how much they can reassure themselves when so many critics pound away on the theme of failure and when the teachers find their daily work ever more fraught with difficulty and uncertainty.

Loss of public confidence and the despair of teachers, eroding legitimacy, will finally undercut the resilience of educational institutions. Schools and colleges have an amazing ability to carry on. No matter how many windows are broken or teachers attacked or classrooms disrupted, someone cleans up, the schedule is reasserted, teachers are back in the classrooms and the whole thing goes on. But somewhere down the line there are limits to the dogged willingness of the devoted group and to the resilience of the institutions that they carry on their backs. If public confidence should continue its downhill slide and teacher despair deepen even more, large segments of the system could fall below a threshold of resilience, where a vicious circle of effects would then ensure an even worse situation for the education of millions.

Part of the problem of legitimacy and resilience is that through long accretion of activities and responsibilities and the assuming of new burdens at a rapid pace in recent decades, the institutions of American secondary and higher education have taken on a great deal of responsibility and work. Public expectations run high, asking schools and colleges to solve national problems of scientific preeminence, unemployables in the work force, disenchanted youth, social inequality, and even the breakdown of community. The functions seem almost endless, as these comprehensive institutions of mass preparation are pushed, and push themselves, to being all things for all young people. The problem is most acute when a single form, the public high school, attempts singlehandedly to meet the increasing spread of group demands and cultural tasks. But a variety of needs can only be served by a variety of institutions. Up to a point, the variety may be provided within a single comprehensive structure, through internal elaboration. But there are limits on how far any organization can be asked to stretch and still function effectively, especially when it is vulnerable to a turbulent environment of contradictory and shifting group demands. There are also limits on how comprehensive any educational organization can be without blandness eroding all sense of purpose and enterprise.

The heavy load of expectation and work of particular schools and colleges, and their growing blandness, can be reduced considerably by reassignment of functions within education itself, particularly to new units with limited purposes. This is one major avenue of reform. But the burdens of socialization could also be shifted in part to institutions outside of education, both to already established institutions of work, politics, and leisure, and to new institutions yet to be developed. We return to such considerations in the concluding chapter of the volume.

6. Biological, Psychological, and Socio-Cultural Aspects of Adolescence and Youth

What biological and psychological characteristics of adolescence and youth should be considered in assessing the relative merits of various institutional arrangements for socializing our young people into adulthood? Whether this question is interpreted to mean "givens" inherent in human development or characteristics resulting from cultural systems so basic to our society that they are unlikely to change profoundly in the foreseeable future makes little practical difference. Therefore, the issue will be addressed here primarily in a unicultural sense, i.e., with respect to adolescence and youth in contemporary U.S. culture.

Physical and Physiological Development

The age period 14 to 24 is characterized by great diversity in (1) the physical and physiological status of persons at the upper and lower ends of this age span, (2) the rate at which physical and physiological changes occur, in terms of both individual differences in their onset and completion and group differences between the younger and older portions of the continuum, and (3) the range of developmental status among individuals of the same chronological age during the earlier part of the period.

At the younger end of this age range most persons, especially males, are in a period of intense physical and physiological development; at the upper end some structural and functional changes continue, but at a very slow pace. Most organs and tissues of the body undergo an adolescent growth spurt, although the extent and timing vary. Among girls the first external sign that the sequence of events constituting biological adolescence has begun is usually the appearance of breast buds. For boys it is accelerated growth of the testes and scrotum. The male spurts in height and penis growth start about a year later. During the peak year of growth in height the average boy's growth rate is greater than it had been since he was two years old. Accelerated growth begins later in the trunk than in the legs, but because the total increase in the trunk is greater, body proportions change in the direction of a higher trunk/leg length ratio. Peak growth in chest and hip breadth usually occur about four months after that in leg length. A few months later shoulder breadth reaches its maximum growth rate followed by trunk length and chest depth. Total hip growth is greater in girls than boys, while the reverse is true of chest and shoulder dimensions.

About 98% of maximal height is attained by the average boy at 17.5 (the average girl reaches this point at 15.5), with small increments continuing into the late twenties. The apex of weight gain is about six months later than the peak of height growth, although gains continue at a more gradual pace to the mid-fifties. About three months after peak growth in boys muscular growth reaches its apex. However, their apex of dynametric strength comes much later (about 14 months after the height peak), and their capacity to increase strength through exercise does not reach a maximum until 25 to 35 years. Although it is not true that the adolescent boy, "outgrows his strength," there does appear to be "a period of about a year when a boy, having completed his physical growth, does not have the strength of a young adult of the same body size and shape" (Tanner, 1962: 204). About the time of the boy's spurt in strength his motor coordination also improves markedly. Performance of simple and complex motor tasks, including athletic feats, improves into the thirties, but evidence for an adolescent spurt is lacking. Increase in strength and in motor coordination and performance occur earlier in girls than in boys but are not, on the average, as great.

Pubic hair may appear with or even before breast buds or accelerated testicular growth, but rapid development usually accompanies the height spurt. Some two years after pubic hair growth begins axillary hair first appears, as does facial hair in boys. Other body hair may also appear at this time but often is delayed until considerably later. The mustache and beard follow a definite sequence of appearance, and the final state—hair along the side and lower border of the chin—rarely takes place until the development of pubic hair and the genitalia is complete.

Concomitant with or preceding these external manifestations are changes in internal organs, body biochemistry and composition, and physiological function. Lymphoid tissue decreases steeply throughout adolescence after reaching its peak at age 10 to 12. Subcutaneous fat has a curvilinear growth curve. The brain and other portions of the nervous system grow rapidly during early childhood but seem to share little in the adolescent growth spurt. However, gradual maturing of function is suggested by dendritic growth in the brain, continued myelination of some nerve tracts and by some physiological measures, e.g., faster reaction times and further maturing of the electroencephalogram (EEG).

Accompanying enlargement of the larynx is deepening of the voice in both sexes. Growth of the larynx is greater in boys, as is their voice change, but the process is gradual, beginning when penis growth is almost completed and often continuing until near the end of adolescence. Development of the apocrine sweat glands and increase in axillary sweating occur at about the time that axillary hair growth begins. Two temporary and troublesome phenomena—acne in both sexes and breast enlargement in males—are not an invariable aspect of adolescence, although some permanent changes do regularly occur in the breasts of boys as well as girls.

The heart, lungs, and most other internal organs participate in the general adolescent growth spurt. As a result of cardiovascular, respiratory and biochemical changes occuring during adolescence, physiological response to exercise becomes more efficient, especially in boys. Most of the endocrine glands show an adolescent growth spurt, but not all increase their rate of secretion relative to body size. Preceding the external signs of puberty by at least a year is accelerated development of the primary gonads, i.e., the testes and ovaries. The growth of these glands is, in turn, in response to increased secretion of gonadotrophic hormones by the anterior pituitary. Under the stimulation of gonadotrophins, differentiation of sperm begins in the seminal tubules, followed shortly by differentiation of the cells that secrete testosterone. Development of the latter is slower, however, so that active sperm are produced before these cells are fully mature. In the average-maturing boy the first ejaculation occurs shortly before 14 years.

Development of the ovaries in girls occurs about two years before testicular growth in males, but their growth spurt is less pronounced, probably because their development is relatively greater in childhood than is that of the testes. Menarche is delayed until some two years after breast development begins and rarely occurs until after the peak of the height spurt. Nor is reproductive maturity synonymous with menarche. Fertility is low for a year to 18 months after menarche, and maximal fertility and lactating efficiency probably are not established until the early to mid-twenties.

In both sexes secretion of androgenic hormones by the adrenal cortex rises sharply at puberty. These hormones are particularly important in girls, in whom they are responsible for the development of pubic and axillary hair.

The sequence of events during biological adolescence is much less variable from individual to individual within a sex than is the chronological age at which these changes take place. Among boys, for example, the normal range of ages for the onset of pubic hair growth is 10 to 15 and for its completion, 14 to 18. Testis growth may begin between 10 and 13.5 and end between 14.5 and 18. The comparable ages for penis growth are 11 to 14.5 and 13.5 to 17. Some boys begin their height spurt at 10.5 and finish it by 13, while in others accelerated growth does not start until 16. In girls the normal range is as great or greater. Pubic hair growth may start any time between 8 and 14, breast development between 8 and 13, and the height spurt between 9.5 and 14.5. Menarche may fall between 10 and 16.5 years. Most physical and physiological changes are highly intercorrelated, although the development of pubic and axillary hair is less closely associated with either skeletal or reproductive maturation than are the latter two with each other. Some aspects of adolescent growth, such as dental and neural development, are virtually independent of other systems.

As the age ranges cited above indicate, most analogous adolescent phenomena occur about two years earlier in girls than in boys. Because of her earlier growth spurt, the average girl is taller than the average boy from about 11 to 14 years and heavier than he from about 9 or 10 until 14.5. Of course, late-maturing boys may be somewhat dwarfed by many girls for an even longer period.

Also clear in the range of ages at which various adolescent phenomena begin and terminate is the fact that some individuals complete their adolescent transformation before other persons of the same sex and age even begin theirs. From about 11 through 16 or 17 years the range of individual differences in physical structure and physiological function at any given chronological age is greater than at any other time in the human life span. To cite but one example, data from a longitudinal study showed an average difference between early and late maturing boys at age 15 of 8 inches and 30 pounds (Jones and Bayley,

1950). Accompanying this size difference were group contrasts of relatively comparable magnitude in body build, strength, motor performance and coordination, reaction time, attractiveness of appearance as judged by adults and peers, leadership roles, self-concepts and other aspects of personal and social behavior (Eichorn, 1963).

Added to the variation within either sex are the differences in maturational rate of the two sexes. Thus, in a classroom of 14- or 15-year-olds the diversity of size and function, with related variation in interest patterns and skills, can span the range from early childhood to adulthood. These intra- and inter-sex differences in the timing of adolescence raise important questions about socialization practices such as age-grading and mixed sex grouping. Because physical size and motor skills play an important role in social acceptance throughout the public-school period, particularly for boys, some youngsters will be advantaged by age-grading while others are handicapped. Some late-maturing boys may not be able to compete successfully until the time has past when skills linked to size, strength, endurance and coordination have considerable social "payoff". Longitudinal data show that that the effects of both advantage and handicap on self-perceptions and interpersonal attitudes can endure long after the physical differences and their social importance have disappeared (Eichorn, 1963). Among girls on the other hand, it is the early-maturing who are most out-of-step with the modal tendency of a mixed-sex age group. Their interests as well as their appearance are well in advance of their age peers of both sexes. Peers and adults may draw derogatory inferences about their moral character, and their well-developed figures may be a source of embarrassment among a class of childlike bodies.

A third source of biological variation among youngsters in educational institutions can result indirectly from individual differences in academic achievement. Although in recent times in the United States accelerated promotion and retention in grade are less common than formerly, these practices and other factors—legally permissible variation in age at starting school, protracted illness, transfer between schools, and language handicap in children for whom English is not the native tongue—increase the variation in chronological and, hence, developmental age within classrooms, particularly in junior and senior high schools and colleges. Thus, although 14 is the modal age for ninth-graders, a few pupils in a given class may be as young as 11 or 12 or as old as 17 or 18. Some 16-year-olds are only in seventh grade while others are in colleges, some are in the full-time labor force, and some are married and even parents.

In sum, chronological age becomes a progressively poorer index of physical and physiological status (as well as of social and academic skills) as children progress from infancy toward puberty. Although this fact may suggest grouping on the basis of some developmental index other than chronological age, e.g., skeletal age or mental age, such an approach is contradicted by other facts. Rates of growth of the skeletal and reproductive systems are very highly correlated and certain social interests are associated with the maturity of these systems, but mental age, academic skills, and emotional maturity are essentially uncorrelated with physical or physiological development and not closely related to social or emotional development. A 14-year-old, for example, may have a skeletal age of 11 and a mental age of 21 or the converse. Further, selection on a maturity basis may have negative implications for slow-maturing individuals that are as adverse in their effects on self-conceptions as are the contrasts resulting from age grading. Arbitrary selection based on chronological age may have less derogatory personal implications, as has been argued by opponents of "tracking" systems in public schools and proponents of arbitrary retirement age.

The existence of biological adolescence also has psychosocial implications beyond those for grouping arrangements in socializing institutions. Prominent among the concerns reported by adolescents are the temporary afflictions of acne, large feet, hands, and nose, and disparaties from peers in size, body build, strength, and skills. Rapid changes in physique and skills influence interpersonal relationships and self-concepts and require psychological integration. Thus, they figure importantly in the "identity quest" of psychological adolescence (see below). In addition, conflicts between generations may be exacerbated by the secular trend toward earlier adolescence.

During the past century (probably since the industrial revolution, Tanner, 1962), each successive generation has reached puberty, begun the adolescent growth spurt, and attained adult size, shape, and physiological function earlier. From infancy through adulthood children are larger than were their parents, but the generational differences are maximal during adolescence, when they amount to about four months per decade not only in size but in reproductive maturity. Average age at first marriage has also decreased during most of the last century, although this fact probably has its source in demographic circumstances (see chapter on Demography) as well as earlier sexual maturation.

Regional, national, and socioeconomic variations in rate of maturing have also been observed. The variables underlying secular and other variations in age at puberty and related phenomena are incompletely understood, but among the variables believed to be influential are genetic inheritance, nutrition, medical care, and housing. Improvement in socioeconomic conditions within a region across time and superior socioeconomic conditions for certain groups within or between regions at a given time have been found to be associated with earlier maturation.

Recent data do suggest an asymptote to secular and socioeconomic trends. The second generation of the Berkeley Growth Study appears not to be more precocious in development than their parents, a group that, on the average, was socio-economically advantaged (Eichorn, unpublished data). Similarly advantaged samples in Denver show no decrease in age at menarche between 1930 and 1965 (McCammon, 1965). Ryder (1971) reports from the study on the Growth of American Families that age at menarche is now the same among different socioeconomic groups in the United States. In Great Britain the socioeconomic difference in age at menarche has also disappeared, although a height difference remains (Douglas and Simpson, 1964). Despite the apparent diminution in generational differences, many parents and other adults must expect the adolescents with whom they deal to be physically larger and more mature sexually than were they themselves at a comparable age. Further, in assessing our socializing institutions we must consider the implications of extending the years of social and economic dependence while the age of biological maturity decreases or at least remains constant. Not to be forgotten in this consideration, however, is the fact that different tissues, organ systems, and physiological functions approximate adult levels at quite different ages.

Psychological Development

Human biological maturation differs from that of lower animals in a number of ways, but particularly in the existence and length of an adolescence period. Man's capacity for learning and his societal and cultural complexities also far exceed those of lower animals. Human psychological adolescence incorporates the interaction of prolonged biological development in an organism with a high capacity for learning dwelling in an environment in which even survival depends upon a protracted period of dependence and upon learning a great deal.

Although adulthood is difficult to define even biologically, probably in no human society is it synonymous with the attainment of adult size and physiologic function. Rates of biological, psychological and social development may, and often do, differ. In most societies adulthood is defined primarily in social terms. The specific terms vary widely, however, as does their linkage to biological or psychological criteria. Probably the most basic contrast between adult and nonadult is between those who are considered capable of providing at least some forms of nurture and those who are considered to require some form of nurturing. In most societies this distinction implies both vocational and emotional skills (working and loving).

The psychology of an individual or a group depends not simply on either the stage of biological maturation or the cultural context, but on the interaction between the two. In the United States the culture of the middle class provides the norm, despite tempering by subcultural variations. This is so not only because the middle class constitutes the largest proportion of the population, but also because in a society with vertical mobility the lower class, the next largest group, aspires to higher status and tends to adopt the value system of the more advantaged group.

As the United States has become an increasingly technological and urbanized society, adolescence and youth (or early and late adolescence) have emerged as clear-cut social and psychological phases. The prominence of these stages has been accentuated by population trends—an increase in total population and, in recent decades, both an absolute and relative increase in the proportion of the population in the age range 12–25. And we should remind ourselves that this social and psychological phenomenon has occurred despite successive generations of decrease in age at physical and physiological adolescence and adulthood.

Our society has been characterized as lacking in *rites de passage* by which to mark transitions toward adulthood. This accusation may be exaggerated. We do, in fact, have a number of status markers along the way to adulthood, although none of them confers instantaneous adult status—a practice of some primitive societies that has been viewed by some observers as conducive to a less stressful adolescence. Inconsistencies in the timing of our rites, e.g., a younger age for being drafted than for voting, are currently under reexamination and change. Whether resolution of such inconsistencies will affect the psychology of youth and interactions between adults and youth remains to be seen.

Laws reflect the minimum ages at which our society regards youth as competent to assume adult roles (e.g., 16 for full-time employment; 18 for marriage and, implicitly, parenthood; and 18 to 21 for full citizenship) but not necessarily normative expectations or behaviors. In fact, less than a third of our youth are in the labor force even at 18, and the median age at first marriage is well over 20. In most sectors of our society parents and other adults responsible for the socialization of the young discourage both early entry into the labor force and early marriage. This attitude stems largely from a desire to promote the best possible future for the young in terms of income, job satisfaction, and a suitable and lasting marriage. Further, the nuclear family style predominant in our society, although better suited than the extended family to an economy involving geographic and social mobility, probably intensifies emotional attachments, making separation of the family by employment or marriage of the young more difficult for both parents and offspring.

What are the psychosocial attributes of adolescents and youth in our society? Those most frequently cited in the developmental literature from psychology, psychiatry, sociology, anthropology, education, and pediatrics may be grouped into the following categories: a high level of cognitive abilities and rapid and efficient learning, vocational preparation and selection, increasing independence and autonomy, strong attachment to the peer group, and an increasingly mature personality integration (the "quest for identity"). Although such categories are useful for purposes of discussion, they and subgroupings of characteristics within them are interrelated. Further, in speaking of the modal or normative attributes two facts should be kept in mind. First, almost all behaviors, attitudes, and the like evolve during the transition from childhood to adulthood and even during the adult years, so characteristics show shifting rather than static patterns throughout adolescence. Second, all members of an age cohort, whether children, adolescents, adults, or the elderly are not alike, and variations from the average must be expected.

Cognitive Abilities. The interaction of different aspects of development is probably nowhere better illustrated than in what has been for some years the most prominent theory of cognitive development, that of Piaget. According to this stage theory of intellectual development, a final qualitative change to adult thought processes, termed formal operations, begins between 12 and 15 years. An operation is a way of acting upon objects or ideas. During childhood, thought processes are predominantly bound to concrete experiences. A variety of concepts are gradually acquired, but a considerable number of variables cannot be considered at one time. At adolescence the individual becomes able to think abstractly with propositions and without the necessity for concrete props, to reason with hypotheses involving multiple variables, and to conceptualize thinking *per se,* both his own and that of others. In the early phases of establishing these mental processes, i.e., about 13 to 14, the ability to test propositions exhaustively is not yet complete, nor is the young adolescent able to differentiate clearly between his own thoughts and those of others. By 15 or 16 the shift to the highest level of cognitive capacity is considered to be completed in the average person in advanced societies.

Piaget and his followers hold that these new thought processes operate in the affective and social domains as well as in intellectual activity. The propensity of the adolescent to construct theories and systems is seen in adolescent commitment to possibilities and the development of a life program, interest in political and social theories and a desire to reform his society, and in building a romance rather than simply "falling in love" as children sometimes do. Whereas the child relates to persons, customs, and institutions he knows directly, the adolescent can grasp society as a whole, its institutional forms, and ethical principles beyond those involved in concrete interpersonal experiences. Reflecting the adolescent's initial inability to distinguish between his own thoughts and those of others are his idealistic zeal to remake adults and their society and his belief that others are as preoccupied with his behavior, opinions, and appearance as he is himself.

For Piaget "the fundamental problem of adolescence is that the individual begins to take up adult roles." Entry into the world of work or serious preparation for it plays a primary role in consolidating the final phase of cognitive development, and this and other adult social roles promote parallel development of the personality. The demands of a job and interactions with coworkers or peers also preparing for a vocation require him to adjust to reality and take into account the thoughts and needs of others. In adopting adult social roles, the individual develops a hierarchical set of values or life plan and constructs a personality. Complementarity of cognitive and personal-social organization (although with a lesser level of abstraction and degree of conflict) is seen by Piaget in youth who go to work early as well as in those whose transition to adult roles involves greater intellectual demands. Young workers adopt or adapt ideologies from their companions and organizations, and girls who marry or are about to are considered to have ideas about married life and their husbands that have the characteristics of "theories."

Although stage theorists make some provision for the influence of environmental circumstances on cognitive development, they emphasize maturational processes and qualitative change. Learning theorists, on the other hand, draw their explanatory concepts from situational contingencies, deny the existence of stages or qualitative shifts, and stress the gradual acquisition of progressively more advanced cognitive skills. They too recognize not only the adolescent's high level of capacity for abstract thinking, for distinguishing between superficially similar objects or ideas, and for dealing with alternatives but also the importance of these abilities in his vocational preparation and personal-social development. However, as determinants of the ability to think abstractly they see such factors as a growing vocabulary of mediating labels, gradual mastery of progressively more difficult concepts, much experience with manipulating both objects and ideas in a variety of situations, and some form of reward for successful efforts in these directions. In sum, the quarrel between stage and learning theorists is not in their descriptions of the abilities of the average adolescent but in their interpretation of how he attained them. Translated into practical implications the two types of theories differ mainly in that learning theories hold greater expectations for the efficacy of remediation of deficiencies through training.

Data derived from conventional standardized intelligence tests also support the notion that a person who has not attained certain intellectual skills by a given age may yet do so. Continued increases in total point score are observed in persons of differing levels of absolute ability and education at least into the early twenties, albeit at a negatively accelerating rate. For some abilities, e.g., reasoning, an asymptote is reached by this age. However, performance on tests of vocabulary and information improves well into adulthood. One may say that experience enhances the fund of knowledge on which to base decisions or make one's contribution to society but not necessarily the capacity to use the information adaptively.

As was noted in the section on biological development, few studies indicate spurts in intellectual growth concomitant with those in physical development. Findings that have been so interpreted show early maturing or larger youngsters to score slightly higher than the later maturing or smaller. However, these differences when present in a sample of adolescents are also seen in adulthood. Thus they seem to be linked not with the rate of biological development but with some other factor, such as socioeconomic advantage, associated with superior levels of both physical and mental status.

Evidence on the notion that abilities become more differentiated (less highly intercorrelated) with age is contradictory. Whether trends toward differentiation that have been observed stem from the nature of the tests used, school curricula or other environmental factors, or from similar trends in interest patterns (see below) cannot yet be determined.

With certain exceptions the adolescent generally proves to be a more rapid and efficient learner than younger children in both laboratory experiments with problems provided by the experimental psychologists and in classroom studies of mastery of school subjects. However, the same statement could be made about 10-year-olds and so on down the age continuum. Such results raise the obvious question of whether introduction of some or all training should be delayed until the age of maximum efficiency. Contraindications come as readily to mind. If learning builds on learning, would the older child be so efficient lacking his previous experience? Are there not matters so useful outside of school at an earlier age that teaching them is advisable? What about motivational considerations? Unfortunately, definite answers to these and related questions are not available.

The adolescent's capacity for abstraction and long practice in learning have prompted some psychologists and educators to ask whether he could not at least be taught more efficiently than is often the case. Most proposals do not question the time needed, but rather the technique. However, cross-national data suggest a quite different approach to the efficient use of students' and instructors' time at all grade levels. In this analysis those who attended school only half time— whether part-days, every other day, or alternate semesters—were found to perform as well on achievement tests as full time students.

Vocational development. In our society economic self-sufficiency is not simply a *sine qua non* of adult status. For most males occupation also sets most aspects of life style for self, spouse, and offspring—characteristics of spouse, marriage and family pattern, income and what it buys, status in the community, satisfactions of personal drives and needs, recreational outlets, conversational style, dress, place of residences, associations with friends, relatives, and acquaintances and their continuity or discontinuity, political and social attitudes, goals, and ideals. Yet by 14, when they are only beginning to form and understand the "self" they are projecting into the future, our young must start to make educational choices that determine occupation and its ramifications. To compound the dilemma they also have little information about the current world of work, even less about future changes, and only haphazard ways of acquiring it.

Rapid technological and social changes render some occupations obsolete and produce new ones, and few if any adult advisors can predict the changes well. Other characteristics of the changing labor scene to which recent generations are having to adjust are the shift from predominantly production occupations to services; increasingly high initial educational requirements (which are costly) and later retraining; growth in size of the typical organization, with concomitants of complexity, formality of structure, and impersonality; and a decline in the work week except for professionals and the self-employed. At least the latter two trends, if not all of them, imply the importance of developing personal-social traits beyond those traditionally advantageous in the job market.

Our complex technological society also offers a welter of possible occupations but few role models for the young. Sons tend to stay in the same socioeconomic rank of job as their fathers, but occupational "inheritance" has become uncommon and most youngsters have little opportunity to observe either their fathers or other adults in their occupational roles. In principle the mass media provide some opportunities for learning about vocations and some models, but the representation of activities is often unrealistic. Further, only a relatively small proportion of current youth seem to identify with public "heroes." Despite increases in the number of school counselors, both professionals and students find this resource unsatisfactory in both quantity and quality.

On the one hand, learning their normative cultural work roles of housewife and mother may be easier for girls because they have the mother directly available as a model with whom they can identify. On the other hand, their task has become increasingly difficult as their adult roles have become more ambiguous. The rate at which females are entering the labor force is rising steeply. Even a decade or more ago females constituted one-third of the labor force, and girls could anticipate working outside the home for 25 years. As of 1966, approximately 25% of all mothers with children under three were gainfully employed; the comparable figures for mothers of children aged 3 to 5 and 6 to 16 are about one-third and one-half respectively.

Given the broad implications of work in our society and the difficulties of coping with them, it is small wonder that vocational preparation, selection, and adjustment constitute a salient aspect of adolescence and youth. Indeed, subjects in one recent large-scale survey considered vocationally related decisions their most critical task, outweighing heterosexual and other aspects of development. Judging by a wide variety of measures, serious concern about these problems begins to appear at about 12 years and increases into the adult years.

Scientists from several disciplines have proposed theories of vocational development differing somewhat in their interpretation of the significance of choices but quite similar in their basic outlines. Before 10, needs and fantasies predominate. Between 11 and 12, preferences are primarily a function of interests, but between 13 and 14 abilities and job requirements come to be considered. The age span 15–24 is an exploratory period, beginning with tentative choices at 15–17 based on simultaneous evaluation of needs, interests, abilities, values, and opportunities. During the transitional phase (18–21) the individual is still working out his self-concept, but he enters the labor market or advanced training and realistic considerations are given more weight. By age 22–24 a specific ocupation has usually been selected, a job secured, and a trial period is under way. If the job proves unsatisfactory, another trial phase may ensue before the person becomes occupationally established. To date, theoretical formulations have been derived largely with respect to males because in our society gainful employment for women is still usually subordinate to family roles and of lower average status. However, the need for parallel studies of women is recognized and will probably become more urgent with continued merging of sex roles.

Much of the data on vocational development between 14 and 24 is based upon the use of occupational aspirations as an index of knowledge about occupations, values attached to them, and evaluation of choices. The general tenor of the results is that vocational plans and goals become increasingly specific, stable, and realistic with advancing age and grade. Without modification, however, this is a deceptive statement. Only the findings on specificity of choice are quite straightforward. Group data show a fairly systematic trend from a relatively high proportion unable to state any preference through broad categories, such as businessman, to an increasing frequency of relatively specialized choices, e.g., accountant.

As might be expected, estimates of stability of choice vary with grade levels sampled, interval between assessments, and type of measure. Patterns of preference expressed on vocational interest tests are highly stable by 25, and they are moderately so even by mid-adolescence. Other measures reveal far less consistency. With broad occupational categories as the measure, about one-third of the sample in a widely cited study were in or preparing for areas chosen shortly before high school graduation when contacted five years later. The use of specific occupations and different time intervals showed 67% changing choices at least once during the last three years of high school and only 11% consistent over the 8-year span from tenth grade to five years after graduation. A continuing study of 127,000 students who entered 246 collegiate institutions in the United States in 1961 found that about 25% changed their long-term career plans and 10% changed their major during the senior year. For youth who enter the job market from high school, the next several years are ones of considerable job change and concomitantly high rate of unemployment. By the mid-twenties, dissatisfaction becomes common among those who have not climbed the occupational ladder as fast as they had expected. In sum, the research evidence indicates considerable change in vocational goals and plans well into the early adult years.

Examination of the factors influencing educational and vocational aspirations and attainments shows the family to be the most powerful. Strong associations have been reported between these criteria and such familial characteristics as father's occupation and education, mother's education and employment, siblings' aspirations and attainments, child-rearing practices, and parental motivation. Besides providing values, models, and direct support the nuclear family has an indirect influence through relatives and friends of the parents and siblings, peers, place of residence and schools. In reports of youth or adults about the most important influences upon their vocational aims parents receive the largest proportion of nominations, with the school, peers, relatives or other adults, and work experience being the others most frequently cited. Peer groups typically are composed of youngsters from homes of similar status and tend to reinforce familial values. Similarly, the parents' freinds are of comparable socioeconomic status and interests. Family income helps to determine not only the likelihood of higher education but also place of residence and, hence, the caliber of lower school attended and the type of neighbors.

Schools and place of residence appear also to have effects independent of those associated with family. For example, lower-class youth who attend predominantly middle-class schools have aspirations more like those of their classmates and teachers. Interview data show that youngsters perceive school as a means toward vocational ends. They quite often mention courses as having stimulated their interest in a field and sometimes mention teachers either similarly or as models or motivators. Counselors are infrequently cited except by college-bound students. Probably the relatively strong influence of the school as an institution is a combination of peer, course, teacher, and counselor influences in addition to the effect of direct job training or educational preparation. Graduation from college has a positive influence on vocational attainment independent of family and personal characteristics (such as IQ and grades). Recent studies also show a positive effect of the cohesiveness of the college peer group on persistence in college, and they show that career choice increasingly comes to resemble the modal choice of the college peer group. Rural as opposed to urban residence is associated with lesser educational and vocational attainment, the latter at least in part because of a lesser variety of job opportunities.

Given the strength of conflicting opinions about the desirability of work experience for the young, one can only wish the supporting data were as strong. Opponents take a protective view, either in terms of preventing mental, physical, or emotional harm or in terms of reducing the competition of a cheap labor supply. Proponents of work experience for the young argue that it contributes to both vocational and personality development and helps to prevent delinquency. On the side of the protectionists are data showing high accident rates among young persons (e.g., those employed in hazardous occupations), a study reporting a reliably lower grade point average among working students than among matched controls (Bateman, 1949), and another study in which eleventh-grade girls who worked were found to have significantly lower scores on the emotional and social scales of an adjustment inventory than did matched controls (Bateman, 1950). Matching in Bateman's first study was on the basis of sex, grade, school, IQ, and father's occupation and in the second on school, grade, and father's occupation. These matching criteria do not, of course, control for a number of other possible sources of the observed differences between working and nonworking groups.

Occupying a neutral ground are data on household chores from two studies. A large-scale survey of children aged 9–17 included measures of work habits, responsible attitudes, and home chores. Both of the former measures showed regular increases with age, but neither was correlated with work experience in the form of home° duties even after years of such training. Instead, responsibility was associated with responsible attitudes on the part of parents. A responsible attitude in childhood was not predictive of later mental health but was related to social outcomes in that outstanding youth in the community had high scores as children while delinquents scored low. A long-term longitudinal study of persons who were adolescents during the depression showed that economic deprivation increased the incidence of participation in household tasks for many adolescents, particularly girls, but this experience had no influence on their adult behavior or attitudes. Employment outside the home, however, had primarily positive concurrent and long-term effects.

According to mothers' reports, responsibility with money was characteristic of 87% of boys and girls employed outside the home, 66% of those paid for home chores, and only 38% of those who had no obligations. As adults boys (but not girls) who had worked outside the home were more likely to save money (80% v. 54%) and to value dependability in their children. Adults who were not relatives saw gainfully employed adolescents of both sexes as more industrious and energetic, and the girls (but not boys) as more dependable. The direction of the influence is not clear, however. Perhaps the more energetic and industrious were more assiduous in seeking jobs. A work-oriented adult life-style was also characteristic of women who had worked outside the home during adolescence. Adult orientation as evidenced by time spent with adults during school-related activities and by expression of interest in adults, was greater among boys and girls who were gainfully employed than among those who had household chores or no home or other duties. Social independence during adolescence had a very low but positive association with gainful employment for boys. More girls who had no work responsibilities of any kind were socially independent than among those who had jobs both in and outside the home (50% v. 25%), perhaps because the latter had such heavy burdons. However, adolescents with responsibilities were not handicapped with respect to popularity. For middle class children responsibilities also did not restrict time for recreation, but working class youngsters were limited in this way.

Also supporting advocates of work experience for young persons is evidence from shorter-term research. Among a sample of ninth-grade boys a measure of acceptance of responsibility was found to be correlated with a history of having obtained gainful employment by individual initiative and working in situations that were relatively free of supervision and that required responsibility. Negro males in grades seven to twelve reported that they felt work experience had been helpful to them in establishing economic independence (68%) and emotional independence (45%), of less help in accepting appropriate sex roles or developing relationships with peers (20% each), and of no effect in seeking or achieving socially responsible behavior. External evidence, however, indicated that work experience may have been helpful in rehabilitating the delinquent boys. Other data suggest that work experience programs under the supervision of the school with related course work in school benefit those of lower ability and academic skills more than their higher standing peers.

In two studies done several decades ago, rural males and high school and college women tended to view work experience as the most important influence upon their vocational choices. However, the level of the association between part-time work and vocational choice was low and may have been an artifact of special conditions; i.e., the limited types of jobs available. In recent years the job choices open to most of the young have become increasingly narrow and may bear little resemblance to long-term career opportunities. Nevertheless, several recent studies have found that the experienced find their vocational choices more satisfactory than do the inexperienced.

Despite compulsory schooling and the limited variety of jobs open to them, young persons are entering the part- or full-time labor force in increasing proportions. Surveys conducted for the Boy and Girl Scouts suggest that youth often regard any work as desirable because they see it as contributing to their sense of worth and identity and as giving them access to more experiences (perhaps in part because they have more money to spend). That this attitude shifts with age may be inferred from research by industrial psychologists showing that job satisfaction declines in the early twenties and that full-time work experience changes vocational values in both men and women. With increasing age a greater preference is expressed for independence and working conditions in which one can be "on his own." Profit, fame and even interesting work are less emphasized.

Another kind of work experience is offered by public or quasi-public programs such as the Job Peace Corps and 4-H projects. Some information bearing on the possible benefits of such approaches is available. For example, over a two-year period Peace Corps volunteers were found to become more toughminded and realistic, independent and self-directed and more sympathetic with the problems of the American Negro. Their major motives for joining were to have a period for self-discovery and reassessment while they were uncertain of their long-term goals yet at the same time to make a worthwhile contribution to society. A mid-western study of students who participated in projects and productive enterprises connected with agricultural and home economics courses indicated that those most active in projects were more likely to enter college or become farm owners. In this case and that of the Peace Corps one must wonder whether the young persons participating were of the sort who would have shown similar attitudes and behaviors even if they had not had these particular experiences.

Although the data are limited and relevant variables often confounded, on balance the weight of the evidence suggests that work experience outside the home is more likely to have positive than deleterious effects. In addition to its long-term implications for life-style summarized at the outset of this section, work seems to have psychological significance for youth as a step toward independence and to contribute to progress toward maturity via personal-social characteristics whether or not it promotes vocational development *per se*. Even rather humdrum gainful employment may yield these benefits. Nevertheless, some findings suggest that when youth perceive their activities as making a real contribution, whether in terms of the kind of task or the real need for it even if routine, the experience is more likely to be a constructive one.

Independence and Autonomy. Two major aspects of developing into adulthood in our society are moving from a childlike emotional dependence on parents to a mature form of interdependence with others and acquiring a sense of self-regulation and direction. Adults cannot count on the support of an extended family in dealing with their day-to-day problems but must carry their own controls and direction with them as they move about the country or up the social ladder. Contrary to much of the lay and professional literature, the process of attaining independence and autonomy in our society does not seem typically to be accompanied by a dramatic struggle between rebellious youth and reluctant parents. Although the research data do show a desire on the part of the young for the externals of individual freedom and a marked increase during adolescence of autonomous behavior (e.g., gainful employment, control of spending money, and dating), they also indicate considerable willingness on the part of parents to accommodate to these desires. More significantly, emotional detachment, as reflected, for example, in relative amounts of time spent with parents and peers and the relative weight placed on the wishes of parents and peers, is achieved much more gradually.

Our society has been indicted, relative to less complex and affluent ones, because it prolongs dependency through extensive compulsory schooling and other legal forms and then expects a quick transition at some point to adult work, family, and citizenship roles. Critics claim that we reward dependency by providing privileges without responsibilities and that we are inconsistent in our demands for both conformity and individuality of behavior and in the discontinuities between childhood and adult status. On the other hand, a prolonged adolescence has been viewed as a "psychosocial moratorium", i.e., a period before the assumption of adult tasks during which the person has time to work out his sexual and vocational identities and a coherent philosophy of life. Psychoanalytic and other observations have been interpreted as indicating more advanced personality development with increasing education and time before entry into full-time employment and marriage or the inverse, i.e., that a rapid rate of physical maturation, early marriage or entry into full-time employment truncates adolescence and inhibits maturation of the personality. However, the possibility that persons who select different routes, e.g., prolonged education *vs.* early employment, may already differ in their potentialities for personal complexity and maturity has not been carefully tested.

Personality Integration. Many professionals and laymen regard Erikson's conceptualization of the "quest for identity" as capturing the essence of adolescence in our culture. Implicit in this conceptualization of the process of personality maturation is the development of a sense of continuity of "self" that includes sex and vocational roles and a coherent and hierarchical sense of values. In a society where sex roles are blurred, vocational roles highly varied, and models with whom to identify scarce, "role diffusion" is a hazard for the developing person.

More prosaic data gathered by researchers working in a variety of frameworks show that during adolescence recreational, vocational, heterosexual, social, and political attitudes and behaviors, with certain temporary exceptions, become more adultlike. Interest patterns become narrower and more focused and some research indicates that this trend arises at least as much from the development of dislikes as from overwhelming enthusiasms. Leisure time activities become more sedentary, e.g., time spent reading rises toward adult levels and participation in athletic and other events moves from active to spectator. The latter trend in particular seems inconsistent with the high energy level of youth, but probably reflects the specialization characteristic of large groups and the way in which heterosexual interest can find expression. Moreover, energies find outlets in more concentrated attention to school, a few sustained leisure time interests, and, often, employment. The amount of time spent "loafing," i.e., without at least ostensibly being engaged in some activity, decreases markedly.

Data gathered in a variety of ways show that preoccupation with bodily concerns is prevalent during early adolescence when physical change is rapid and often accompanied by temporary afflictions such as acne and obesity. Also, youngsters become more perceptive about the ways in which others—peers and adults—view them. Masculinity and feminity as reflected on interest tests rise steeply, reaching a peak during the high school period and then subsiding. Sexual activity also increases markedly, in terms of frequency of experiences by an individual and of the number of persons engaging in some form of sexual behavior, especially among boys. The relative influence of biological and social factors on such interests and behaviors has been a topic of considerable debate.

As adolescence progresses, self-preoccupation shifts toward personal traits and values, vocational aims, and heterosexual roles. Moral standards become more internalized and individualized and concern about philosophical, ethical and political issues rises. Despite the public prominence of some youthful social and political "activists," participation in citizenship roles is not, on the average, any greater than among adults. However, concern and responsibility for others, our ideal for healthy adulthood, typically become stronger and more highly channeled when the individual has achieved some measure of independence, autonomy, and "identity."

Overview. Among the characteristics of adolescents and youth growing into adulthood in our society that have implications for institutional arrangements directed toward their socialization are:

(1) great heterogeneity within and among individuals with respect

to the rate of physical, intellectual, and social development, particularly between 14 and 17 years, including a temporary disjunction between the average maturity of males and females;

(2) a level of cognitive and physical abilities that, on the average, closely approximates those of adults by mid-adolescence;

(3) increasing differentiation of interests and abilities;

(4) changing patterns of preferred peer group arrangements that reflect growing heterosexual interests as well as emancipation from parents;

(5) increasing desires for independence, autonomy, and a sense of "identity" that often seek expression in gainful employment as well as in informal social interactions.

The global impression gleaned from the research literature is that the family, school, and peer group are the primary socializing agents in our society, with the mass media playing an increasing role and the influence of the church perhaps less apparent than it really may be. In terms of the various roles to which the young must be socialized, attention to parenthood is conspicuously lacking. Most of our youth get very little experience, much less direct tuition, in child-rearing. Systematic vocational training occurs almost exclusively in or through the school, with work experience being largely a function of individual circumstances and initiative. The family figures predominantly in socialization toward work roles, but neither it, the school, nor the wider community seems to offer as much conscious attention to, or facilities for, this function as may be desirable. At least in part this situation may result from lack of certainty among adults about values, goals, and needs.

From existing data and theories both support for and contraindications to a variety of institutional arrangements can be marshalled. Examples of divergent approaches to which this statement applies include: age segregation vs. age heterogeneity; age grouping, developmental grouping, or self-selection of groups; "spiked" vs. "broadfront" learning; self-directed vs. other-directed activities; and total vs. partial institutional arrangements. Probably the greatest lesson here is that the sometimes contradictory needs of individuals for both inner- and outer-directed activities and the great range of difference in abilities and interests among individuals require variety and flexibility in institutional arrangements. Our institutions need to be evaluated in terms of how we can improve the options open to the young in preparing for adulthood.

7. Youth Culture

The phenomenon of "adolescence" was named at the turn of the century by G. Stanley Hall. (1904) It signalled the emergence of a period of life beyond childhood but before adoption of adult responsibilities. Those children who did not go directly into the labor force, but continued into high school occupied this emerging stage of life. As this fraction of the child population who stayed on in school continued to grow, the period of adolescence began to encompass the whole age group of 13 or 14 to 17. When this happened in the 1930s and 1940s, a distinctive pattern of life began to emerge, around the high school. Some sociologists (Gordon, 1957; Coleman, 1961) described this pattern of life in the 1950s as a pattern in which high school athletes, cars, clothes, and dating played an important part and began to write of an "adolescent society" or an "adolescent culture." Since then, there have been ongoing disputes about whether there existed an adolescent culture, or whether teen-agers were not more adult-oriented than appeared from descriptions of the adolescent culture. (See, for example, Elkin and Wesley, 1955, and Gottleib, 1963). Was there a distinctive adolescent culture or subculture? The debate probably existed because on the one hand, it was obvious that for some teen-agers, a world of their own in which adults played only background roles did exist, while others were oriented to adults in their immediate vicinity, and pursued a style of life in anticipation of adult responsibilities. But it was certainly true, at least by the 1950s, that there were some adolescents in every high school who were highly involved in the social system of adolescents, and who developed distinctive cultural norms toward schoolwork, relations between the sexes, athletics, music, clothes, and other items.

But during the 1960s and 1970s, a new phenomenon developed, one that was named by Kenneth Kenniston (1970) : the phenomenon of youth. Kenniston pointed out, as Hall had done for adolescents seventy years earlier, that there was emerging a new period of life, after adolescence but before assumption of adult responsibilities. He called this period "youth," and the term youth has come to be more and more widely used for a segment of the population, some of whom are adolescent, some of whom are beyond adolescence, but not yet in full independent adult status. The term "adolescent" and the period of adolescence has been in part absorbed by this more inclusive category of "youth." As college attendance grew in the 1960s, this segment came to include a larger and larger fraction of the post-high school age group, along with the high school age group).

With this expansion in the 1960s came a set of distinctive patterns of activity associated with youth, but a more diverse array than those of the adolescent society in the high school. These patterns include style of dress, ranging from high involvement with new fashions to studied rejection of accepted norms of appropriate dress. They include new forms of music, and sometimes associated with it, drug use. They include small intense subgroups, with content ranging from religious and mystical belief to political activity. These and other attributes can be said to describe a "youth culture," not because they constitute a homogeneous culture, nor because they characterize all youth, but because taken together, they are activities initiated by youth and pursued more by youth than by adults. It is still the case that many young persons are little involved in the "youth culture," and are fully occupied in preparation for adult responsibilities. But the youth culture in all its varieties nevertheless exists, and it is important to examine it in some detail.

This examination will not attempt to describe youth culture in all its facets. That would entail a study of the rock music culture, the hippy culture, the athletic crowd in high schools, the motorcycle cult, the surfers, the new left, the drug culture, the Jesus cult, Hare Krishna, mysticism, the college campus culture, and others, some international, others highly localized. Indeed, a description of the present varieties of youth culture would be quickly incorrect because the culture changes rapidly. Rather, we will aim to examine certain elements that recur, certain characteristics that are held in common. The value of this examination lies in the fact that these common elements derive from the special position that young people find themselves in today. It is not a position initially created nor sought by youth, but one imposed on them by the structural forms that their environments have come to take. Because these structural forms are called into question by this report, it is important to examine their effect on the youth culture.

Inward-Lookingness

One element that characterizes all segments of the youth culture is *inward-lookingness*. Young people, whatever segment of the youth culture they choose, look very largely to one another. Their friends are other young people and a large fraction of their communications come from young people. Even the goods and services they consume have increasingly come to be provided by young people. In popular music, for example, nearly all the popular musical entertainers—whether rock bands or pop singers—are part of the youth culture itself. In contrast, the entertainers of twenty years ago, whose audience was youthful as it is today, were seldom young themselves. The revolution in clothes fashion, which began in England in the sixties, is a revolution in which the young are themselves the designers and the boutique owners. The New Left rejects the Old Left nearly as much as it rejects the Old Right, and looks for its popular heroes among the young themselves: Jerry Rubin, Bobby Seale, Huey Newton, Rennie Davis.

The change that has occurred is a striking one: in politics, in music and popular entertainment, in clothes, even in movies. Not only are the producers producing for a youth taste; the producers and consumers are both part of the self-contained youth culture. This has been a change—in all these areas—during the past twenty, or perhaps even ten, years.

Perhaps the change in the process can be seen most clearly in clothes fashions. Beginning in the early 1960s, there was a new source of fahion. The styles began with miniskirts, moved to hotpants, to no-bra fashions, cheap fake furs, midis, maxis, and so on. The old high fashion, which is now nearly gone, had its center in Paris, with clothes designed for women in their thirties and at the top of the fashion and financial ladder. It trickled down, in income and in age, through copies made in mass production and sold in every woman's shop. The revolution in fashion began in London's Carnaby Street and King's Road, where young designers created new designs and sold them to the young. The miniskirts, and their successors, began there, among the young, and spread throughout Europe and America, trickling up in age this time, rather than down.

It is no accident that this fashion revolution began in London rather than New York, because the distribution system there is less controlled by corporate enterprise. Clothes are less sold in the U.S. pattern of large stores and chains whose buyers order in quantities from large manufacturers. The young could more easily break into the women's clothing market with small-scale operations.

But whatever its problems of gestation, the central characteristic of the revolution in women's fashion was that it was a revolution by the young, for the young. Youth looked toward youth rather than toward adults for its fashion.

At least three aspects of youth's position in society brought this about: First, the large number of youth, beginning with those who turned 14 in 1960 and 20 in 1966 and are now in their late twenties. They were born in 1946, the beginning of the baby boom, and they were the first wave of a tide that continues to make the youth fraction of the population much larger than it was in 1950 or 1960.

Second, as youth continue their education for longer and longer periods, they are together with other youth and segregated from adults. Adults, meanwhile, have more and more come to work in large organizations where youth are not present. Adult women have increasingly left the home and neighborhood, where they were the keepers of the mores, and have followed the men into work organizations. Thus not only are there fewer adults for youth to look to as models, and as points of reference; youth and adults are more segregated than ever from daily contact with one another.

Finally, a third change in the position of youth helps sustain this inward-lookingness, though it is not directly responsible for it. This is their increasing affluence. Young people's economic position in the household has passed through three stages: in the first, their labor was needed to help support the family, whether on the farm or in the factory. Second, as families came to breathe more easily, the youth were freed to continue their education. Finally, families have enough money so that they can afford to let their young spend some of it, on things they want. Youth now have a large portion of the discretionary income of society.

Thus youth can back up their tastes with money. They can buy the records they like and the clothes they like, can go to the movies they like, can pay for underground newspapers if they like. Their inward-lookingness need not be confined to finding their popular heroes among youth, or to conformity with norms laid down by their peers; it can be expressed also by the power of their dollars.

Psychic Attachment

A second element that characterizes the culture of youth is similar to the first, but not the same: it is the *psychic attachment* of youth to others their own age. Today, for many youth, their most intimate psychic bonds are with one another. The evolution of the dating pattern probably shows this best, for this pattern shows the increasing psychic need of the young for one another over the past half-century. Traditional societies, whether rural America or pre-1960 Europe, show little in the way of "dating" at all. The practice developed in the high schools and colleges of America, first among a small elite in the colleges in the 1920s and 1930s as a pattern of courtship fitted to the campus life in which large numbers of marriageable young were thrown together on their own. Scott Fitzgerald's novels contain the flavor of that early period. A sociologist, Willard Waller (1937:727–34), named it the "rating and dating" system. It moved down to the high schools on a broad scale in the 1940s, where it replaced the parentally supervised and much less intimate outings, gatherings, community dances, and parties (which often included not only youth but adults as well). In high schools, dating became not so much a pattern of courtship as an opportunity for intimacy and closeness. In the 1950s the dating system began to break down, under the force of a new phenomenon that developed out of it: "going steady." Going steady reduced the uncertainty inherent in the competitive market of the dating system, and simultaneously intensified the psychic intimacy that had been begun by the dating system. Going steady appears to provide for teen-agers the same kind of psychic support that the intense husband-wife relation in the nuclear family provides in modern society: a psychic haven in a society where other relationships have become increasingly distant.

But in the late 1960s and early 1970s, going steady is being followed by a new pattern, which is enhanced by the drug culture, in both high school and college; a pattern of closeness, intimacy, and extreme openness among a small group of close friends, often around a marijuana joint which passes from one to another. Another pattern, the commune, has developed as well for a small fraction of youth. Although it derives in part from other sources, it can be seen as a kind of end point in the search for psychic warmth that began with dating and rating systems.

This evolution of social patterns has a single thread running through it: the increasing need for close relations, for the psychic support and security of another or others very close. Those needs have always existed for young persons, and for persons of all ages. But the difference now is that young persons turn much more to other young persons than they once did. A flavor of another time and place is given in a description by Elizabeth Bott (1971) of young married working-class women of London's Bethnal Green shortly after World War II. These young women had their closest ties to "Mum," their mothers. The time they spent during the day and during the evening was with Mum, the talking they did was with Mum, their joys and sorrows they shared with Mum. The men they married were necessary to the household, but their psychic support came from Mum.

The distance between Bethnal Green and modern youth in America is a very great one. The psychic needs of young women may be filled by a "Mum" in Bethnal Green. But in America in which kinship structure is weakening in each decade, and in which even the nuclear family provides little psychic strength for its teen-age members, the needs must be met from outside. As the psychic strength of the family has dwindled, the evolution of the dating system and the ultimate emergence of the very close circle and the communal group has supplied those same needs.

This element of a psychic need for closeness increasingly unfilled by the family is apparent not only in the evolution of the dating system and in communal groups. It probably is an important stimulus to the use of soft drugs and to the religious movements among the young. It is an aspect of youth's current situation which helps spawn activities that are very unlike, but tied together by this one need.

The Drive Toward Autonomy

A third element that runs through all segments of the youth culture is a *press toward autonomy*. This manifests itself in a high regard for youth who successfully challenge adults, or who act autonomously of adults. Rock groups injecting direct allusions to LSD and marijuana in their songs, political apostles such as Stokely Carmichael and Abbie Hoffman, youthful actors who represented in their roles the independence of youth, like Jimmy Dean, have enormous attraction for the young, even those who oppose the specific things they stand for. Part of the regard in which football players and other athletes have traditionally been held during high school lies in the fact that they can capture the attention and respect of adults, and that the fortunes of the school depend on them more than on most teachers in the school.

The situation is like that described in this passage written about Negroes in Chicago in the 1940s (Drake and Cayton, 1946) :

> If a man "fights for the race," if he seems to be "all for the race," if he is "fearless in his approach to white people," he becomes a Race hero. Similarly any Negro becomes a hero if he beats the white man at his own game or forces the white world to recognize his talent or service or achievement. Racketeer or preacher, reactionary or communist, ignoramous or savant—if a man is an aggressive, vocal, uncompromising Race Man he is everybody's hero. Even conservative Negroes admire colored radicals who buck the white world. Preachers may oppose sin, but they will also express a sneaking admiration for a Negro criminal who decisively outwits white people. Even the quiet, well-disciplined family man may get a thrill when a "bad Negro" blows his top and goes down with both guns blazing at the White Law.

This passage has striking applicability to youth relative to adults.

Substitute "youth" for "Negro," "adult" for "white man," change a few phrases, and the passage could be directly applied to youth today. The reason lies in the essential similarity between youth's position relative to adults today, and the position of Negroes in relation to whites described in the 1940s study. Youth are a subordinate nation, and any youth that can stand up to adults is regarded with a certain amount of respect, awe, and admiration.

This widespread regard for youth who successfully challenge adults or act autonomously is not entirely new, but it has grown over the years. As late as the 1950s and early 1960s, the crowd of boys that were most rebellious against adults were, in high school, not only regarded as rebellious and antischool by most teen-agers; they were regarded with disdain, and some pity. They were the crowd that was unaccepted by the "in" crowd in the school, they were "turned off" by the school and society, they were the "black leather jacket" group, or the "black boot" crowd, and were regarded as "drapes" by the teen-agers who were part of the leading crowd. They were always from poorer backgrounds than other students, they were the residue of working-class students who had not been captured by the adult-oriented adolescent society and by the promise of school and the upward mobility it would bring. Today, there are four changes: the alienated culture has expanded in size, now doing its own capturing of middle-class youth who are turned off by the school and society; it no longer has the distinct boundaries that once isolated it from the majority, but has fringes of people who are in and out of it; it is often the front-runner in forbidden activities like drugs which many other youth pick up later; and it is regarded not so much with disdain by the majority of teen-agers, as with some awe for what is seen as courage in rejecting the school and the society, and for engaging in illegal but partially approved activities.

A quotation from a high school girl in 1960 about the value climate in her school suggests the contrast with today (Coleman, 1961:120):

> At—, a good reputation is important. . . . Neat dressing is taken into consideration too, but a girl would not be blackballed [from the high school sorority] unless she were a really impossible dresser. I think neatness is stressed the most. In a way this means all-aroundedness. If a girl is a lot of fun, dresses fairly neatly, has a good reputation, wants to get in, she can get into a sorority, provided no girl in the sorority has a personal grudge against her.

This quotation could certainly characterize the value climate in some youth cultures today; but it has a distinct pre-1960s flavor, reflecting the more positive orientation of the youth of that time to norms encouraged by the adult society.

The special position within the youth culture of those youth who can hold their own with adults (whether in competition with them, as in athletics, or in opposition to them, as in political action or campus confrontation) is characteristic of any subgroup in society that sees itself as a subgroup and in a subordinate position as a subgroup. The respect paid to these members derives from the fact that they overturn, in their small way, that subordinate position. They take out of the hands of the superordinate group—the adults in this case —a small portion of the control they hold over the subordinate group.

The change that has come about in the 1960s and 1970s is a change from a nascent and mild form of this response, which gave prestige to athletes who could draw adults' attention and control the school's fortunes, to one which gives prestige to youth who challenge adults in direct confrontation. In the earlier stage, the norms of the adolescent society (for there was no "youth culture" before the 1960s) were enough guided by adult social norms that direct contravention of adult norms gained not respect but condemnation by most other young people. The change that has occurred results in part from a strengthening of the self-definition of the group as a distinct subgroup in society. That is, youth now see themselves more as a specific group with specific interests than at earlier times. It results in part from an increased deviation of norms of youth from those that adults in their homes and schools and colleges encourage them to hold. The social sources of that increased deviation are important to recognize.

There is one major change in society in recent years that is more responsible than any other for this increased deviation. This is a change in communication. The change has two components: First, there is an absolute increase in the fraction of society's total communications that are carried through the mass media. Second, there is a proliferation in the number of channels through which information flows in the mass media, and a resulting greater diversity of communication in the media. The first occurred through television, which captures a larger portion of people's time and attention than any other medium ever did. The second occurred through a proliferation of media channels that cater to minority tastes. The proliferation has occurred in three media: movies, radio, and newspapers. Movies before television sought a mass audience and catered to a mass taste. When television came and drew off the mass audience, movies began to appeal to minority tastes. One of these was that of an audience that had least deserted movies for television: the unmarried youth audience. Probably because movies offered privacy from family which television did not, young people never stopped going to movies, as did adults, and the moviemakers began to design movies to appeal to teen-agers.

The second medium in which channels proliferated was radio. Again, as television drew off the mass audience, radio stations began to search out minority tastes. As they did so, and thus specialized, they began to increase in number, through new stations, both in the broadcast and FM band. Many of these stations are now "youth" stations, which play a form of music attended to by youth alone. In addition, some of the "talk" shows are youth-oriented, dealing with problems of interest to youth: drug problems, sex-related problems (VD, contraception, pregnancy, abortion), problems with police, problems of dress, problems with school, and with parents. ("Talk" shows are a new form of radio, invented by a disk jockey in the 1960s, in which listeners phone in to an announcer and discuss an issue of concern to them or one that has been raised previously on the show. Both sides of the conversation are broadcast). These stations inevitably have become a form of communication among youth, with the disk jockeys sometimes acting as crusaders, sometimes merely as a medium through which some youth express their interests.

Most recently, in the late 1960s and 1970s, has come a new kind of station: the "alternative medium." This is a station (sometimes on the broadcast band, more often on FM) that is run by young people, is tolerant of and expresses the tastes of one or more of the deviant cultures among youth, and takes an antiestablishment position in news reports and in disk jockey discussions. The main fare of these stations is music, but sandwiched in is discourse that expresses youth interests and tastes. The use by youth of these as direct communication media is reflected by the fact that on some such stations, rides to other cities, or riders wishing a ride to other cities, are announced, with telephone numbers, so that listeners can make their own ride arrangements. The advertisers on these stations are ordinarily local boutiques and other stores catering to youth, and manufacturers of products that youth buy. (One such station carries advertisements for roach killers, the advertisers recognizing that many of the station's young audience live in old roach-infested apartments).

It is interesting, as an aside, that just as the corporate structure of clothes merchandising in the United States prevented the emergence of a fashion revolution that broke out in London, the corporate structure of broadcasting in England has prevented the radio revolution that has begun in the United States. In England, the only stations are state monopolies (the First, Second, and Third Programmes), which have not responded to the interests of youth. Attempts to create youth-oriented channels have led to stations being created on the mainland (Radio Luxembourg is the best known), and stations located on off-shore islands. The latter have led to periodic wars with the coastal police.

The final medium in which there has been a proliferation of channels has been newspapers. As the mass newspapers have shrunk in number, most cities being served by only one or two independent newspapers, an underground press has blossomed. With the *Village Voice* in New York as a long-standing prototype, semiunderground and underground newspapers have grown up in most large cities and many small ones. A few have a national circulation, some have a citywide circulation, some are college-campuswide, some are circulated within high schools, and finally some have begun within business organizations. The topics are New Left and Black Left politics, drugs, sex, and mysticism. They provide, probably as much as any other single medium, a nationwide communication network among antiestablishment youth.

The two components of change in communication in American society, increased attention to mass media and a proliferation of channels has been newspapers. As the mass newspapers have shrunk norms, and values for youth. Until this change, which provided communications directed at youth by youth, young persons' communications with one another were largely restricted to the face-to-face contact. Deviant norms could spring up, and did, in specific schools and neighborhoods, but there were no mass media to link the youth together in different localities and provide national and international resonance to strengthen those norms. Information and directives from parents, from school authorities, and from the mass media controlled by adults, exercised a partial monopoly of communication, shaped the elites among youth, and held the alienated antiestablishment culture down to a small minority, disapproved by the youth who were "important." That has not completely changed, but it is changing, and it will change even more as youth gain a firmer grip on those communication channels that have come to serve them in recent years. These media strengthen and maintain those norms of youth that deviate most from those held by the mass of adults, and thus as these media consolidate their position, the antiestablishment norms will strengthen relative to others.

A note should be added here about the interaction between the adult counterculture and the strengthening of youth counterculture. Before the middle 1960s, the deviant subcultures or countercultures among young persons subsisted on their own. They sprouted from the alienation created by the school and the adolescent society within the school, and provided a haven for those youth who could not meet the school's demands and were unaccepted by the dominant teen-age crowd. But as television more fully focused attention on national and international events, and as the proliferation of channels in the mass media took place, minority and antiestablishment expression among adults grew. It found a ready audience among some youth, and provided them with both content and justification for their antiestablishment orientation. Thus as the communication channels opened up in society, those norms in the youth culture that had been kept confined to an unsuccessful minority gained strength from the newly deviant adult expressions. It is probably true also that the content of events strengthened both the expression of deviant opinion by adults and the responsiveness to it by youth. In particular, the Vietnam War, which threatened youth more than any other segment of the population, provided such content. But the essential change of the 1960s was the proliferation of mass media, which both allowed the expression by adults of deviant opinion and provided youth with their own channels which resonate to the antiestablishment and antiadult norms of youth.

Concern for the Underdog

A fourth element that is common to youth in nearly all segments of youth culture is a *concern for the underdog*. Such a concern does not come naturally to children and youth; they can be, when unsocialized, savage and sadistic as animals, without compassion. Anyone who has watched the savagery of young children knows that concern for the underdog is hardly present at early ages.

Concern for the underdog among youth finds its expression mostly in political support: in sympathies for the Third World, in political alliances with blacks and with women, in the pilgrimage of youth to the South in the early 1960s to open it up for blacks, in sentiments antagonistic to the corporate structure of society (a sort of modern-day populism), in greater sympathy for a convicted criminal than for the system of justice that convicted him, in a relaxed attitude toward stealing from large corporations, in a general antiestablishment political stance. It also manifests itself in other ways. A larger proportion of youth than of other age groups hold an anticompetitive ethic, because in competition someone must lose, and many youth are sensitive to this. Sympathy for the underdog is also a large component of the "idealism" of youth that is often noted. More youth will give to a cause if that cause is the aid of poor people. Youth will disproportionately contribute to Bangladesh relief or Biafran relief, but not to the Community Chest or medical charities.

It is a strong thread indeed which can link together political support for blacks, contributions to Bangladesh, and stealing from corporations. This support for the underdog is strong among youth, and it derives directly from the underdog position of youth themselves in modern society. Excluded from the central institutions of society, the organizations in which men and women work, brushed aside into schools "to prepare themselves," given no opportunity to view matters from a position of authority and responsibility, youth of all social classes are outsiders in society. They have, as a consequence, the political views characteristic of outsiders.

This was not always so. In the past, the central institutions of society were families, not work organizations, and the "outsiders" in society were those of all ages who belonged to families that were outsiders. Young and old from lower classes were outsiders and united in their alienation; young and old from middle and upper classes were insiders, and united in their support for the existing system.

But even beyond that, youth at ages that are now in school or college were at work or otherwise occupying adult roles. This was true not only for the lower classes in society; sons and daughters of the well-to-do often completed education by 17 or 18. Thus youth in their late teens and twenties were not outsiders, but were already directly involved in society. True, they were not often in positions of authority, because the hierarchical lines in work organizations were stronger in the past. But not all youth were on the bottom; their starting position usually depended on their family or origin, so that positions of authority were less age-graded, more class-graded, than they are today. Even those who were on the bottom had a serious responsibility for carrying out their work on which other men depended. And because men lived a shorter time, often dying in their prime, positions of greater responsibility were opened up to men at an earlier age.

Thomas Jefferson wrote the Declaration of Independence when he was 33; in earlier days, responsible positions in many areas of life were common to youth, as ship captains, generals, captains of industry, statesmen, union organizers. Today, youth's positions of responsibility lie principally in sports.

It is not even necessarily true that being kept at school prevents experience with positions of authority and responsibility. The British boarding schools, which are remarkable sociological institutions in many ways, create within them an artificial hierarchy so that by the time a young person leaves school at 18, he has been, during his final year, in a position of rather strong responsibility and authority in his house. This experience gives the young person a very different perspective on authority and responsibility than he had just a year or two before.[1]

The political repercussions to society of keeping a large and able fraction of its members as outsiders, with no history or experience of responsibility, until well after they are politically active, are certainly great. It creates a special political bias, in which many of the most able members of future elites become politically active while still in an outsider's status, still able to view the world only from the position of an outsider. It creates a warmhearted, sympathetic, and open political stance, one which focuses on certain principles like equal opportunity and civil rights but ignores others, such as honesty, reward for merit, and the rule of law.

Interest in Change

Closely related to the concern by many youth for the underdog is a fifth element: *interest in change.* Youth show a generally greater interest in change per se than do adults. The difference between youth and age in their support for the status quo is nothing new, and has been the source of much social change throughout history. But it is useful to mention this difference here, because it results from somewhat the same social source as does youth's concern for the underdog: youth's being an outsider. An outsider has no stake in the existing system. Just as lower classes have less stake in any economic and social system than do upper classes, youth have less stake in the system than do their elders.

Now although this difference has always existed, it has been increased in recent years by a structural change in society as a whole: a shift from a society in which statuses are ascribed to one in which they are achieved. As society becomes more achievement-oriented, a young person inherits less in the way of social position and job from his father's social position and job; he is more nearly on his own, starting out perhaps with educational advantages, but with only those. Thus it is not the case that children directly "inherit" their father's social position to the degree they did in the past. They begin at the bottom, and work their way up, first in the educational system, then in the occupational one. The system of occupational status and income is more highly correlated with age, with the young having lower status jobs and lower income, and the old having higher.

---

[1] It is this aspect of the social structure of the British boarding schools that has led to most of the criticism of them, for the older boys (or girls) often abused their authority. That is now largely past.

This structural change in society toward achieved statuses and away from those ascribed by virtue of kinship greatly intensifies the difference between youth and age in support of the status quo. The young have less at stake than their counterparts did a generation or two ago, and the old have more at stake. This means an increase in the relation between age and the left-right dimension of politics, the young being more left than the young of some years ago, and the old being more right.

Conclusion

What is important about these elements that characterize youth culture is that they have their origins in the relation of youth to the rest of society. Youth are segregated from adults by the economic and educational institutions created by adults, they are deprived of psychic support from persons of other ages, a psychic support that once came from the family, they are subordinate and powerless in relation to adults, and outsiders to the dominant social institutions. Yet they have money, they have access to a wide range of communications media, and control of some, and they are relatively large in number.

All these elements combine to create the special characteristics of the youth culture. It is not the "nature of youth" to show the particular characteristics that youth culture shows: it is their natural response to the somewhat unnatural position in which they find themselves in society. In other times and places, youth show different characteristics, because they are in a different relation to society. A description of an English farming village in East Anglia (Blythe, 1969) shows this. In the words of a teacher in the school:

> The children are very involved with their parents' work and with adult gossip. Quite little boys will know the technical names of tractor attachments and what is going on in the fields at a particular time of the year and the girls talk together like grown women. Neither seem to want their childhood.

In that society, the position of the young is very different from that in modern industrial society. They are, many would say, too much a part of the adult world. They want to hurry through their childhood to arrive at adulthood. In modern industrial society, nearly the opposite has begun to occur: having been forced to create and live within a youth subculture, an alternative culture, many youth are reluctant to leave it, reluctant to become assimilated into the adult culture from which they have for so long been segregated.

PART 3:   ISSUES

Introduction

Of the various themes that have recurred in the foregoing papers, two are paramount. First, segregation from others of different ages has increasingly come to characterize the social and economic position of youth in our society. This segregation takes many forms. One is separation from younger and older children outside the family. In schools, age grading and specific institutions such as the junior high school and high school have effectively removed teenagers from significant institutional contact with those under age 12 or 13. High schools and colleges operate to split the youthful age group into two groups, 14–17 and 18-upwards, with members of each group segretated from institutional contact with the other.

As part of this separation of older and younger children, there is a declining degree of contact between children and youth even within the family. The range of ages in families today much less fully approximates the age range of society as a while than was once true. Today, siblings are usually close together in age.

Another form of segregation of youth in our society is segregation from adults. There is a low degree of contact with adults in working situations outside the school and family. To the extent that youth has been removed from the labor market, the number of occasions on which they meet adults in working situations contracts. There is as well separation of youth from nonspecialized contacts with adults outside the family. Young people tend to meet adults in highly specialized relationships. In schools, for example, teachers are encountered primarily as instructors in specific subjects rather than as persons. As schools have become more specialized and as teachers have embraced the ideal of professionalization, this has become more and more the case. The separation of youth from adults is even more pronounced in their lack of contact with elderly people. Nuclear family structure and formal retirement ages have tended to force elderly people into isolation from other age groups in our society, youth included.

These aspects of segregation of youth are accompanied by a youth culture. While the youth culture does not embrace all young people, nor even exclusively young people, it rests on the social and psychological detachment of youth. Those who take part in the youth culture view themselves as "outsiders" and distant from the "system" or "establishment." Taken in conjunction with all the other aspects of segregation already mentioned, the strength of the youth culture raises serious questions. For youth culture has provided many young people with a pleasing surrogate for maturity, just as their attachment to the youth culture often conceals a negative assessment of maturity and a positive preference for continuation of the irresponsible position in which they have been held as youth.

It should be clear that the segregation of youth in our society differs from the element of hierarchial distance that traditionally marked the relationship of young and old. Segregation does not involve the subordination of youth in matters of etiquette or social address. On the contrary, the institutional segregation and psycho-social detachment of youth in our society co-exist with the democratization of social relationships between young and old. Adults today usually adopt an informal, egalitarian mode of address toward the young. It is likely that the very segregation of youth promotes more earnest efforts by adults to address youth on the latter's terms, just as the stiff and formal character of traditional relations between groups was compatible with the institutional and social intermingling of age groups in daily life. Put differently, an authoritative personal relation of adult to youth occurred when it was the primary way to establish the subordination of youth; with the segregation of youth into subordinate institutions, personal authority has become unnecessary as a way to establish hierarchy.

A second theme that has recurred in the background papers of Part 2 has been a shift in the options available to young people. As consumers young people have more options open to them than ever before. Grand tours of foreign countries were once the exclusive prerogative of sons of noblemen; now a broad segment of middle class youth enjoys foreign travel along with the ability to gratify its tastes in clothes, music, and a multitude of forms of entertainment. Similarly, educational opportunities at all levels have expanded in the 20th Century. Young people today are far more cosmopolitan in outlook than their predecessors.

While new options have opened up to young people in areas of consumption, leisure, and education, opportunities have declined in other areas. Opportunities to carry out responsible work outside the home, to engage in efforts that are important to the welfare of others, have been deferred until the end of an increasingly long period of schooling.[1] This is shown only in part by labor force statistics. For example, in 1971 almost half of the 16-to-19-year olds in the nation found some kind of employment. But over the last half century, the proportion of young people at work has declined sharply.

Moreover, recent changes in occupational requirements have especially excluded youth from some of the most challenging jobs. The explosion of certification requirements in recent decades has effectively barred nearly all young people from professional occupations, teaching included. In the past, when a college degree was not a prerequisite to professional education and when professional education was less demanding and affected fewer occupations, a young man intending to be a doctor or lawyer could begin in his late teens or early twenties. More generally, in the second half of the 20th Century the proportion of jobs which require education has increased greatly in our society, effectively closing these jobs to young people. In other words, the discrepancy between the kind of work available to youth and to adults is greater now than in the past when few jobs, whether held by youths or adults, required either explicit certification or a high level of education.

Taking these two trends together, the earlier onset of consumption opportunities has been accompanied by a deferment of productive opportunities and responsibilities.

A corollary of the deferment of economic opportunities has been a decline in options concerning the path to adult working life. Social and sometimes legal pressures make it difficult to resume education after several years out in the job market. This difficulty is certainly one of the bases underlying the frequently-heard demands for greater "relevance" in education.

Many educators and others have recognized the divorce of work and education. For much of the 20th Century, beginning with Progressive Education, the answer to this dissociation has been to diversify the school so that it comes to incorporate "real life" situations. Young people have been enouraged to experience in the microcosmic setting of the school the kind of situations which, presumably, they will confront in adulthood.

While this approach is not without merit, it has its drawbacks. First, it places an enormous administrative burden on the schools, which find themselves besieged by demands to incorporate the latest trends, some-

---

[1] This pattern differs somewhat for women, because of increasing movement into the paid labor force.

times the latest fads, into the curriculum. Secondly, however earnest the efforts to recreate the world in the school, the school is not the world, and is not perceived by students as "real." There is not the discipline of a production goal to impose standards, and in its absence, the vocational work often becomes "makework." Or if a student botches a job in a vocational course, he is not fired from the school; in fact the compulsory educational laws demand that he be kept in school. Similarly, if he puts in an extra effort, his rewards are confined to grades, which impose a motivation and discipline only for a fraction of young people.

Segregation and the shift of opportunities available to youth have grown out of some of the most basic forces of 20th Century society. Family values no longer sanction, as they once did, the early commitment of youth to productive activity. Trade unions and professional organizations, for understandable reasons, fear large scale incursions by youth into their labor markets. Humanitarian sentiment opposes the exploitation of youth. Professionalization and bureaucratization have sharply narrowed the range of youth's contacts with adults outside leisure pursuits. The forces that have isolated young people and cut off certain options once available to them have not, thus, been necessarily mean or reactionary. Paradoxically, they have been, at least in original intent, enlightened and altruistic.

Yet it seems equally clear that we have reached a point in history in which these forces are spinning out of control. What was once done to protect youth from manifest exploitation now serves to reinforce the "outsider" status of youth. Ideas and institutions that once served explicit and genuine needs, and in some cases still do, have uncritically been extended to the point where they deprive youth of experience important to their growth and development.

If society's treatment of its youth is to go beyond the school into a new phase involving design of environments appropriate for youth's development, direct attention is necessary to a number of issues. In the pages below, we discuss these issues and some of the consequences of resolving them in one direction or the other. Such an examination, of which the pages below constitute merely a start, is a useful precursor to the social inventions and social experimentation that can shape environments fruitful for youth.

1. *Segregation from Adults vs. Integration with Adults*

Our society has changed in the past century from one in which the young of this age (14–24) were in frequent and continued contact with persons older than they to one in which adult contacts are confined to parents and teachers. The age segregation is extensive enough to deprive youth and adults from effective contact with another, yet not complete enough so that the young are required to establish institutions and activities to serve their own needs. Thus many of the disadvantages of age-segregation are present, without many of the advantages.

a. Benefits of segregating youth from adults: In the past the segregation of the young into schools was in part carried out as a protection for the young and in part as a custodial agency to free adults. It was protective for the young to shield them from the harsh work activities of adults and from the predatory behavior of adults who were often seen as coarse and unfit as associates of youth. The family and the school were seen as proper places for youth, and efforts were devoted to insulating them from other institutions less beneficial to them. This protection remains codified in child labor laws and school attendance laws of today. For adults, the school kept the young in custody, freeing adults for more efficient production in their work organizations.

Both these benefits still exist to some degree. School is a healthier place for the young than are some of the institutions occupied by adults. And any institution that placed adolescents in extensive and continued contact with adults would remove some of the protection of youth that schools were designed to provide. But the harsh labor from which children were protected has vanished in many workplaces, and elaborate legal machinery has been developed to shield youth from exploitation.

The custodial benefit to adults, which allows them to get on with their work more efficiently, remains as well. If age segregation of youth were eliminated, so that all the young currently in school were injected into workplaces populated by adults, many of the average adult's contacts on his job would be with young persons, whose current counterparts are in school. The age-segregation that adults currently experience on their jobs, and which some find enjoyable, they would no longer have.

The benefit to youth of extreme age-segregation, such as would be found in a self-contained community of youth (as a boarding school could become), is the necessity for youth to fill roles currently occupied by adults: construction, purchasing, cooking, care of grounds, etc. Such roles are valuable training-grounds for adulthood. This benefit can arise in a variety of types of self-contained youth communities. It is found both in a community like Summerhill, at the extreme of unstructured freedom, and in a school like Eton, at the extreme of hierarchical structure.

In addition to these benefits to youth and adults of segregation between the two, there is a benefit for social change. Youth that are in close and continual contact with adults are often in close and continual supervision by them. This, and the close contact itself, leads youth to be near-replicas of these adults and less free to bring about social change. A degree of segregation from adults increases the change that a new generation can bring about. Adults often regard youth-initiated change with some fear, but it is one of the major means by which societies change to meet new conditions.

b. Benefits of age integration: The fundamental benefit to youth of integration with adults is the incidental experience in every day activity. When adults go off to work institutions from which the young are excluded they not only carry out work there; much of their living is done there as well. By enclosing adults' activity within these confines, work organizations increase their own efficiency, but at the expense of the incidental learning and experience that youth would otherwise have. So long as other institutions (such as the community and the extended family) made up some of these deficits, the fact was not apparent. But it is evident now that a major means by which skills, culture, ideas, and information is transmitted is vanishing as direct contacts between youth and adults in structured situations decline.

In addition to the benefit to youth, age integration between youth and adults brings a benefit to adults. Some work situations have become routine and dull to persons in them. If a larger portion of adults' everyday environment, on the job or off it, were in association with youth, the interaction would be a livening one, which could be beneficial to the adult as well as the young person. This is not to say adults would freely choose it, because there are psychic comforts from associating only with one's age mates. The balance of psychic gains and losses to adults from age segregation remains an open question which research could illuminate. It is clear at this point, however, that there are both psychological gains and losses from age-homogeneous environments.

An additional benefit to society of social integration between youth and adults is that it facilitates social order and lessens the social conflict between ages. The daily contact between youth and adults in common activities leads each to see the point of view of the other and reduces the explosive potential inherent in the isolation of youth.

In this discussion of the benefits of age segregation and integration, we have implicitly recognized what should be made more explicit: that integration of youth with adults would not only modify the lives and activities of the young: it would modify the lives and activities of adults as well. Placing youth in the hands of teachers for increasing periods of time has meant a way of life for adults that rarely includes youth other than their own children. If that is to be changed, the way of life must change as well.

Considering both the benefits of segregation and the benefits of integration, it appears to us that those of integration of youth with adults outweigh those of segregation. Such age-integration requires structure to insure protection and development of the young. But throughout history the very continuation of society has depended upon the intimate intermixture of adults and the young. This intermixture is now threatened by the weakness of the family unit, which reduces the intermixture not merely outside the family, but even within. The question of how this integration might be accomplished we will defer to a later point when concrete alternatives are considered.

2. Age Segregation Among the Young

A somewhat different issue lies in the degree of age segregation of youth of differing ages, and the segregation of youth from children. Because of the way our schools have developed, there is a high degree of age segregation within them, each year being largely segregated from those on either side. In addition, schools have sometimes been made to cover smaller age spans (e.g., the creation of the junior high school) to reduce the purportedly demoralizing influence of older youth upon younger. High school students are institutionally segregated from college students, and only in college do friendships appear with some frequency across grades. This age segregation was not so great in the past, even within schools, because of the smaller number of students served by schools in rural areas. Several grades were often taught in one room, and children had greater association with others older or younger than they.

Changes in the family have also contributed much to the increase in age segregation among the young. The number of children in a family has declined except for a period after World War II. Current families have a small number of children, closely spaced. Thus there is less cross-age association within the family, further reducing experience of youth with younger children.

In sum, current institutions have resolved the issue of age-segregation among youth in one direction, partly by intention, partly by changes in population density, partly by changes in family structure. Despite this premature resolution, it is important to evaluate the benefits of age segregation among the young and the benefits of integration.

a. Benefits of segregation among youth of different ages.

Some of the benefits of age segregation are straightforward. It is administratively simple and natural, if a school spanning 6 years of age has 600 children, with 100 children for each year of age, and each teacher can handle only about 30, to make the division by age, with each teacher's class age-homogeneous. This is especially so if children are all expected to occupy the same role, as recipients of information and skills from the teacher. Classes of children homogeneous in age are easier to handle as a mass, just as are classes homogeneous in I. Q. The one-room schoolhouse or 3-classes-in-a-grade schools of rural areas of the past were seen as makeshift, necessary only because of the scarcity of pupils.

Age homogeneity also reduces the unfair advantages that older children take of the younger, simply because older and younger are infrequently in contact. Age heterogeneity among the young requires some kind of structuring, else the anarchic lack of structure results in a survival of the fittest, meaning the oldest. But all this is more true among children, where a year of age makes a large maturational difference, than among youth, where the difference is less large (except for the spurt of puberty, which ordinarily comes before age 14, which marks our starting point; see Part 2).

b. Benefits of integration across ages among youth.

The principal benefits of age integration among children and youth arise through the experience a young person gains with others outside his age group. But those benefits are ordinarily realized only in a structured situation in which age carries with it certain responsibilities, not simply the privileges arising from greater physical strength. When this kind of structure does occur, two things are learned by the older. The first is experience with and knowledge about children of different ages, especially quite young children, with whom they may otherwise have no contact until parenthood arrives. The second is learning how to take responsibility and discharge it effectively. This is a situation that young persons seldom find themselves in, and for this reason is an especially valuable form of activity. But the learning does not take place automatically; it depends on the care, supervision, and structure within which the responsible young person carries out his action. Without such supervision, it can lead to sadism, ineffectiveness, or mutual frustration of the young person and the children for whom he is responsible.

As these comments indicate, the structuring of a system in which youth are integrated with children offers some important benefits. But they are benefits that depend on a better articulated system of relationships between adults and youth and between youth and children than ordinarily occurs in schools or elsewhere in society. Summer camps constitute perhaps the most frequent example of such a relation. Junior counselors are often as young as fourteen; counselors may be high school seniors or college freshmen. In some camps, only the director and the camp nurse have passed their 21st birthday. The example of camps and the example of a few schools in which older children and youth have some responsibility for younger children, shows that such systems of relations are not so difficult to arrange. What seems to militate against this structure in schools are two elements: First, there is the fact that youth are, up to age 16, compulsorily in school, and thus cannot be forced to accept active responsibilities, but can only be required to perform in the relatively passive role of "student." Second, students in school and college are supposed to be there "for their own benefit," to learn, with teachers paid either by society or their own tuition, to "make them learn." It is not seen as fair to divert the child from his own learning to take responsibility for others. The effect of this dual argument is to prevent that kind of development, whether it is called learning or not, that occurs through the assumption and discharge of responsibility, and that kind of understanding, whether it is called learning or not, of the way younger children respond to attention. In this, middle class youth are more deprived by society than are lower class youth, for the greater need for child care help of older siblings in lower class families gives their youth more experience in taking responsibility for children than occurs in middle class families.

It appears to us that the benefits of age integration of youth with children in relations involving responsibility far outweigh the benefits of age segregation. We do not mean to imply that there should never be age-homogeneous settings, whether social or intellectual. But the relative absence of settings involving age integration with role relations that include responsibility of youth constitute a serious and increasing gap in the experience that society owes its youth. Thus we believe that future environments for growth should include settings in which older youth can have responsibility for the young to provide an opportunity that is largely missing for youth in today's society.

3. *Grouping of the Young by Stage of Development*

Young persons of the same chronological age differ widely in their rates of physical, social, and cognitive maturation. In addition, the physical maturation of boys is, at puberty, about two years behind that of girls. The result of these varying rates is that youth grouped by chronological age, and introduced to certain experiences by chronological age, will differ widely in their mental, physical, and social levels of development. Yet if one of these other criteria is used for grouping, for example, physical maturity, then the differences in mental development, social development, and chronological age will be great. In fact, if any of these four criteria of development are used for grouping, there will be wide variation on the others.

The issue is just what principle of grouping is most beneficial for youth. At present, chronological age is the primary principle of grouping in schools, with mental maturity a secondary principle, through "ability-grouping." We know that this procedure creates some distress and very likely permanent impacts on self-concept, for example, of boys who achieve their physical growth late and girls who receive theirs early. But we do not know that the use of physical maturity or social maturity as grouping principles would be better.

Therefore, the first question pertinent to this topic that should be addressed in designing environments for growth is what principle or principles should be used in grouping young persons in activities. This question is related, however, to a second, third, and fourth. What total range in stage of development should exist within a set of young people engaged together in activities (for example, what age range)? What interdependent roles should exist among the young in these activities? And what should be the degree of self-selection into age-level grouping or other grouping by young people themselves?

These are complex questions related to some of the other structural issues considered earlier. But the different component to which this issue draws attention is the various types of development according to which young persons can be grouped—and the fact that the correlation between these different modes of development is not high. We wish to open here an issue that current institutions—the schools—have prematurely closed by using one-year chronological age grouping among youth.

4. *The Patterning of Self-development and Productive Activity*

Experience indicates that young persons need both activity directed toward self-development and useful activity directed toward the outside on which others depend. Neglect of the first results in an unskilled adult, impotent to deal with a complex world. Neglect of the second leads to a frustration of the idealistic, creative, and constructive impulses of youth. For most persons these two activities, directed inward and outward, take the prosaic forms of school and work (though school does not always bring self-development, and work does not always constitute productive and useful activity). The patterning of these two activities in the past involved for many youth a daily mixture, with his duties in the home and elsewhere balancing the self-development toward which school is directed. For many youth at present, however, the pattern is self-development until the end of full-time schooling, followed by useful activity in the form of a full-time job. There are many indications, however, that this is not the best environment for growth. At least four other alternatives exist, all of which have been proposed in one form or another. These four constitute alternatives in the construction of environments for growth.

Alternative 1: "Continuing Education"

A pattern that has developed widely in the United States, and to some degree in other advanced industrial societies, is continuing education on a part-time basis. In every metropolitan center, and in many places outside metropolitan areas, evening classes for adults can be found. These range from classes devoted to basic skills held in high schools to courses for graduate university degrees. For many adults who have full-time jobs, these courses appear to fill a very important need. The heavy demand for these courses indicates the strength of adult interest in continuing education beyond that provided by full-time schooling. And the wide range of content and level of these courses indicates that the interest is broadly spread from the least to the most educated persons and from the most technological to the most humanistic activities.

But this alternative serves only the needs of those who have left full-time education. The closest analogue for youth who are still in full-time education is a part-time job—but part-time jobs cannot be had for the asking in the same sense that an evening course in the local college or high school can. Thus continuing education as it now exists in the United States is in essence more an environment for growth for adults than for youth.

Alternative 2: "Recurrent Education"

A pattern termed "recurrent education" has been under discussion in Europe since the term was introduced by Sweden's Olaf Palme in 1970. This pattern implies alternating full-time work and full-time education, with the interleaving spaces at the individual's option. As formulated, the pattern implies entry into the labor force before university but return to full-time education after a period of time.

Again, a pattern of this sort has evolved in the United States, through youth taking a year or two years out of school between high school and college, or between two years of college. This spontaneously-initiated pattern (which still encompasses only a small fraction of youth) appears to have developed from the dissatisfaction of youth with the prolonged insulation from the world created by their extended status as student.

The principal problem with this pattern as it now exists in the United States is that it receives no institutional supports beyond the willingness of some colleges to allow deferment of entry or automatic reentry after being out a year or two. The occupational structure does not always have a supply of full-time jobs appropriate to this period that youth can easily enter. Nor has there developed a system of national service or public service with opportunities for youth from age 16 on. In the absence of such opportunities work-interspersed recurrent education rarely seems a feasible option, and many youth feel they must remain in school until they can move from it onto the career ladder toward their ultimate aims.

Alternative 3: "Career Education"

A third alternative that has developed in schools and is increasingly discussed at the Federal level in the U.S. Office of Education is career education. Present developments lead from the traditional "vocational training" toward an expansion of the range of careers, including arts and professional fields.

The Federal discussions and proposals go beyond vocational education as carried out in the schools. Some programs of career education shift the central focus of education from the school to the workplace or home. Whether the overall benefits of this shift outweigh the benefits of incorporating career education in the schools is too early to know. However, one cost of occupational learning within an educational setting is that the focus remains on learning, that is, on self-development, and the constructive activities are treated only as means to that goal rather than as an end in themselves. This does not, of course, deny the value of well-designed career education in the schools. It says only that the other alternatives in the recently-developed Federal plans for career education offer benefits that should not be overlooked.

Alternative 4: "Learning at Work"

A fourth alternative consists of an intimate and daily intermixture of learning and work similar to that produced by career education in schools but instead in a work setting. This alternative also exists in several forms today, ranging from cooperative education programs in high schools (in which the young person spends half of each day at work on a job and half at school) to educational programs in a work organization for which the worker gets released time. And there now exists in Federal agencies an intensified interest and some plans toward the further development of these programs. As with career education programs in the schools, the existing programs are sometimes implemented well, sometimes badly. Their essential difference from vocational education in schools lies in the fact that the work is performed for a purpose and is not merely a diversification of learning, and it is performed in a setting with adults engaged in similar work.

Work-study programs of this sort are seldom designed to capture the idealistic and altruistic impulses of youth; the external purpose for which the work is done may not be a purpose of the young person himself. Indeed, in a differentiated work organization it is unlikely to coincide with his own purposes. Nevertheless, the intrinsic satisfaction of doing useful and constructive work provides rewards even in the absence of a common collective purpose. On the other hand, some of the proposals for a national service program or public service program for youth involve a mixture of learning and work that is intended to be for some common good. To satisfy the dual needs for activity directed inward and outward, some such environment, involving both learning and some public service work directed toward a shared goal, would be optimum. But environments of this sort are now seldom available to youth.

5. Role-Segmentation vs. Community

Another set of issues concerns a youth's position in the institutions of socialization:

1. How much continuity with one set of personal relationships in

a single institution should he have before leaving it and moving to another? This is an issue of continuity vs. mobility.

2. How encompassing should a given institution be? The range extends from the all-encompassing institution of the boarding school to a system like work-study programs in which he spends a portion of the day in one institution and a portion in another.

At one time neither of these questions could properly be raised. Other problems dominated. The family's and community's needs dictated how long the child spent at home with the family; whether there was to be a school, and if so, what form it would take; how long a young person would stay at school; and whether his family moved so that he had to change schools. Today both questions must be asked. School organization is an open question, perhaps as much as it has ever been. In public school there are numerous patterns, among them K–12; K–8 and 9–12; K–6 and 7–9 and 10–12; K–4 and 5–8 and 9–12. In addition, there is a variety of new arrangements designed to facilitate school integration. Some involve a student spending a portion of a day or week in one school or one out-of-school setting and the remainder of his school time in another.

At one extreme of the dimension at issue here, the young person is in a close community and at the other he is in a role-segmented society similar to that of the larger society. Each of the extremes of role-segmentation and community has its defects. But it is not sufficient to say that because of this "the" solution is somewhere between these extremes. The young people unsuccessful in one might be successful in the other. Further, a solution somewhere between these extremes (which is what the typical high school and college are) may have just as many defects. Perhaps there is a strong relation between the personality characteristics of the young person and the degree of segmentation or communalism in which he can be successful. We suspect that for the majority of youth, the development of segmented institutions, each covering a portion of his activities, will be more beneficial. But at this point it is necessary to recognize the importance of such a dimension or set of dimensions and the importance of learning the consequences of each pattern for youth of various backgrounds and personalities.

6. *The Scope of Formal Schooling*

One of the implications of the set of social changes we have described is that the non-school portions of a youth's environment have dwindled in scope and force while the school portions have increased.

One consequence has been to introduce into schools some things that were once outside in the form of extra-curricular programs, work-related programs, community projects, and other activities. This is one kind of solution: to bring into the school certain of those non-cognitive activities that are deemed valuable to the development of youth or at least those activities for which there is some demand on the part of youth or the community.

Another solution, however, is to take the opposite approach: to confine formal schooling to those cognitive skills that are traditional to it and to devise new organizational arrangements outside the formal structure of the school for those non-academic activities important to the movement into adulthood. Such an approach very likely implies a reduction in the time spent in formal educational settings, rather than the increase inherent in the first solution. An example of this solution is cooperative education programs in high school in which a young person typically spends half his day in school and half on the job working for an employer. Recently other programs with a similar structure have been initiated. In Minneapolis, for example, an "urban arts" program consists of a half day spent outside the school learning music, ballet, or other arts and a half day inside the school devoted to academic activities.

Although the usual approach with non-academic activities has been to enlarge the scope of the school to incorporate them (as with vocational education), some examples exist of the opposite solution, involving adjustments in the social structure outside rather than inside the school.

a. Benefits of incorporating non-academic content into schools: In effect, the school has always stood to inject those activities into the lives of children and youth that are important to their development but missing in their everyday environment. When literacy and reading were absent from the environment of most young persons, as they still are for some, schools acted primarily to fill that gap. If we find now that certain other activities important to becoming adult are missing from young persons' lives, then the school is the most obvious place for these activities. School is the sector of society that can be explicitly designed to meet the needs of the young, while the restructuring of other sectors of society is a difficult and compromise-ridden task. This same principle holds for supervision of the ongoing everyday activities: supervision and control to insure that these activities benefit youth is much easier inside than outside school walls.

b. Benefits of pursuing non-academic activities outside school: The central defect of the school for activities other than transmission of academic knowledge and skills is that schools are not well organized for other activities. Schools are apart from society while the non-academic portions of becoming adult, such as gaining the capacity to take responsibility and authority, learning to care for others who are dependent, acquiring the ability to take decisive action, learning how to work, achieving a sense of self respect, are directly part of society. The school may try to simulate those activities of society that bring about these capabilities, but it has not to date shown great success in its attempt to do so.

The essential difficulty of schools in handling activities other than academic learning is the position of the child or youth within the school. He is a dependent, and the school is responsible for shepherding his development. Yet if youth is to develop in certain ways involving responsibility and decision-making, then the responsibility and dependency are in the wrong place. To reorganize a school in such a way that young persons have responsibility and authority appears extremely difficult, because such reorganization is incompatible with the basic custodial function of the school.

Various means have been used to change the child's or youth's role in the school from that of passive dependent student to that of active responsible person. The most successful ones are voluntary and freed from the custodial aspect of the school's activities. In high schools extra-curricular activities including school newspaper, music, drama, debate, athletics have provided some escape from the role of student. Similar activities but with wider scope and greater independence occur in colleges. One example within the classroom is the tutorial or helping activities of older children toward younger ones, an activity that has been attempted in a few schools. But the most characteristic end result of experiments of this sort in schools has been a return to the old pattern of dependency of the young person in the school. In fact, the history of bringing non-academic activities from real life into the school is marked with a transformation of those activities to the point where the young person is once again in the role of student, learning cognitive material that can be tested by traditional academic paper-and-pencil tests.

In contrast, there are organizations outside the school that have been able, with apparent ease, to devise activities involving actual performance, even including tests of performance. One of the oldest, which is widespread both in Western and Socialist countries, is Scouting. The activities of scouts are traditionally linked to the outdoors, and tests of performance (cooking, firebuilding, construction, swimming, etc.) rather than tests of academic knowledge are used. For farm youth, 4-H Club projects provide similar roles of responsibility, decision-making, and rewarded work. Junior Achievement has, for a few youth, provided similarly for enterprenurial activities, and in summer camps youth move into positions of developing responsibility at an early age. A federal program, the Neighborhood Youth Corps, has sometimes engaged youth in projects of real benefit to the community. Outdoor programs like Outward Bound have also been able to put youth in roles other than student.

In short, when non-cognitive activities are created for youth as ways of developing personal qualities important to a satisfactory adult life, the incorporation of them within schools places an enormous strain that is often resolved by a reversion to student role for youth and to teacher role for adults. The prospects of success for such activities appear far greater when carried on outside the school.

Examining both sides, we feel that the benefits of incorporating non-cognitive activities into schools are far fewer than those from organizing them outside schools. The principal benefit of the former path appears to be organizational "neatness" and insurance that all youth will be "covered" by such activity. But the costs are the distortion of such activity to fit the organizational characteristics of a school, a distortion that strikes at the very heart of the activity.

7. *The Legal Status and Rights of Youth*

Persons below the age of majority, the age at which one is deemed legally competent to assume responsibility for his person and property, are subject to various disabilities not imposed on adults. At the same time, persons below the age of majority are accorded certain protections denied to adults and are exempt from some of the legal obligations of adulthood.

The age of majority has traditionally been set at twenty-one. Since the adoption of the 26th Amendment to the Constitution establishing eighteen as the voting age, some states have reduced the age of majority to eighteen. In a few states youthful offenders, even though above the age of majority, receive special treatment when found guilty of breaches of criminal law.

Primary responsibility for control and protection of persons under the age of majority is entrusted to parents or guardians. Under the doctrine of *parens patriae,* however, public authority, in the form of local, state, or federal government, intervenes to require obedience to parents, to protect children and youth from undesirable parental conduct, and to compel young people to perform some duty (such as attending school) imposed by the state.

The problem is at what point do societal controls over youth cease to be legitimate protections of the welfare of young people and become instead unwarranted constraints. From one perspective protection becomes unwarranted constraint when agencies such as schools, juvenile courts, correctional institutions, shelters for the neglected, and institutions for the handicapped and mentally retarded fail to discharge the educational, benevolent, and therapeutic functions entrusted to them. Just as young persons are entitled to secondary protection by social institutions against neglectful and abusive parents who are intended to be their primary agents of protection, they are entitled to protection against neglectful and abusive social institutions. Recent court decisions indicate increased respect for the minors' constitutional right to due process and equal protection of the law. Various proposals have been made for establishing children's advocates or ombudsmen at various levels of government. The 26th Amendment will bring stronger representation of the interests of young people into the process of government and will presumably increase pressure for more equitable and responsible treatment of youth.

Some aspects of the issue, however, are not easily resolved because the borderline between protection and constraint is not sharp. Perhaps the best examples are child labor and school attendance laws which act to protect youth under 14, 16, and 18 (depending on the kind of labor and other conditions) from the harmful effects of some work and to keep them in school to learn. Yet those same laws act as constraints that hold young people in environments that for some may be unproductive and unhealthy (e.g., preventing them from leaving school when that environment becomes a fruitless one). Is a fixed minimum age criterion for terminating school and beginning work appropriate? It is certainly not feasible to examine in every instance the school environment and a potential work environment and then decide the case on its merits. But it seems likely that a better means can be found for assuring the rights of the young person to some degree of self-determination while protecting him from exploitation by others.

PART 4: ALTERNATIVE DIRECTIONS FOR CHANGE

Introduction

In the preceding parts of this report, we have attempted to establish a frame of reference for discussion and debate to help move society from the second, schooling, phase of its treatment of youth to a third phase that includes schooling but is not limited to it. In this third phase, environments for youth must be designed in such a way that the broad objectives stated in Part I are met. But in meeting these objectives, the issues discussed in Parts 2 and 3 must be addressed. That is, the social inventions and social experimentation necessary to create appropriate environments can be developed only through specifying the objectives that they should satisfy and diagnosing the current conditions surrounding youth. Although we have only begun that task here, it is useful to indicate some changes that can be first steps toward appropriate environments for youth. This Part is devoted to suggesting such changes.

Some changes proposed in this Part would resolve certain of the issues of Part 3 in one way, some in the opposite way. Some are compatible with certain directions of society's development, some with other directions. Because it is not clear what directions society will take, and because it is not evident just what consequences a given proposed institution would have, we suggest a diverse array of changes. We believe all are worthy of serious trial; we cannot know enough about any one of them to recommend that it be universally adopted. Further, no single environment for youth's transition to adulthood would be beneficial to all youth or to the society. Indeed, the recent emergence of such a single monolithic pattern—unbroken schooling for many years finally truncated by a sharp shift to full-time work—has reduced effective opportunity for those who would find different paths more fruitful.

Consequently, these proposals are made from the premise that diversity and plurality of paths to adulthood are important for the youth of any society. Each of the proposed changes brings some of the benefits and incurs some of the costs discussed in Part 3, through the explicit stance it takes on those issues. And each is designed to address some of the objectives of environments for youth discussed in Part 1. But the proposed changes are not neutral with regard to the objectives; they are specifically designed to address those objectives for which schools as currently constituted are least well suited. It is useful to examine briefly just what those objectives are, to show the intended thrust of our proposals.

The Unmet Objectives in Current Environments for Youth

Schools are the principal formal institutions of society intended to bring youth into adulthood. But schools' structures are designed wholly for self-development, particularly the acquisition of cognitive skills and of knowledge. At their best, schools equip students with cognitive and noncognitive skills relevant to their occupational futures, with knowledge of some portion of civilization's cultural heritage, and with the taste for acquiring more such skills and knowledge. They do not provide extensive opportunity for managing one's affairs, they seldom encourage intense concentration on a single activity, and they are inappropriate settings for nearly all objectives involving responsibilities that affect others. Insofar as these other objectives are important for the transition to adulthood, and we believe they are, schools act to retard youth in this transition, by monopolizing their time for the narrow objectives that schools have.

In general, the proposed directions of change are intended to break that monopoly, through environments that complement schools. Thus the proposals do not address problems and deficiencies of schools in the development of cognitive skills. They do address the objectives that schools omit, by proposing institutional structures that aid these objectives.

As a general class (with the exception of the first proposal, intended to encourage intense and self-motivated concentration) these institutional structures place youth in a different role from the student role. This different role involves either responsibility for his own welfare, or responsibility for others' welfare; it involves orientation to productive and responsible tasks; where it involves learning, it is learning through action and experience, not by being taught. Most of the proposed institutional structures also are designed to reduce the isolation of youth from adults, and from the productive tasks of society. This is intended both to bring about a greater degree of personal responsibility of adults for the development of youth, and to remove from youth some of the insulation that impedes the transition to adulthood.

These are the general directions in which most of the proposed changes are intended to go. But each of these proposals addresses specific objectives, and it is to the connections between the proposals and the objectives that we now turn.

The Proposed Changes and the Unmet Objectives

The first set of changes proposed below are changes in the school structure. These are changes designed in one way or another to allow the school itself to fulfill some of these previously-ignored objectives, although we feel the school's capabilities are limited in this. By expanding the roles of a young person in school beyond that of student, to include that of tutor, for example, the school becomes not just a place for self-centered skill development and learning, but also a place in which young persons engage in constructive activities benefitting younger children. The creation of a wider range of activities outside the classroom but administered by the school as an "agent" of youth is intended to provide the young person the possibility of managing his affairs within a structured setting. The possibility of differentiated schools (or subunits within schools) with choice among them, concentrating on different areas of activity (e.g., music, performing arts, science, physical education, crafts) is intended in part to provide a setting more conducive to intense concentration on a chosen activity than do current comprehensive schools. And the reduction in size of schools or substructuring of large schools is intended to encourage personal involvement of adults in the school with youth, as a set of personal resources on which youth can draw in times of difficulty.

The second set of proposed changes, which bring young people into work situations sooner, are intended to contribute to several of the objectives discussed in Part 1, but primarily to the second class of objectives, the experience of responsibilities affecting others. A work situation can involve interdependent and collective tasks, experience with others differing in background and in age, and the experience of having others dependent on one's actions. Our general belief is that environments which provide a significant amount of serious and responsible work experience are much more likely to meet these objectives than are the narrower environments of school that most youth find themselves limited to. In addition, such work settings are intended to provide, to a much greater extent than reducing school size, the opportunity for adults outside schools to become enough involved with young persons that they constitute personal resources to whom the young persons can turn in times of stress.

The next set of proposals concern youth organizations and youth communities. The intent of such organizations and communities is to provide experiences of leadership, responsibility, interdependent activity, and self-management. They are not effective settings for the development of cognitive skills and cultural tastes, nor for intense concentration on a single activity.[1] Like most institutions, they are valuable settings only for certain activities, and thus only for a subset of objectives. It is important, in the design of environments for youth, to have an orchestration of such partial institutions, rather than the total and encompassing institution that the school has become.

The next two proposals concern reduction of constraints on the young against work. They are intended to increase the opportunity for youth to act responsibly, in moving toward independence and self-management. The implementation of these proposals is meant to facilitate the broader participation of youth in society's institutions beyond the school, and to facilitate the scond set of proposed changes mentioned above (bringing young people into work situations).

The next proposal is a pilot introduction of vouchers for youth at age 16, which they can use for education or training. This places resources for further training directly in the hands of youth, who will experience most directly the consequence of their use or misuse. The aim of this proposal is to create the opportunity, earlier than it now exists for many youth, for taking responsibility for the management of their affairs. It is predicated that not only will such responsibility develop the capability in youth of managing their own affairs, but that youth themselves will more often use these resources for activities that will make them capable adults than would public agencies directly subsidized by public funds to "serve" youth.

A final proposal concerns an expansion of the presently miniscule opportunities for public service or national service by youth, from age 16 on. Public service activities are activities designed to directly benefit other segments of the community. The intent behind such service lies in the second class of objectives: the experience of responsibilities affecting other people. The work is ordinarily inter-

---

[1] A. S. Neill (1963), the founder of Summerhill, the English prototype of unstructured youth communities, says in his book *Summerhill* "The children of Summerhill are not much interested in book learning."

dependent, directed toward collectively-held goals, it often involves work with persons of different backgrounds and different ages, and it usually provides an experience of having others dependent on one's actions. Thus it is a direct complement to the self-development objectives of schools.

Altogether, it is important to emphasize that no one of the proposed changes is intended to accomplish all the objectives of environments for youth. The design of such environments is a more complex and differentiated task than the society and communities have yet recognized, and cannot be accomplished within a single structure like the school. At the most general level, the proposed changes in this report are for a differentiated set of institutions within which young people develop, rather than a single encompassing one, as is now the case.

However, it is not the intent of our report to recommend immediate and large-scale changes in these institutions. In the case of each of the proposed changes, only experience will show 'whether the benefits it brings are sufficient to make it valuable for youth and thus for society. Further, this experience should be gained through explicit experimental design and systematic collection of data rather than in traditional casual ways. In this way the necessary feedback from social experiments or pilot social policies can occur and lead to their modifications, or to their extension on a wider scale. If this is to occur, three points should be recognized: 1) Each of these proposed changes should take place only in pilot or experimental form; 2) When such pilot policies are initiated, careful monitoring and evaluation are necessary to guide modification; and 3) The design of the pilot program should anticipate extension to broad policy change, so that its consequences are not limited to an evaluation report.

The Information Base for Social Policy

Traditionally, the information base for changes in social policy has been provided by testimony from parties interested in the proposed legislation, sometimes augmented by a review of research that is relevant to the proposed policy change. Only recently have other sources of information begun to play some part in social policy. This is explicitly-designed social research, program evaluation, and finally social experimentation, in which the policy change is instituted on a pilot basis, with some experimental design that provides information about the likely consequences of the proposed policy. The recent income maintenance experiment is one example of social experimentation; another is a set of proposed experiments for the demand and supply of housing under a program of housing allowances for families with low incomes.

For most of the proposals made in this section, social experiments or pilot programs with evaluation are the appropriate recommendation. Most of these involve changes in the institutions through which youth pass in their movement to adulthood. For institutional changes, there are few guidelines from the past on which to base a policy, and a recommendation for major policy changes in the absence of such information is hardly warranted.

The fact that this section consists largely of proposals for social experimentation or pilot programs should not be regarded as merely a call for "more research." The pilot programs are proposed as precursors to full-scale policy changes. They are necessary precursors simply because the full-scale changes require more than present information or information from analysis of existing institutions.

If these social experiments or pilot programs are to serve their purposes, it is important that they be preceded by careful planning which includes not only experimental design and evaluation of results, but also looks toward the next phase of full-scale implementation. It is important also that the social experiments be designed and executed well in advance of strong social pressure for a policy change. Otherwise, it is not possible to obtain results from the experiment or pilot in time to affect the policy itself. In health insurance, for example, experiments now being designed concerning different types of plans will probably not be executed and analyzed before the pressure for a national health insurance program builds up to the point that some program is enacted in the absence of appropriate information.

At the same time, something can be learned from data on existing institutional arrangements. One of our proposals (No. 8) is to carry out such research in a more systematic fashion than at present. Such ongoing research will not only record the functioning of existing institutions, but as there come to be changes, will monitor the effects of these changes as well.

Measurement of Objectives

As pilot programs of social change are instituted, it is important to insure that they be evaluated on a full set of objectives such as those discussed in Part 1, and not solely on the narrow objective of increasing cognitive skills. Indeed, most of the proposed changes are intended to implement non-cognitive objectives. But evaluation on these objectives is only possible if measures are developed for non-cognitive objectives analogous to those that now exist in school grades and standardized tests for cognitive skills. One important deterrent to incorporating these broader objectives in society's responsibilities toward its youth is the relative absence of measurement. Most of the required measures are performance measures, and just like the physical performance measures used in the armed forcs or task performance measures used in occupations or in youth organizations, they can be developed. For other objectives, such as those involving responsibilities for others, the best criterion for meeting the objectives may turn out to be the time spent in the activity. It may also be necessary to develop quite different kinds of measures for capabilities developed in experiential learning and those developed in non-experiential learning (primarily classroom learning).

The task of developing such measures is not a simple one, but its importance is great. Without such measures the criterion of success of an activity reverts to its effect on cognitive skills, since standardized measures exist there. Yet those criteria are precisely the ones that are not relevant to most of the changes proposed here. It is in part the absence of non-cognitive measures that makes the usual list of school objectives meaningless. And it is explicit attention to measures that cover the breadth of the objectives stated in Part 1 which can guide environments for youth toward those objectives.

1. *Change in School Structure*

Later proposals involve some youth moving out of the traditional school setting, part or full time, into other environments. The present section discusses changes in the school, for it is the central institution for most youth, and will continue to be for many. These proposed changes are intended to achieve some of the objectives of environments for youth other than the traditional ones of increasing cognitive skills and knowledge. These proposals are in part designed to encourage certain existing innovations in schools, for in some school systems there are innovations that move in the directions we propose.

As described in Part 2, American secondary education is increasingly a world of large urban districts composed of large comprehensive schools, with students assigned to schools according to the neighborhoods in which they live. We noted growing problems of this institutional arrangement: little consumer choice; the heavy weight of bureaucratic and professional controls; the large size of single-grade student strata; segregation by class, race, and ethnicity;

overloading of institutional capacity by an excess of expectations and functions; and the institutional blandness that can follow from ambiguous purpose and amorphous structure.

A school that is large, amorphous, and bland is likely to have the unintended consequence of promoting socialization by the youth culture. The assembling of large numbers of youth along age-and-grade lines encourages them to create worlds of their own. At the same time, the increasing specialization and segmentation of teaching encourages teachers, the only adults in the setting, to withdraw from those worlds. And there is little linkage provided by a sense of common purpose and a community of experience. The school has always been a setting, it is fair to say, in which there is some natural struggle between adults and youth. But the large comprehensive school changes the nature of the struggle from largely informal conflict and accommodation between teachers and students to a more formal one in which one major bloc feels impelled to elaborate rules and add more agents of control—even the police—while the other side, or a good share of it, moves collectively to avoid the rules and to weaken the will to participate and learn. Students, like members of work groups, will produce when they feel it is in their interest to do so and when their group norms call for achievement (Boocock, 1972, p. 312). If youth culture is growing stronger, as we believe it is, then the group norms of the young become more powerful in contending with the formal systems. Therefore, now more than ever before, it is important to think of the capacity of educational settings to encourage self-interest in achievement and group norms that support a learning climate.

We suggest four routes of change.

(a) *School diversity and student choice.* The typical pattern for American high schools is comprehensive schools with fixed attendance areas, designed to be alike and differing only on the dimension of "quality." There is little possibility of a young person choosing a special activity on which to concentrate his attention, and then finding a school setting within which that concentration is encouraged. Yet such a specialization allows intense personal concentration, strengthened by the fact that it is a common interest. This kind of bond ordinarily occurs in regular schools only in extra-curricular activities, in the long hours of common struggle that it takes to produce a play or a concert or a winning athletic team.

Two elements are necessary for this possibility of voluntary commitment and self-motivated concentration to occur. One is the development of genuine specialization among high schools, including but not limited to academic specialties, and the other is free choice by youth among high schools.

This proposal goes directly against the trends in American education toward comprehensive schools. The specialized schools of the past were eliminated in one community after another (even largely so in New York City, where they were most fully differentiated). Comprehensive schools seemed to have advantages of mixing students, allowing easy transfer from one curriculum to another, and in general, providing a democratic equality of opportunity and treatment. But these supposed advantages have been negated in many locales. Comprehensive schools drawing from black lower class neighborhoods or white upper middle class areas are very different. By specializing overtly in student body, they specialize covertly in curriculum. The comprehensive school becomes a narrow school, vainly trying to be like the others, but passively specializing around neighborhood input.

In many areas where the supposed benefits of comprehensiveness have been lost, the advantages of moving toward deliberate specialization in school purpose will probably outweigh the disadvantages. The advantages lie in the greater encouragement of intense concentration on an activity that can occur in specialized schools. Specialized schools have a clearer mission, they can build organizational competence and identity around their more restricted focus, and they can attract students and faculty of appropriate and mutually-reenforcing interest. For example, they can concentrate on excellence in music, art, performing arts, science, humanistic studies, or different industry sectors (medical services, educational services, printing and publishing trades, broadcast media). And there are other advantages. A school specializing in one major area of study can draw students from a larger geographic area, helping to attenuate the existing specialization by narrow geographic base that commits all neighborhood youth to the one public school. Such a school can set admissions policies that encourage representatives from various social groups.

New forms of specialization can be developed in quasi-alternative schools. We earlier described the short life of most alternative schools to date, both those that have been organized inside the public school framework and those organized outside it. But alternative schools that will survive can be organized. Some trials toward this end are now under way in public school systems. If their results are carefully monitored, a viable pattern may emerge that can be widely used.

A move from passive to active specialization in American secondary education is a move to encourage administrative leadership and staff imagination. The rewards for simple imitation are reduced and con-

forming to one model is not the road to success. Instead, the staff
of a school must unite in an effort to make their own combination
work, and compete against other schools who are offering other patterns. And each district needs to determine its own optimum mix of
comprehensive and specialized schools, offering an opening for creative leadership in the system as a whole. A shift to deliberate design
of institutional variety becomes then not only the ground for genuine
student choice among public schools but also the ground for genuine
institutional leadership. Particularly in a country as large and varied
as the United States, innovation, and adaptation of new ideas to the
uniqueness of each context, is best designed at the local level. Although superintendents, principals, and teachers will need the help
of researchers to monitor and evaluate new and altered forms of
schooling, they themselves must be responsible for choice of institutional alternatives.

(b) *School size.* Experimentation with new educational settings and
the redesign of old ones should pay attention to school size
as experienced by participants. From the rural school consolidation movement to the call by Conant (1959) for larger and more
comprehensive high schools, as reviewed in Part 2, American schools
have been growing larger. This change has occurred in the face of
some findings and experiences that raise serious questions about the
benefits of large schools. Youth in large schools are more often passive spectators of action, less often participants, more often followers,
less often in leadership roles than youth in small schools (Barker,
1962). Also, when a high school is larger than about 500 students,
teachers no longer know the names of students they do not teach,
and the principal no longer knows students by name. At about a
thousand students, the principal becomes unable to distinguish
whether a particular young person belongs to his school. Such tentative findings at least suggest the existence of critical thresholds in
interaction, impersonality and control. Large size also brings greater
segregation of students by age and academic track, and specialization
of teachers by grade level and subject-matter. Small size brings
greater relations among the young differing in age and ability, less
teacher specialization, and more personal relations all around.

The problems of large organization occurred earlier in higher
education than in secondary education, because in the great student
expansion of the last two decades colleges and universities were allowed to grow to the huge sizes reported in Part 2. Recent national
reports on the state of higher education have pointed to size as a
serious problem. The Carnegie Commission on Higher Education
(1971) has attempted to state maximum and minimum sizes for

different major types of colleges and universities. The "Newman Report" (Report on Higher Education, 1971) has argued vigorously that huge size and comprehensive organization are seriously weakening American higher education. The community colleges, which we noted in Part 2 shared many features and problems of the secondary level, have not escaped this new criticism. Their original purposes seemed dependent on small scale (in deliberate contrast to the public university and growing state colleges), but rapid growth has turned them in the direction of mass counseling and distribution centers.

Careful experimentation and monitoring of effects will be needed to inform us of the advantages and disadvantages of small and large educational units—for different kinds of students, at different levels of education, and in contexts that vary on many characteristics other than size. The effects necessary to examine are not limited to academic nor psychological ones, but rather outcomes for the whole range of objectives toward which environments for youth should aim.

One possible approach is to attempt to combine the advantages of the large place at its best (economies of scale, a wide array of programs, the excitement of an educational city) with the advantages of the small place at its best (a sense of deep involvement, interpersonal trust and loyalty, a unifying and motivating institutional tone). Two directions of change seem particularly fruitful to pursue. One is dual membership in the small and the large through small units within large schools. The possibilities for creative inventions and adaptations here are very large, with some interesting plans already underway that are in need of serious study. The second direction is dual membership in the small and the large through attendance in two distinct schools. Participation can be split, in various combinations of hours and days and weeks, between large comprehensive and small specialized schools.

Finally, there remains the possibility that small schools are better than big schools, and small colleges better than large colleges, across a profile of effects (on colleges, see Feldman and Newcomb (1969), Chap. 11, and Clark, et al (1972, Ch. 10)), But the benefits of small size have lain in what are often described as "intangibles": the quality of the relationships, the motivation created, the involvement in common goals. Attention to measurement is necessary in order that these "intangible" effects be compared to the hard facts of the financial benefits of large scale and the gains in esoteric knowledge of having experts at hand. Clearly, the more intractable educational problems of the day do not lie in the provision of sufficient expertise. Rather, the problems are seemingly rooted in broader aspects of the relation between the schools and the young, with stronger cultures of youth contending with strong formal systems in ways that are adverse to learning, and with teachers withdrawing from personal involvements with students. Small scale may be a helpful and even a necessary social response to these problems, serving to link teachers and students in reasonably integrated systems of learning.

(c) *Role-diversity for youth in schools.* A third strategy for modifying existing educational structure involves reshaping a portion of the time in school so that the young person is not wholly occupied as a student but learns in ways that assist others and himself. This direction of change means among other things a re-examination of the pros and cons of various extracurricular activities, taking more seriously those activities, especially in the arts, in journalism, and in athletics, which allow participation and performance that is within the school but outside the strictly academic role.

Our particular proposal concerns the activity of tutoring or teaching by young people in school. Teachers in various settings have, of course, long used some students to assist in the instruction of others. As noted in Part 2, teachers in one-room schoolhouses and other very small schools were virtually forced to use older students as aides. But large size has diminished those informal arrangements, and the concept of student-as-tutor has only recently been revived in the teaching of slum children. We propose that part-time teaching should be seriously explored as an activity favorable to the growth of youth, with experimentation designed both at local and national levels.

Role diversity within schools runs contrary to certain other directions for change suggested in this report. For example, where systems move in the direction of narrowing the scope of formal schooling to the strictly academic, then the role diversity for youth that we believe valuable will be found in participation in old and new institutions outside the schools. But if the school continues to dominate the time and energy of youth, as it undoubtedly will in many locations in the country, then it seems important to change it in ways that will allow the young to widen the range of rewarding educational experiences.

(d) *The school as agent for the young.* If a larger social setting—the community or city—were seen as the environment, or a set of environments, for the growth of a young person, then the school could come to take on a new role of planning and facilitating the best use of the learning components of the larger system. In this approach, the school would delegate a portion of its present custody to other institutions. Time in school could be cut by reducing school functions to the more strictly academic ones. But school personnel would then also plan to be the main agents of the young, acting in their interests in employing other institutions of the community. The school would purchase a set of services for youth, making it an important potential source of social change.

There may be an inherent conflict in this dual role of the school in teaching and in acting as a disinterested agent for youth development. Nevertheless, some secondary schools have programs that move in this direction. Cooperative education, involving half-days spent at work, is a widespread example. Programs that involve middle-class youth engaged in public service activities have been developed in a few places. Some purchase of teaching services by the school through performance contracting has also been attempted. However, in the absence of a general conception of a new role for the school as agent for youth and the flexibility in the use of school funds that would follow from such a conception, the evolution is heavily constrained.

Our proposal here is for the explicit introduction of this new conception in an experimental program, together with broad evaluation of the existing programs that have this character. Such a conception would be favorable to, and in some cases necessary for, the directions of change to which we now turn.

2. Alternation of School and Work

One way of providing youth with opportunities for acquiring experience in the assumption of responsibility and facilitating their contact with adults prior to the termination of education is to encourage movement between school and workplace. Some movement of this sort has recently come into being in career education programs, initiated by the schools or at the Federal level, and our proposal is intended to strengthen and broaden this development.

Without considering major modifications in educational or occupational institutions, two patterns of alternation of school and work may be examined. In the first of these patterns, the young person leaves school for a period of time such as a semester, for full-time employment, returning to school subsequently. In colleges, this pattern was initiated by Antioch College, and exists also in a number of engineering curricula. But at the high school level the patttern does not exist.

The experience of veterans who resumed their education after the Second World War suggests that even an extended hiatus need not carry any penalty of difficulty in picking up the academic thread again, although obvious selective factors suggest caution in generalizing from that experience. Prospective employers may be reluctant to invest time in training an ostensibly short-term employee, but data on job mobility of the young suggest that at present most first jobs are short-term.

The second pattern of alternation of school and work consists of half-time schooling and half-time employment. This pattern, limited largely to manual jobs, exists in many schools as federally-funded "Cooperative Vocational Education" for youth 16 and over, and more recently for 14- and 15-year-olds as "Work Experience and Career Exploration Program" (WECEP) .[2]

The most conspicuous limitation of these programs is the limitation to terminal education, making the program incompatible with education beyond high school. Limitations also exist in attitudes of school personnel, for the programs are ordinarily seen as "programs of last resort." The proposal here, however, is for school-work alternation for college preparatory programs as well as vocational programs. The aim of such programs should not be primarily to "learn a skill," but to gain experience in responsible interdependent activity—and the importance of such experience is not limited to youth with manual labor destinations.

To make such arrangements feasible from the standpoint of the organization of the school time table, there are scheduling problems. But these have been solved for existing cooperative education programs, and can equally be solved for students in non-vocational education.

With the first pattern of school-work alternation also (periods of full-time schooling and full-time work) , there are scheduling problems. The conventional summer vacation from school is anachronistic, reflecting our agricultural past. If the school year were organized on a year-round trimester basis, with each student spending one of the three trimesters in employment and two trimesters in school, the alternation we are suggesting would be realized. Side benefits would arise from a more efficient use of school physical plants and year-round employment of teachers.[3]

Both these patterns of school-work alternation seem to offer sufficient benefits for aiding the transition from school to work to justify the scheduling and organizational arrangements that would make the two activity patterns possible. The patterns currently exist for some students in vocational programs, and are beginning for a broader range of students through new career education programs. Our proposal is that

---

[2] One evaluation of work-study programs (WECEP) for 14 and 15-year-olds in Illinois shows that 46% responded "better than before" to a question "How do you get along with strangers and older people now that you are in the program?" See Weisman, 1972.

[3] Synanon, a residential community in California which educates its own children, operates with monthly alternations for its teen-age children, intermixing academic schooling, work experience, and extended ventures of an Outward Bound sort into nature. Kibbutzim in Israel have a regular school year, but carry out an alternation of school and work during the school year by establishing work responsibilities for youth like those of adults, but for a shorter period each day.

these be carefully evaluated in terms of the objectives discussed in Part 1, and that experimentation be carried out with such programs for young people in nonvocational tracks.

2.1 The Specific Experimentation Proposal

a. The work-study experimentation should have these characteristics:

1. For the pattern with a half day of work and a half day of school, the program should build upon present Cooperative Vocational Education Programs (for ages 16 and over) and Work Experience and Career Exploration Programs (for ages 14 and 15) in high schools. In design of the augmentation, the experiment should use existing evaluations of these programs.

2. These programs should be augmented by a wider range of occupations, and be made compatible with a college-preparatory high school curriculum. (The sufficiency of half a school day for a college preparatory program is shown by the experience of high schools operating on split shifts or double shifts because of overcrowding.)

3. For the pattern with a trimester in school and one out, the program should probably begin with age 16. A school schedule should be converted to a trimester basis, with cooperating firms having full-time jobs that are successfully filled by different young persons on their work trimester. College preparatory curriculum, as well as others, should be compatible with the work program.

4. Wherever possible, random selection of applicants to the program should be used when the program is oversubscribed, to allow using the nonselected students as controls to show effects of the program.

b. The results to be studied should include:

1. Comparison of selected and nonselected students on:
   a. The second class of objectives discussed in Part 1, involving the assumption of responsibilities affecting others, and the ability to engage in joint or interdependent work with others. In addition, performance measures on work-related skills should be used.
   b. Subsequent work histories and employer ratings.
   c. Attitudes toward school, self, and work.

2. Comparison should also be made between youth employed in these arranged programs and youth with similar amounts of

experience in part-time or summer work, to learn what is
gained, if anything, compared to ordinary labor force hiring
of teen-agers.

3. Assessment should be made of employers' experiences, and the
incentives necessary to induce employers to participate in the
program. For such programs to be extendible to general school
policy, they must be of interest both to youth and employers.

4. Cost accounting of the program is necessary to learn additional
costs beyond regular high school.

3. Work Organizations that Incorporate Youth

Educational and work institutions are almost wholly distinct. There
were some good reasons for that in the past, but in the present and
future there are good reasons for a closer connection. These reasons lie
in the second class of objectives for youth, experience with responsibility affecting others, and in the creation of settings that involve closer
personal relations between adults and youth.

For a closer connection to be achieved, one strategy is to add educational functions to organizations that have a central work purpose.
With this strategy, organizations modified to incorporate youth would
not have distinct and separate "schools" within them to which youth
are relegated. Persons of all ages in the organization would have a
mixture of learning and working roles, with only the proportions of
the mixture varying with age. All but the youngest persons would
have a third role as well, teaching. Although there would be some
persons in the organization with primary responsibility for teaching or
directing the learning of young persons, a large portion of the teaching would be done by persons whose primary responsibilities were in
other work.

In addition, new techniques in teaching offer especially valuable opportunities for this kind of institutional arrangement. At present, these
lie principally in televised or video-tape instruction. Such instruction
has reached operational practicability (as the Open University in
Britain and instructional programs on a smaller scale in the United
States make clear), and its existence eliminates many of the needs for
a school in a building with teachers in classrooms. The young person,
rather than finishing high school, can enter a firm in which he spends
a certain fraction of his time at work and a certain fraction at self-
instruction. With televised instruction, the necessity of a classroom full
of students to economize on the teacher's time is no longer present,
and scheduling can be fitted to a work schedule.

Such a transformation of a work organization would have differing degrees of difficulty in different kinds of organizations. Organizations involving the performing arts, especially music, would be among those that could most easily modify themselves. Others providing personal services, such as hospitals, are similarly modifiable, with youth engaging both in the work of the organization and in the tasks of learning that are presently carried out in schools. But many kinds of governmental offices, manufacturing organizations, and retail sales firms will be appropriate as well. In manufacturing firms there are manual activities, office work, research and laboratory activity, all of which can provide valuable experience for the young. Whether the work accomplished is seen as a by-product of the development of young persons or this development is seen as a by-product of the productive experience is not important. What is important is that in such a setting both these things take place.

Introduction of youth into work organizations of the sort that we are describing will bring a loss of efficiency in its central activity of producing goods or services. At the same time, the participating organization is providing for its youth the sort of academic opportunities now provided by schools and colleges that allow opportunities for advanced training in purely academic settings. This service should be compensated from public funds, as schools now are, offsetting the reduced efficiency in productive activity. Whether the reduced efficiency would be only partly offset, exactly offset, or more than offset by payments equal to public funds now spent in public schools can be learned only through experimentation.

Such organizational responsibility for the development of youth can be taken by business firms, government organizations, and non-profit organizations, and the responsible agents can be both management and worker's organizations (unions and professional associations). It is important that the design of youth's schedule of activities and the implementation be jointly in the hands of management and worker's organizations if that design is to be appropriate.

This mixture of school and work in a work organization is difficult to introduce in American society because schools are in the public sector, while most work is in the private sector, in firms that are subject to market competition. Without some kind of mixture between the principles behind the public-sector organization and the private-sector organization confronting a market, an organizational change of the sort proposed here can hardly take place. For a firm to carry out public educational functions necessarily increases its costs and makes the firm non-competitive in the markets where its products or services are sold. Only if the educational activities are publicly supported, as they currently are in schools, can firms afford to add such functions. The form of this support could be either direct government payment through contract or a similar mechanism or vouchers in which the youth themselves are, with their families, the purchasers of educational and training services. Close attention would be necessary in the pilot or experimental programs to learn whether the youth activities tend to become segregated into specialized sections of the organization. If this occurred the intended benefits of the activity of course would be lost. If not, then further information is necessary to learn just what differences such a changed environment makes in the lives of those youth within it.*

3.1 The Specific Experimentation With Youth in Work Organizations

a. The social experiment under consideration here should have the following characteristics:

1. The experiment should cover a number of cities (for demonstration effect), with participating and control high schools in each city.

2. Eligibility to youth of age 16 and over, with each youth at age 16 from the high schools included in the experiment given the alternative of finishing high school through his regular school or shifting to employment-with-school, in one of the participating employer's organizations.

3. High school diploma awarded through use of GED high school equivalency test. Higher credits and degrees awarded through college level equivalency tests.

4. Formal courses available that allow continuation into various streams of post-secondary school of the young person desires, and for post-secondary courses within the work organization.

5. Work in the organization like that of adults, with the same daily schedule except a portion of that schedule reserved for formal instruction, with the youth paid by the organization for the time worked, and the work organization paid from public funds for the time he spends in formal instruction.

6. The experiment should involve a set of participating employers who agree to reserve a given number of jobs for participating youth.

7. Wherever possible, selection should be randomized. If there is oversubscription by youth to the program, selection should be

---

*See Coleman comment.

randomized within school and age, to allow comparability of subsequent measures on selected and non-selected youth.

b. The outcomes to be measured should include:

1. Comparison of selected and non-selected youth, and of youth from high schools in the experiment and those from control schools, on:
    a. Ability to assume responsibilities affecting others, and to engage in joint work with others.
    b. Other objectives discussed in Part 1, though these are not the principal intended effects of the change.
    c. Work histories at least to age 25.
    d. Subsequent educational experience.
    e. Attitudes toward work and toward formal instruction.
2. Employers' experiences with these youth in productivity, absenteeism, and promotability.
3. Comparison of the schools in the experiment with control schools, in:
    a. Rates of absenteeism and school discipline problems, by age of student.
    b. Rates of dropout from school.
4. Cost-accounting of the program.

4. Youth Communities and Youth Organizations

The preceding proposals represent an attempt to counter the trend toward increasing specialization of organizations in society. But that trend, and the age segregation it implies, may not be reversible. Two existing patterns for the development of youth that are compatible with specialization and age-segregation are the youth community and the adult-sponsored youth organization.

Although youth communities differ radically in the supervision they have, even within specimens of a given type (e.g., boarding schools), the assumption has been that there is something to be gained by youth living together and developing a greater or lesser degree of self-government. To the extent that self-government has characterized such communities, the additional assumption has been that youth can learn those attributes necessary for adulthood not from the example of adults but from experience with problems—from being thrust into practice of responsibility. Youth communities in which adults provide ultimate authority but not daily direction differ from current colleges and high schools not in the proportion of youth within them, for college and high school communities are made up almost entirely of youth. They differ instead in that youth are not merely clients to be served, but provide most of the services, exercise most of the authority, and carry most of the responsibility for the functioning of the community, from seeing that the laundry is done to hiring outside expertise in the form of teachers.

A second type of youth society is the adult-sponsored youth organization. Such organizations are not residential, and they receive their goals and direction principally from adults. Adult-sponsored youth organizations embrace a number of activities, but seldom formal education. Broadly speaking, such organizations may be classified as follows:

1. Organizations designed to transmit non-cognitive skills and moral qualities by finding non-economic but still valuable roles for youth to play, e.g., Boy Scouts, Girl Scouts.
2. Occupationally-oriented youth organizations which seek to prepare youth for future economic roles, e.g., 4-H, Junior Homemakers.
3. Clubs which seek essentially to organize recreational activities for youth, e.g., P.A.L., Y.M.C.A., Boys Clubs of America.

This crude classification should not obscure the existence of some overlap in function, or the fact that some of these organizations, like the Y.M.C.A., have modified their goals in the last century. In addition to these organizations, there is a set of semi-organized youth groups including street gangs with no adult supervision and gangs with street workers.

Several advantages can be derived from attempting to utilize youth communities and youth organizations to achieve goals outlined earlier in this report. The principle of self-government which has appeared in some youth communities can lead to early assumption of responsibility and management of one's affairs. Adult-sponsored youth organizations have had goals covering most of the objectives of environments for youth other than cognitive skills. At the same time, several limitations exist in youth-communities and adult-sponsored youth organizations as these are now constituted. Traditionally, the most widespread type of youth community has been the boarding school, confined mainly to children of the wealthy and located mainly in the East, and often rigidly hierarchical in structure. Adult-sponsored youth organizations also suffer from restricted clienteles, but for different reasons. The single-sex character of some of them sharply reduces their appeal to youth beyond early adolescence. And organizations like 4-H have not been successful in urban or suburban areas. Finally, many adult-sponsored youth organizations are now suffering from a confusion of purpose, having experienced a weakening of their original commitment to the value of crafts or nature study as ways to build character without having settled on a new set of goals.

Two proposals appear to us useful in the area of youth communities and adult-sponsored youth organizations:

4.1 Youth Communities

We propose the pilot introduction of such communities in nonresidential settings, each of which would contain within it the classroom activities of a school, but only as one of its activities. Certain of its activities would be directed toward community service or social action, and also possibly toward production of goods or services for a market. Such organizations, it is clear, would be "youth communities" only in the sense that they would be largely self-governing. Although there is value in the residential principle, in practice it puts sharp limitations on the scope of youth communities.

a. Members of the youth community should be selected randomly from among volunteers, and both sets followed to compare the effects of the youth community with those of the school from which members were drawn.

b. Eligibility should begin at the level of freshmen or sophomores in high school.

c. The program should differ from current "alternative schools" in having primarily an outward focus engaging in community service activities, with school learning being a secondary goal.

d. Measurements comparing members with non-selected youth should include:

1. Measures of development of community members on the objectives discussed in Part 1.
2. Measure of performance in the next setting, post-secondary education or work, to learn how the transition is facilitated or inhibited by membership in the community.
3. Drop-out rates and other measures of participation level.

e. Cost-accounting of the program, for comparison with regular schooling.

4.2 Youth Organizations

With respect to adult-sponsored youth organizations, we suggest that the government support as a customer certain of their activities directed toward public service. Several of these organizations view some of their present efforts as involving public service. Extension of these services would be necessary to the point that they produce goods and services which can reasonably be purchased by the government. This role of government as purchaser of public services from youth organizations must be worked out in detail if it is to succeed (e.g., what services are to be purchased, what overlap exists with current public services, what range of organizations is eligible). But if designed appropriately, such purchase of services could be of benefit both to youth and the community that receives the services, without introducing government control or administration of the youth organizations. It could also aid in the extension of these organizations among lower-class youth who are presently much less well served than middle class youth.

a. The principal questions to be asked of this experiment are the effect of the purchase of services on expansion of youth organizations and the types of youth atttracted into the program. The effectiveness of those organizations toward the objectives discussed in Part 1 should not be at issue here, because that effectiveness can be as well studied with existing youth organizations.

b. In addition, the community-service benefits of the purchase of services should be weighed against the costs, to compare the costs of these services purchased in this way to those obtained in the usual unrestricted markets.

5. *Protection vs. Opportunity for Youth*

As described in Part 3, the young are subject to a number of legal constraints designed to protect them from exploitation in the adult world. These include compulsory school attendance to age 16 and being barred from some employment below the age of 14, 16, or 18, depending on the employment. In addition, the structuring of most work into full-time jobs, the increasing set of employee benefits which reduce employers' incentives and ease of hiring casual labor, and the legal minimum wage provisions create additional barriers to youth's productive activity. These constraints and barriers protect youth from the potential harm, but they also make it difficult for many youth to have experiences that would be beneficial to their growth and development. They enforce the isolation of youth from adults and from adult responsibilities, increasing the difficulty of creating environments for youth that involve serious responsibilities affecting others.

The rights of youth to protection and rights of youth to opportunity are, we believe, for most youth presently unbalanced in the direction of too little opportunity.[4] There is general agreement that current child labor standards, both federal and state, need to be reviewed and revised in the interest of flexibility, individualization, and the opening of wider opportunities for work experience and employment. Procedures for issuing state employment certificates to those eligible for them should be simplified and steps should be taken to make provisions in the federal Fair Labor Standards Act relating to learners and apprentices effective. Regulation of working conditions for young workers is a legitimate and necessary form of protection. But the longstanding legal provisions related to working conditions require overhauling in view of technological changes, advances in safety devices, and changes in business methods and social customs.

At present, youth under age 18 experience some of the same barriers as handicapped workers: they require special insurance, have minimal job flexibility because of state and federal regulations, and impose extra administrative procedures upon the employer. Furthermore, these restrictions may fall more heavily upon lower-class and black youth than middle-class youth. Labor-force statistics show that middle-class youth, though they need the jobs less, and although they stay in school longer, manage to find part-time work earlier than working class youth.

5.1 Administrative Constraints

Our first proposal is that at both the state and federal levels, there be careful review of the occupational restrictions and administrative procedures designed to protect youth from adult exploitation and from hazardous occupations. Many of these occupations have changed character, and for them the aims of protection have reduced the rights of opportunity Cumbersome administrative procedures that offer no protection but have the effect of reducing opportunity are inexcusable. There are, to be sure, hazardous occupations from which youth should continue to be protected. For these, the federal and state enforcement is often lax, and the rights of youth to protection are being disregarded. If occupations are appropriately reclassified and the administrative inhibitions to youth employment streamlined, then enforcement can focus on the truly hazardous occupations and on

---

[4] This obviously is not true for a small minority such as childlren of migrant agricultural laborers. But increasing protection for this minority is not incompatible with increasing opportunity for the majority now excluded from opportunity. See *New Generation* (1971) for discussion of the necessity for increased protection of migrant labor children.

the truly exploitative activities, increasing both the protection and opportunity of the young.

5.2 Dual Minimum Wage

In addition to this general proposal, we propose that there be broad experimentation with a dual minimum wage, lower for youth than for adult workers.* A flat minimum wage rate has two deleterious consequences: first, it constricts the number of jobs available to the young, particularly in the 14 to 18 age range and for those with little experience, since their productivity may be significantly below that of experienced and mature workers. To the extent that the minimum is set at a relatively high level and is effective, it will discourage the employment of the young whose productivity is not yet sufficiently high.

Second, and perhaps more important, is its effect on the incentive to employers to provide general training on the job for the young. Such training is costly to the employers, and to the extent that it is general rather than specific and hence transferable to other jobs and employers, it will be supplied by employers to the young only if it is offset by lower wages during the initial training periods. This is the rationale behind the variety of formal and informal apprenticeship arrangements in the labor market. A high and uniform minimum wage level discourages such arrangements and transfers the training to the schools, which are not the best places for it.

For these reasons, we propose experimentation with various forms and levels of a dual minimum wage before any general increase in the minimum wage is enacted at the federal level. Although the consequences of existing minimum wage legislation for young workers are not well known, the consequences of a general increase seem clearly to fall differentially upon the young. Earlier studies, summarized in Kalachek (1969) and BLS Bulletin No. 1657 (1970), were largely inconclusive. More recent studies, incorporating a longer period of rising levels and extended coverage, detect a larger effect particularly after the depressing effect of the minimum wage provisions on the labor force participation rates of teenagers is allowed for (see in particular Mincer and Hashimoto, 1970, and Kosters and Welch, 1972).

---

*See Bremner dissent.

6. *Vouchers to be Employed by Youth*

From the point at which compulsory education ends—age 16—our society subsidizes the activities of those who choose to stay within the educational system. Such a subsidy makes the young person's decision of whether to remain in school less sensitive to the actual benefits he or she expects to receive from school, since the subsidy is lost upon leaving high school or college. In turn, this makes the institutions themselves less attentive to providing experiences that youth regard as important enough to pay for. The more heavily subsidized the activity from the outside, the greater the danger that youth are there for a free ride, and that the institution is indifferent to the actual benefits that activity should provide.

There are several undesirable consequences of the fact that the subsidy decision is made by those who do not directly experience the consequences of the decision—that is, local school boards, state legislators, Congressmen, and parents of youth. First, most types of subsidy are available only to those who take a prescribed path, a path which may not be the best one for a particular young person. For example, graduate school is highly subsidized by federal and state governments. To receive this subsidy, a young person must have completed college and choose to continue beyond college. College is subsidized as well. But to receive this subsidy, the young person must have completed high school and choose to enter college. In short, the system of subsidies provides a set of inducements to youth for following a very narrow path, strongly biasing their choice of activities in the direction of the path society has decided is "good for them."

Similarly, the middle class and more affluent families in effect "bribe" their children to continue education by making the transfer of funds conditional on specified school attendance. This contributes to the feelings by a young person of being pushed in a direction that is only marginally desirable for him and thus to an inefficient use of college resources by those youth who would never invest their own funds in college. It contributes as well to a deferral of responsible choice by the young person, undermining some of the most important objectives of environments for youth.

Many of these problems would be alleviated if educational support were vested directly in the young person. One way of doing so is through the use of educational vouchers for the period following compulsory education (from age 16), rather than direct subsidy to high schools and colleges from governments. Such vouchers, perhaps equivalent in value to the average cost of education through four years of college, would be given to the young at age 16, to be used at their discretion for schooling and other skill acquisition at any subsequent time of their life. That is, they should have a wide range of use, and they should not lose their value if they are not used in continuous sequence. Any unused portions should be added to the individual's social security base and be reflected in payments (annuities) he would receive on retirement.*

The principal advantages of such a plan are two. First, it would leave the major educational decision in the hands of youth themselves, who would be spending their "own" money in the directions they saw to be profitable, and with a commitment and responsibility for making its use productive. Second, it would equalize the subsidy to all youth that now goes only to those who attend college. The present system of subsidies discriminates in favor of those who are able to attend college and interested in doing so—a discrimination generally in favor of those from higher income families. Expenditure of the vouchers should be limited to institutions designed to engender some skill, with the institutions subject to some criteria or standards of the sort developed for GI benefits.

The experience our society had with the GI Bill after World War II, which included a similar though less broad program of educational benefits, is generally regarded as highly successful. Those educational benefits were available for, and used for, a very wide range of training activities, outside college and within, for blue-collar and white-collar occupations.

Such a voucher system would, of course, sharply modify the methods of financing the current system of higher education. Some of the changes, such as the fact that investments are being made by those who actually experience the consequences of the investments, are desirable. Others might be less desirable. It appears to us, all things considered, that the benefits of flexibility, responsibility, and equality of opportunity are valuable enough to warrant experimentation with such a plan on a wide enough scale to learn its potential.

6.1 The Specific Voucher Proposal

One method of defining the population for an experimental voucher program is to encompass all youth of the designated ages in a given geographic area. Another is to select a sparse random sample in a number of localities (e.g., through lotteries). The former method is used in the design for educational vouchers at the elementary school level initiated by OEO. It is necessary if the experiment is to examine

---

*See Davis dissent.

the response of educational and training institutions to the vouchers. But in the present case, the voucher is to be for later ages, from age 16 on. For these ages, the choices are not limited to a geographic locality, so that the experiment cannot measure the institutional response. Given this, it is probably most feasible to sample sparsely in a number of localities, with some dense sampling in a few localities to test the effects of the total cohort's receipt of vouchers. Thus the specific characteristics of a voucher experiment should be:

1. Random sample in several localities, relatively small in size (about 5000 per year for three years).

2. Voucher given to youth at age 16, usable for training or education from that point on.

3. Value of vouchers should be sufficient to cover total educational costs through four years at a publicly-supported university.

4. A procedure must be established for determining eligibility of the particular institution for voucher use, whether in the public or private sector.

5. If the recipient attends a public institution, he is to be charged full costs, not merely tuition.

Measures of effects should consist primarily of comparision of voucher recipients and non-recipient youth selected by a comparable random procedure. Measures should focus on early educational and occupational history, and should include also measurements on objectives described in Part 1. No study of institutional response to the vouchers is possible with this experimental design, and none is necessary to examine the effects of interest.

7. Opportunities for Public Service

Many youth who expect to graduate from college have begun, in the past few years, to take one or more years out at some point before completing their education. Some do so after high school, some during college, and a few do so (through with more difficulty) during high school itself. Many colleges have accommodated to this, allowing a student automatic re-entry after staying out one or two years or deferment of entry after admission from high school. High schools have not so accommodated. and a young person who is "tired of school" before completing high school becomes a simple dropout. Certainly a portion of the motives of youth in taking a period out from school lie in the areas touched in this report: a dissatisfaction with school, with isolation from the real world, with always being asked to prepare, never being asked to do. And a portion of their objectives in doing so are some of those discussed in Part 1: gaining the experience of responsible activity affecting others; interdependent work with others toward commonly-held goals; the management of their own affairs.

But for few youth are there opportunities to which they can direct their energy and make some kind of contribution to society. For many, the year they spend away from school is an uproductive one.

Although there have been programs of national or public service for youth in recent years (Peace Corps, VISTA, Teachers Corp, Neighborhood Youth Corps, Job Corps, Youth Conservation Corps, University Year in Action), and although the best of these have been extremely successful, there are four defects in the national service opportunities that currently confront youth.

1) They provide a very small number of opportunities. The Peace Corps had about 8500 volunteers in service in 1971 of all ages. All national programs for youth taken together provided less than 20,000 man-years of opportunity per year. For comparison, the total number of youth aged 18 is currently about 4,000,000.

2) Some of those programs that have been most successful in employing the energies of youth have shifted their focus to older persons with well-developed skills. The Peace Corps is the best example.

3) Nearly all programs are not available to persons below the age of 18. Thus for most youth wishing to defer college entrance, they are not a feasible alternative. Nor are they a feasible alternative to high school completion for dropout potentials.

4) Most formal programs require a 2-year commitment, which is twice the time period that most of those who are interrupting their education are ready to make.

7.1 The Specific Proposal for Public Service Opportunities

a. We propose the development of programs with these characteristics:

   1. A much higher level of funding of successful youth programs, to increase the opportunities available beyond the miniscule number that now exist;

   2. Availability to youth age 16 to 24, with parental consent where necessary by law;

   3. Commitment required for only one year, but with option for extension to two;

4. Service opportunities primarily within the United States, in both urban and rural areas;

5. Concentration first on those areas of activity that create least conflict with the adult community, whether jurisdictional disputes with labor unions or class conflict through activities of advocacy. If public or national service programs are to have a fair test of their ability to aid youth's transition to adulthood, they should not, in the early period, be saddled with conflict beyond that they will unavoidably or accidentally create.

b. Measurement:

Results of the public service programs should be examined in the two areas representing the dual objectives of the programs: effects on the participants and effects of the work on the target goal. Since the public service is designed to be of value to the society, it gains its justification in part from this value. Specifically, the measures should include:

1. Cost-benefit or productivity analysis of the work performed.

2. Effects on the participants:

a. Extensive research has been carried out on the effects of Peace Corps experience on volunteers, as well as other youth public service and volunteer programs. This work should be used as a starting point in designing a study of the effects of the public service programs recommended above, keeping in mind the objectives discussed in Part 1.

8. *Research on Ongoing Processes Among Youth*

In addition to the social experimentation discussed above, research on existing institutions can give more information than we presently have on the effects of various environments in which youth find themselves. The value of this research is not as a substitute for social experimentation or pilot programs. Ordinarily, a policy creating institutional change is sufficiently different from existing practice to have special and somewhat unpredictable consequences. These consequences should in most cases be studied in pilot programs before the policy is implemented on a full scale.

But research on existing institutions derives its value from two facts: the existing variability of environments and activities of young persons, which provide "natural experiments," and can allow comparative analysis; and the fact that the periods of youth are short, making it possible to observe effects rather quickly. The period of youth is a period of rapid change, bringing relatively quick payoff to research on young persons.

A major thread running through our discussion and recommendations is the suggestion that current institutions serving youth are incomplete in certain specific ways. This led to recommending, among the proposals, an expansion in opportunities for work-experience, age-integration and puublic service. These recommendations are based on two assumptions: a) that the suggested experiences are in fact valuable, and b) that they can be had at little or no cost to academic achievement provided by the current schooling institutions. The latter implies that there is slack, redundancy, or diminishing returns in current schooling, which would allow these additional experiences to be substituted for some schooling without loss.

Because we are uncertain about the validity of these assumptions, many of our recommendations are couched in experimental terms. But much can be learned also from the operation of existing institutions and from "natural experiments" that have occurred in the past. The following appear to be important and worthwhile research topics, transcending in many cases, the confines of this report:

1. We know very little about the cost of part-time work to academic achievement, or the returns from such work in terms of subsequent job availability and accumulated work experience. Several of currently available bodies of data on the young, such as the National Longitudinal Surveys (Census-Ohio State), Youth in Transition (University of Michigan), and Project Talent data should be analyzed with such questions in mind.

2. The benefits and costs of interrupting schooling are not well known. Both the current experience of youths who postpone their entrance into college and the effect of past events, such as the impact of World War II on post-war educational and occupational experiences, should be examined.

3. The experience with national service programs such as the Peace Corps, should be reviewed and systematized.

4. Existing research on the economic returns to schooling should be pushed further into asking more specific questions as to where, for what type of schooling, and at which age level, these returns really are.

5. An ongoing representative panel of young persons of age 14–24 should be established to study the general characteristics of successive cohorts of youth. The panel would consist of separate cohorts, which would be followed until they leave this age period and then resurveyed again, intermittently, throughout their lifetime. A detailed methodology has been developed for longitudinal studies involving separate age co-

horts in the Census Bureau and elsewhere, and this methodology should be employed for the study of youth. Through careful analysis, it is possible to study the changing experiences of successive cohorts, as well as the changes that occur in the life history of a given cohort. The existence of such a panel can also be of value in assessing the effects of changes in the institutions that affect youth, as new programs and policies are initiated. In an earlier period, the Current Population Survey was initiated in the Census Bureau to provide sensitive indicators of the state of employment throughout the country. That survey has come to be an immensely valuable information base for a wide variety of social policies. It is evident now that a youth panel, maintained just as continuously and systematically, can provide a wealth of information for social policies that affect youth. And since much social change occurs through the entry of new generations into the population, such a panel can provide a sensitive indication and anticipation of social change.

6. Discussions of the desirability of various alternative environments for youth are very much hampered by the lack of appropriate instruments to measure the impact of social institutions on those within them. Often, measurement is limited to measures of academic success (graduation and test scores) and economic success (income and occupation). These measures do not capture all important aspects of an institution's impact. More research is needed on non-cognitive measures of personal development and on more direct measures of social well being. The fact that we can neither measure not agree on a definition of what constitutes a good life should not deter us from trying to improve the measures we have and to develop new ones.

Comment and Dissents

At several points in Part 4, certain members of the Panel disagreed with the general position of the Panel, or felt sufficiently strongly about an issue to wish to make a comment at some variance with the general body of the report. Those points are recorded here.

a. Comment by Coleman on Section 3.

The proposal to encourage and support some work organizations to sufficiently modify themselves to incorporate youth is, I think, an important one. Experimentation with new forms of social organization to reverse the movement toward increased specialization is necessary if society is to be free to evolve in those directions. But the recommendation in the text stops short of the kind of major experimental innovation that I believe is warranted. That is, a logical extension of the organizational changes recommended is the age-balanced organization. In most societies of the past, the basic social unit was the extended family. The family was a multi-purpose unit, engaged in production, consumption, and raising the young. As productive activities have come to take place in formal bureaucratic organizations, which are single-purposed, many of the incidental activities that aided in bringing children to adulthood are no longer available to the young. The time of adults is more and more confined within formal organizations, as more and more adults work within them. The age segregation of both the young and the old results primarily from, the narrowed purpose of these productive organizations of society.

One means by which the increasing age segregation of the society can be reduced is to broaden the functions of these single-purposed organizations, encompassing both the young and the old. Their efficiency as productive organizations would thereby be reduced; but the external costs they presently impose on society by relegating the young and the old to special institutions with specialized personnel in attendance would be gone.

Such an age-balanced organization would include day-care centers, classrooms, and places frequented by the elderly. But persons of all ages other than the very young would in addition engage in some activities with those of other ages: working, teaching, learning. The age structure of the organization would reflect that of society as a whole, something like this:

In an organization of 1,000 persons:

0–4	90
5–13	180
14–17	80
18–24	110
25–64	440
65+	100

It is interesting to note that very recently something approximating age-balanced organizations has come into existence in a few areas of the economy. These are communes organized to engage in a given productive activity. In book publishing, for example, there now exist on the west coast two publishing communes that have recently developed. Although these communes are not presently age-balanced, their mode of organization is such that over time, they will become so if they continue. Older religious communities, such as the Bruderhof, which manufactures children's toys for a commercial market, have long been age-balanced productive organizations. The proposal here is not for the creation of such residential communities, but for age-balanced organizations that operate on a regular workday schedule.

The modification proposed here is not intended to transform such organizations into "participatory democracies" in which all ages have equal voice. The productive functions of the organization will continue to require hierarchial organization if they are to survive in the marketplace. The sole organizational changes will be those necessary to incorporate the new functions—and of course, these changes will not be negligible. What the proposed transformation is intended to do is to bring down to humane size the organizational units responsible for care of the young and the elderly and to facilitate the daily contact of persons of different ages.

Nor is the idea of an age-balanced organization a demand for "age quotas" in organizations. There are many organizations of society for which the possibilities of creating an age-balance are not great. The point instead is that the subsidy that society now pays to schools to contain its young can well be paid to work organizations and their unions that are willing to reorganize themselves to create an age-balance. Again, as in the recommendation in the text, the public support of this activity could take different forms. The government might be the client, paying the organization through contract for the provision of certain services to the young and old that are now provided outside work organizations. Or the young and old themselves could come to be the customers, through a voucher redeemable by organizations that become age-balanced and appropriately restructured themselves. But whatever the fiscal mechanism, what is important is to create the conditions within which age-balanced organizations can develop. Inherently, this means the use of public funds in an organization that is otherwise engaged in marketable products and services.

b. Dissent by Bremner on Section 5.
This dissent is concurred in by Davis.

This is a dissent from the dual minimum wage recommendation. It is made on the following grounds: (1) The impact of minimum wage laws on youth employment and unemployment is still a moot point (See U.S. Department of Labor, 1970, p. 187–189, and Perella, 1972, p. 17); (2) Setting a lower minimum wage for youth may have adverse social effects, which the Panel has not considered (see Cohen, 1971); and (3) The subminimal wage permits employers to pay young workers a lower wage than adults for the same job performed under the same conditions, solely because of their age. The justification is that cheapness will encourage employment of youth, but this is at the possible cost of adult workers' employment. If the same justification were offered for a subminimal wage for other under-employed groups such as blacks or women workers, its unfairness would be readily apparent.

c. Dissent by Davis on Section 6.
This dissent is concurred in by Bremner.

Vouchers presume a capability to select appropriate opportunities for skill development, and this capability is often not present in youth or their families. In addition, possibilities of exploitation by recipients of vouchers are pronounced. Finally, there is a need to insure against racial and social discrimination or segregation, particularly because tax money is involved.

References

ABBOTT, GRACE
    1938   The Child and the State. Chicago: University of Chicago Press.

ALCOTT, AMOS BRONSON
    1960   Essays on Education (1830–1862). Edited by Walter Harding. (Gainesville: U. of Florida Press, Scholarly Facsimiles.

ALCOTT, WILLIAM A.
    1839   Confessions of a School Master. Andover: Gould, Newton & Saxton.

ALLMENDINGER, DAVID F., JR.
    1968   "Indigent Students and Their Institutions, 1800–1860." Unpublished Ph.D. Thesis, Department of History, University of Wisconsin.

AMACHER, F. and R. FREEMAN
    1972   "College-Trained and Other New Labor Market Entrants, 1950–60," Study Paper No. 2, M.I.T. Center for Policy Alternatives (unpublished).

AMERICAN CIVIL LIBERTIES UNION
    1968   Academic Freedom in Secondary Schools. New York: American Civil Liberties Union.

BACHMAN, J.G.
    1970   Youth in Transition, Vol. II: The Impact of Family Background and Intelligence on Tenth-Grade Boys. Ann Arbor: Institute for Social Research.

BACHMAN, J.G., S. GREEN and I.D. WIRTANEN
    1971   Youth in Transition, Vol. III: Dropping Out—Problem or Symptom? Ann Arbor: Institute for Social Research.

BARCLAY, DOROTHY
    1962   "Challenge to Education: The Poor." New York Times Magazine, June 3.

BARKER, ROGER G., ET AL
    1962   Big School-Small School: Studies of the Effects of High School Size Upon the Behavior and Experiences of Students. Lawrence, Kansas: Midwest Psychological Field Station, University of Kansas.

BARNEY, HIRAM H.
    1851   Report on the American System of Graded Free Schools. Cincinnati. Printed in the office of the Daily Times.

BATEMAN, R. M.
    1949   "The Effect of Work Experience on High School Students as Revealed by the Bell Adjustment Inventory," Journal of Educational Research, 43, 261–269.

    1950   "The Effect of Work Experience on High School Students' Scholastic Achievement," Occupations, 41, 129–148.

BATTLE, KEMP P.
    1907   History of the University of North Carolina. Raleigh: Edwards & Broughton.

BECKER, GARY
    1967   Human Capital and the Personal Distribution of Income. Woytinsky
             Lecture No. 1. Ann Arbor: University of Michigan Press.

BLACKSTONE, SIR WILLIAM
    1872   Commentaries on the Laws of England, Vol. 1 Thomas M. Cooley. (ed.),
             Chicago: Bancroft.

BLYTHE, RONALD
    1969   Akenfield, Portrait of an English Village. New York: Delta Books.

BOOCOCK, SARANE S.
    1972   An Introduction to the Sociology of Learning. New York: Houghton
             Mifflin.

BOSTON SCHOOL COMMITTEE
    1882   "Second Annual Report of the Superintendent of Public Schools," in
             Annual Report of the School Committee of the City of Boston, 1882.

BOTT, ELIZABETH
    1971   Family and Social Network. New York: Barnes and Noble.

BRONSON, WALTER O.
    1914   The History of Brown University, 1764–1914. Providence; the University.

BRUCE, PHILIP A.
    1919   History of the University of Virginia, 1819–1919. New York: Macmillan.

BURN, JAMES D.
    1865   Three Years Among the Working Classes in the United States During the
             War. London: Smith Elder.

CALHOUN, DANIEL H.
    1965   Professional Lives in America: Structure and Aspiration, 1750–1850.
             Cambridge: Harvard University Press.

CALLAHAN, RAYMOND E.
    1962   Education and the Cult of Efficiency. Chicago: University of Chicago
             Press.

CARNEGIE COMMISSION ON HIGHER EDUCATION
    1971   New Students and New Places. New York: McGraw-Hill.

CARRIGAN, THOMAS CHARLES
    1911   "The Law and the American Child" Pedagogical Review (June 18)
             122–83.

CARTER, A.M.
    1971   "Scientific Manpower for 1970–85," Science (April 9).

CLARK, BURTON R.
    1960a   The Open Door College: A Case Study. New York: McGraw-Hill.
    1960b   "The 'Cooling-Out' Function in Higher Education." American Journal
             of Sociology 45 (May): 569–76.

CLARK, BURTON R., PAUL HEIST, T. R. McCONNELL, MARTIN A. TROW, AND GEORGE
    YOUNGE
    1972   Students and Colleges: Interaction and Change. Berkeley, Calif.: Center
             for Research and Development in Higher Education, University of
             California.

CLARK, KENNETH
    1957   "Present Threats to Children and Youth." Draft report, May 31. Manu-
             script in the office of the National Committee on the Employment of
             Youth, New York City.

CLARK, RUFUS W.
    1863   Lectures on the Formation of Character, Temptations, and Missions of
             Young Men. Boston Jewett and Co.

COHEN, ELI E.
1971   "Protection vs. Opportunity," New Generation, Vol. 53, No. 3, Summer.

COLEMAN, JAMES S.
1961   The Adolescent Society. New York: Free Press of Glencoe.

COLEMAN, JAMES S., ET AL
1966   Equality of Educational Opportunity. Washington: U.S. Government Printing Office.

CONANT, JAMES B.
1959   The American High School Today. New York: McGraw-Hill.

CREMIN, LAWRENCE A.
1961   The American Common School: An Historic Conception. New York: Teachers College, Columbia University.

DAVIS, KINGSLEY
1935   Youth in the Depression. Chicago: University of Chicago Press.

DAVIS, MAXINE
1936   The Lost Generation. New York: Macmillan.

DEMOS, JOHN
1970   A Little Commonwealth: Family Life in Plymouth Colony. New York: Oxford.

DOUGLAS, J. W. B., AND SIMPSON, H. R.
1964   "Height in Relation to Puberty, Family Size and Social Class," Millbank Memorial Fund Quarterly Bulletin, 42, 20–35.

DOUVAN, ELIZABETH AND JOSEPH ADELSON
1966   The Adolescent Experience. New York: Wiley.

DRAKE, ST. CLAIR, AND HORACE R. CAYTON
1946   Black Metropolis. New York: Harcourt-Brace.

EDDY, DANIEL C.
1855   The Young Man's Friend. Boston: Graves and Young.

EICHORN, D. H.
1963   "Biological Correlates of Behavior," in H. W. Stevenson (ed.), Child Psychology, Yearbook, National Society for the Study of Education, Part I. Chicago: University of Chicago Press.

EISENHOWER, DWIGHT D.
1955   "Annual Message to the Congress on the State of the Union, January 7, 1954." P. 22 in Public Papers of the Presidents—Dwight D. Eisenhower, 1954. Washington: U.S. Government Printing Office.

ELKIN, FREDERICK, AND WILLIAM WESTLEY
1955   "The Myth of Adolescent Culture," American Sociological Review, 20.

ENSIGN, FOREST C.
1921   Compulsory School Attendance and Child Labor. Iowa City: University of Iowa Press.

EX PARTE CROUSE
1838   4 Wharton (Pa.) 9

FARBER, BERNARD
1972   Guardians of Virtue: Salem Families in 1800. New York: Basic Books.

FOWLER, NATHANIEL C.
1910   Starting in Life. Boston: Little.

FEARN, R.M.
1968   Labor Force and School Participation of Teenagers, unpublished Ph.D. Dissertation, University of Chicago.

FELDMAN, K. A. AND T. M. NEWCOMB
1969 The Impact of College on Students. San Francisco, Calif.: Jossey-Bass.

FREEMAN, R.B.
1971 The Market for College-trained Manpower. Cambridge: Harvard University Press.

FROTHINGHAM, OCTAVIOUS B.
1874 Theodore Parker, A Biography. Boston J. R. Osgood.

FRYER, DOUGLAS
1931 The Measurement of Interests in Relation to Human Ability. New York: H. Holt.

IN RE GAULT
1967 387 U.S. 1.

GORDON, C. WAYNE
1957 The Social System of the High School. New York: Free Press.

GOTTLIEB, DAVID, AND TOM REEVES
1963 Adolescent Behavior in Urban Areas. New York: Free Press.

GREER, COLIN
1972 The Great School Legend: A Revisionist Interpretation of American Public Education. New York: Basic Books.

GRILICHES, ZVI
1970 "Notes on the Role of Education in Production Functions and Growth Accounting." In W. L. Hansen (ed.), Education, Income, and Human Capital. New York: National Bureau of Economic Research.

HALE, EDWARD EVERETT
1855 "The State's Care of its Children," pp. 22–26 in Edward E. Hale, T.V. Moore, and A. H. Grimshaw, Prize Essays in Juvenile Delinquency. Philadelphia.

HALL, G. STANLEY
1904 Adolescence: Its Psychology and Its Relations to Physiology, Anthropology, Sociology, Sex, Crime, Religion, and Education. New York: Appleton.

HALL, R.E.
1970 "Why is the Unemployment Rate so High at Full Employment?" Brookings Papers on Economic Activity, No. 3. Washington: Brookings Institution.

1972 "Turnover in the Labor Force and the Prospects for Achieving Low Unemployment Rates," Statement before the Joint Economic Committee, U.S. Congress, October 17.

HAMBURGER, MARTIN
1971 "Protection from Participation is Deprivation of Rights," New Generation (Summer):1–6.

HAMMER V. DAGENHART
1918 247 U. S. 251.

HANDLIN, OSCAR AND MARY
1971 Facing Life: Youth and the Family in American History. Boston: Little.

HAVIGHURST, ROBERT J.
1963 "Urban Development and the Educational System." Pp. 24–45 in A. Harry Passow (ed.), Education in Depressed Areas. New York: Teachers College, Columbia University.

HAWES, JOEL
1828 Lectures Addressed to the Young Men of Hartford and New Haven. Hartford: O. D. Cooke.

HOLL, JACK M.
1971   Juvenile Reform in the Progressive Era: William R. George and the Junior Republic Movement. Ithaca: Cornell University Press.

HOLLINGSHEAD, AUGUST DE B.
1949   Elmtown's Youth: The Impact of Social Class on Adolescents. New York: Wiley.

JANOWITZ, MORRIS
1969   Institution Building in Urban Education. New York: Russell Sage Foundation.

JONES, M. C., AND BAYLEY, N.
1950   "Physical Maturing Among Boys as Related to Behavior," Journal of Educational Psychology, 41, 129–148.

JOUGHIN, LOUIS (ED.)
1969   Academic Freedom and Tenure: A Handbook of the American Association of University Professors. Madison: Univ. of Wisconsin Press.

KELLEY, FLORENCE
1882   "On Some Changes in the Legal Status Since Blackstone," The International Review, 13 (August):83.

KALACHEK, E.
1969   The Youth Labor Market (Policy Paper No. 12). Ann Arbor, Mich.: Institute of Labor and Industrial Relations.

KENDALL, AMOS
1872   Autobiography. Edited by William Stickney. Boston: Lee & Shepard.

KENNISTON, KENNETH
1970   "Youth, A (New) Stage of Life," American Scholar, 39, 4 (Autumn), p. 631.

KETT, JOSEPH F.
1971a   "Adolescence and Youth in Nineteenth-Century America." Journal of Interdisciplinary History 2 (Autumn) :283–98.
1971b   "Growing Up in Rural New England, 1800–1840." Pp. 1–14 in Tamara K. Harevan (ed.), Anonymous Americans: Explorations in Nineteenth-Century Social History. Englewood Cliffs, N. J.: Prentice-Hall.

KING, IRVING
1914   The High School Age. Indianapolis: Bobbs-Merrill.

KLEINFELD, ANDREW JAY
1971   "The Balance of Power Among Infants, Their Parents, and the State," Family Law Quarterly, 5 (March):106–7.

KLOAK, DALE B.
1972   "Working Children and Youth," Children Today (March-April) :24–25.

KOSTERS, M. and F. WELCH
1972   "The Effects of Minimum Wages on the Distribution of Changes in Aggregate Employment," American Economic Review (June).

KRUG, EDWARD A.
1964   The Shaping of the American High School. New York: Harper.
1972   The Shaping of the American High School, Vol. 2, 1920–1941. Madison: University of Wisconsin Press.

LATHROP, JULIA S.
1912   "The Children's Bureau," Proceedings of the National Conference on Charities and Corrections: 33.

LEBERGOTT, STANLEY J.
1964   Manpower in Economic Growth: The American Record since 1890. New York: McGraw-Hill.

LINDSLEY, PHILIP
1825   An Address Delivered in Nashville, January 12, 1825, at the Inauguration of the President of Cumberland College. Nashville: J. Norvelle.

LYND, ROBERT S. AND HELEN M.
1929   Middletown: A Study in Contemporary American Culture. New York: Harcourt.

MASSACHUSETTS COMMISSION ON INDUSTRIAL AND TECHNICAL EDUCATION
1906   Report on the Commission (April). Boston: Wright & Potter.

McCAMMON, R. W.
1965   "Are Boys and Girls Maturing Physically at Earlier Ages?" American Journal of Public Health, 55, 103–106.

McENTIRE, DAVIS
1960   Residence and Race: Final and Comprehensive Report to the Commission on Race and Housing. Berkeley and Los Angeles: University of California Press.

MEAD, MARGARET
1928   Coming of Age in Samoa. New York: William Morrow.

MINCER, JACOB
1970   "The Distribution of Labor Incomes: A Survey with Special Reference to the Human Capital Approach," Journal of Economic Literature (March).
1972   "Youth, Education and Work," National Bureau of Economic Research.

MINCER, JACOB and M. HASHIMOTO
1970   "Employment and Unemployment Effects of Minimum Wages," Winter Meeting of the Econometric Society, Detroit (unpublished).

MORISON, SAMUEL E.
1965   Three Centuries of Harvard, 1636–1936. Cambridge: Harvard Univ. Press.

MURRAY, WILLIAM D.
1937   The History of the Boy Scouts in America. New York: Boy Scouts of America.

MUSGROVE, FRANK
1965   Youth and the Social Order. Bloomington: Indiana University Press.

NATIONAL EDUCATION ASSOCIATION
1962   Education and the Disadvantaged American. Washington: National Education Association.

NEILL, A. S.
1963   Summerhill: A Radical Approach to Child Rearing. New York: Hart.

NEW ENGLAND MAGAZINE
1832   "Choice of Profession." New England Magazine 3 (August): 138

NEW GENERATION
1971   Children and Work: Protection and Opportunity. Vol. 53, No. 3.

NIXON, RICHARD M.
1970   "Remarks to the Participants in the 1969 Youth Program, February 7, 1969." P. 81 in Public Papers of the Presidents—Richard M. Nixon, 1969. Washington: U. S. Government Printing Office.

NORTH CAROLINA v. JONES
1886   95 N.C. 588.

OLIVER ET AL. v. HOUDLET
1816   13 Massachusetts 237.

ORGANIZATION FOR ECONOMIC COOPERATION AND DEVELOPMENT
1970   Development of Higher Education, 1950–67: Analytic Report.

O'SHEA, MICHAEL V.
1909   Social Development and Education. Boston: Houghton.

PANEL OF CONSULTANTS ON VOCATIONAL EDUCATION
1963   Education for a Changing World of Work. Washington: U.S. Government Printing Office.

PARSONS, JAMES R.
1900   Professional Education. Albany: J. B. Lyon.

PERELLA, VERA C.
1972   "Working Teenagers," Children Today, May-June.

PERRY, G.
1972   "Unemployment Flows in the United States Labor Market." Brookings Papers on Economic Activity, No. 2. Washington: Brookings Institution.

PHILLIPS EXETER ACADEMY
1869   General Catalogue of the Officers and Students of Phillips Exeter Academy, 1783–1869. Cambridge: Welch Bigelow.

PRINCE, HEZEKIAH, JR.
1965   Journals of Hezekiah Prince, Jr., 1822–1828. New York: Crown.

PRINCE V. MASSACHUSETTS
1944   321 U.S. 158.

REPORT ON HIGHER EDUCATION
1971   Washington, D.C.: U.S. Government Printing Office.

RIESSMAN, FRANK
1962   The Culturally Deprived Child. New York: Harper

ROOSEVELT, FRANKLIN D.
1941   Letter to Joseph Cadden. President's Official File (January) 3910, FDR Library. Hyde Park, N.Y.

ROSS, DOROTHY
1972   G. Stanley Hall: The Psychologist as Prophet. Chicago: U. of Chicago Press.

RUDOLPH, FREDERIC J.
1962   The American College and University: A History. New York: A. A. Knopf.

RYDER, N. B.
1969   "The emergency of a modern fertility pattern: United States 1917–66," pp. 99–126 in Fertility and Family Planning (eds., S. J. Behrman, Leslie Corsa, Jr., and Ronald Freedman), Ann Arbor: University of Michigan Press.
1973a   "Two Cheers for ZPG," Daedalus (forthcoming).
1973b   "Notes on American Fertility," in Keyfitz, Nathan (ed), Statistical Problems in Population Research, Honolulu: East-West Center, University of Hawaii, (forthcoming).

RYDER, N.B. and C.F. WESTOFF
1971   Reproduction in the United States: 1965. Princeton, Princton University Press.

SCHOULER, JAMES
1895   A treatise on the Law of Domestic Relations, 5th ed. Boston. Little Brown.

SCOTT, COLIN A.
1908   Social Education. Boston: Ginn.

SHEA, J.R. and R.A. WILKENS
1971   "Determinants of Educational Attainment and Retention in School." Paper presented at the 1971 Annual Meeting of the American Educational Research Association. New York City.

SHELDON, ELEANOR BERNERT AND RAYMOND A. GLAZIER
1965   Pupils and Schools in New York City: A Fact Book. New York: Russell Sage Foundation.

SHERMAN, DAVID
1893   History of the Wesleyan Academy at Wilbraham, Mass., 1817–1890. Boston: McDonald & Gill.

SIZER, THEODORE R., JR.
1964   Secondary Schools at the Turn of the Century. New Haven: Yale Univ. Press.

SIZER, THEODORE R., JR. (ED.)
1964   The Age of the Academies. New York: Teachers College Press.

SPENCER, HERBERT
1890   Social Statics. New York: Appleton & Century.

STEVENS, ROBERT
1971   "Two Cheers for 1870: The American Law School." Perspectives in American History 5: 405–548.

STORY, WILLIAM WETMORE
1847   A Treatise on the Law of Contracts Not Under Seal. Boston: Little Brown.

TANNER, J. M.
1962   Growth at Adolescence (2nd ed.). Oxford: Blackwell Scientific Publications.

1970   "Physical Growth," in P. H. Mussen (ed.), Carmichael's Manual of Child Psychology, Vol. 1. New York: Wiley.

TAYLOR, HENRY L.
1900   Professional Education in the United States. Albany: Univ. of the State of New York.

THOMAS, H. SCOTT
1903   "Changes in the Age of College Graduation." Report of the (U.S.) Commissioners of Education, 1903. 2:2199–2206.

THOMAS, WILLIAM I.
1923   The Unadjusted Girl, with Cases and Standpoint for Behavior Analysis. Boston: Little.

TINKER V. DES MOINES INDEPENDENT SCHOOL DISTRICT
1969   393 U.S. 503.

TOCQUEVILLE, ALEXIS DE
1945   Democracy in America, Vol. 2, trans. Henry Reeve, Phillips Bradley (ed.). New York: A. A. Knopf.

TRATTNER, WALTER I.
1970   Crusade for the Children: A History of the National Child Labor Committee and Child Labor Reform in America. Chicago: Quadrangle.

TUCKER, LOUIS
1962   Puritan Protagonist: President Thomas Clap of Yale College. Chapel Hill: University of North Carolina Press.

TYLER, WILLIAM S.
1895   History of Amherst College during Its First Half Century, 1821–1871. New York: F. H. Hitchcock.

U.S. BUREAU OF THE CENSUS
1960   Historical Statistics of the United States, Colonial Times to 1957. Washington: U.S. Government Printing Office.

1969   Current Population Reports, Series P–20, No. 185, "Factors Related to High School Graduation and College Attendance: 1967," Washington, D.C.: U.S. Government Printing Office (July).

1970   A Century of Population Growth: From the First Census of the United States to the Twelfth, 1790–1900. Baltimore: Genealogical Publishing Company.

1971   Current Population Reports, Series P-20, No. 222, "School Enrollment: October, 1970." Washington, D.C.: U.S. Government Printing Office (June).

U.S. BUREAU OF THE CENSUS

1971   Current Population Reports, Series P-20, No. 229, "Educational Attainment: March, 1971." Washington, D.C.: U. S. Government Printing Office (December).

1972   Current Population Reports, Series P-23, No. 40, "Characteristics of American Youth: 1971." Washington, D.C.: U.S. Government Printing Office (January).

1972   Current Population Reports, Series P-25, No. 476, "Demographic Projections for the United States: 1972." Washington, D.C.: U.S. Government Printing Office (February).

U.S. BUREAU OF EDUCATION

1880   Legal Rights of Children. Circulars of Information, No. 3. Washington, D.C.: U.S. Government Printing Office.

U.S. CHILDREN'S BUREAU

1967   The Story of the White House Conference on Children and Youth. Washington, D.C.: U.S. Government Printing Office.

U.S. COMMISSIONER OF EDUCATION

1897   Report of the Commissioner of Education, 1895–96. Washington.

U.S. v. DARBY

1941   312 U.S. 100.

U.S. DEPARTMENT OF HEALTH, EDUCATION, AND WELFARE

1971   Projections of Educational Statistics to 1980–81. Washington: U.S. Government Printing Office.

1972   Digest of Educational Statistics, 1971. Washington: U.S. Government Printing Office.

U.S. DEPARTMENT OF LABOR

1969   Special Labor Force Reports, No. 111, "Employment Status of School Age Youth, October 1968." (Reprint No. 2634) . August. G.P.O.

1970   Career Thresholds, Manpower Research Monograph No. 16. Vol. 1 by Herbert S. Parnes, Robert C. Miljus, and Ruth S. Spitz. Washington: U.S. Government Printing Office.

1970   Special Labor Force Reports, No. 121, "Empoyment of High School Graduates and Dropouts in 1969." (Reprint No. 2684). August. G.P.O.

1970   Special Labor Force Reports, No. 122, "Education of Adult Workers: Projections of 1985." (Reprint 2685) . August. G.P.O.

1970   Special Labor Force Reports, No. 124, "Employment of School Age Youth, October 1969." (Reprint No. 2694). September. G.P.O.

1970   Special Labor Force Reports, No. 125, "Educational Attainment of Workers, March 1967." (Reprint No. 2696). October. G.P.O.

1970   Youth Unemployment and Minimum Wages, BLS Bulletin No. 1657. Washington, D.C.: U.S. Government Printing Office.

1971   Career Thresholds, Manpower Research Monograph No. 16, Vol. 2 by Frederick A. Zeller, John R. Shea, Andrew I. Kohen, and Jack A. Meyer. U.S. Government Printing Office.

1971   Special Labor Force Reports, No. 128, "Students and Summer Jobs, October 1969." (Reprint No. 2710). G.P.O.

1971   Special Labor Force Reports, No. 131, "Employment of High School Graduates and Dropouts in October 1970." (Reprinted No. 2737) May. G.P.O.

1971   Special Labor Force, Reports No. 132, "Young Workers and Their Earnings, October 1969." (Reprint No. 2744) . July. G.P.O.

1971   Special Labor Force Reports. No. 135, "Employment of School Age Youth." (Reprint No. 2752). August. G.P.O.

1971   Years for Decision, Manpower Research Monograph No. 24. Vol. 1 by John R. Shea, Roger D. Roderick, Frederick A. Zeller and Andrew I. Kohen. Washington: U.S. Government Printing Office.

1972   Career Thresholds, Manpower Research Monography No. 16. Vol. 3 by Andrew I. Kohen and Herbert S. Parnes. Washington: U.S. Government Printing Office.

1972   Special Labor Force Reports, No. 143 "Usually Weekly Earnings of American Workers, 1971," (Reprint No. 2795). G.P.O.

U.S. v. GREEN
1824   26 Fed. Cas. 30

VAN WATERS, MIRIAM
1925   Youth in Conflict. New York: New Republic.

VASSAR, RENA L. (ED.)
1959   The Life of Silas Felton, Written by Himself, in Proceedings of the American Antiquarian Society 69, Part 2.

VENN, GRANT
1964   Man, Education, and Work. Washington: American Council on Education

VEYSEY, LAURENCE R.
1965   The Emergence of the American University. Chicago: University of Chicago Press.

WALLER, WILLARD
1937   "The Rating and Dating Complex," American Sociological Review, 727–734.

WEISMAN, LAWRENCE
1972   School, Community and Youth, mimeographed. Southern Illinois University, Carbondale, Ill.

WELCH, F.
1971   "The NBER Approach to Human Resource Problems." In the 1971 Annual Report of the National Bureau of Economic Research, New York City.

WERTENBAKER, THOMAS J.
1946   Princeton, 1746–1896. Princeton: Princeton University Press.

WHITE HOUSE CONFERENCE ON CHILDREN, 1970
1971   Report to the President. Washington, D.C.: U.S. Government Printing Office.

WHITE HOUSE CONFERENCE ON YOUTH, 1971
1971   "Preamble." Recommendations and Resolutions Washington, D.C.: U.S. Government Printing Office.

WILLINGHAM, WARREN W.
1972   The Number Two Access Problem: Transfer to the Upper Division. Washington: American Association for Higher Education.

WINGATE, CHARLES F.
1898   What Shall Our Boys Do for a Living? New York: Doubleday & McClure.

WISHY, BERNARD
1969   The Child and the Republic: The Dawn of Modern American Child Nurture. Philadelphia: University of Pennsylvania Press..

WOLFLE, DAEL
1971   The Uses of Talent. Princeton University Press.

Index

Adolescence: cultural detachment during (*see* Youth culture); physical development during, ~~91–97~~ psychological development during, 97–111; psychosocial implications of, 96, 99; interest of society in, 22–26; "vestibule stage" of, 40–41; vocational development during, 102–8
Adolescence (Hall), 22
Adolescents. *See* Adolescence; Youth
Age-grading (age-grouping), 9–29 passim, 81–83, 134–36
Age-integration: in age-balanced organizations, 178–79; benefits of, 134–35, 174; as characteristic of nineteenth-century society, 10–13; through grouping by stages of development, 136; in schools, 82–83; of youth with adults, 132–33
Age-segregation: vs. age-integration, 132–33, 134–35; among youth in institutions, 81–83, 87, 127, 133–35; benefits of, 131–32, 134; dependency of youth as result of, 81; effect of in families, 127; modern, vs. traditional, 128; patterns of development compatible with, 163; proposed reduction of, 177–78; as result of changes in family structure, 133; types of, 127; youth culture as result of, 81, 128; of youth from rest of society, 28, 80–81, 127. *See also* Age-grading; Segregation
Alienation of youth. *See* Youth; Youth culture
"Alternative schools" (communal grouping), 86–87
American Youth Act, 39–40
Apprenticeships, 12, 13, 14, 22, 168
Armed forces, 65, 67

Baby boom, 50–53; average number of births during, 48
Bill of Rights (for youth, 1971), 41
Birth control, 61–62
Birth rate. *See* Fertility rate

Child labor, regulation of, 31, 35–38, 43–44; humanitarian campaign for, 19, 24;

legislation on, 24, 26, 31, 35–36, 43. *See also* Employment
Children, rights of. *See* Youth, rights of
Children's Charter (1930), 32–34
Clark, Kenneth (quoted), 40–41
Cognitive abilities, 3, 99–102
Cohort size, increase in, 46–50. *See also* Youth population, growth of
Colleges: rise in population of, 24–25, 26. *See also* Institutions, higher educational
Communities, youth, 148, 163–64, 165. *See also* Organizations, youth
Community vs. role-segmented society, 140
Community colleges, 88–89
Conant Report, 77
Contexts for youth. *See* Environments (of youth)
Cultural detachment of youth. *See* Youth culture
Culture, youth. *See* Youth culture

Demography of youth, 45–64; and absorption of baby boom by society, 50–53; and increase in size of youth group, 46–47; and limitations of statistical appraisals, 64; relation of changes in, to unemployment and extended schooling, 72–75; in schools, family status, and jobs, 53–58; trends in marriage and parenthood, 58–63
Dependency (of youth), 15–16, 53, 65, 67, 81
Depression (Great): effect of on youth, 26–27
Dropouts, 68, 72

Economic independence (for youth), 3, 14–15, 53, 54, 63, 67
Economy: effect of stabilization of population on, 49
Education: academic and non-academic activities in, 141–43; alternative types of, 137–39; compulsory, 24–25; consequences of recent trends in, 75; "cooperative," 137; effect of industrializa-

Education (*continued*)
tion on, 19–20, 21; effort expended in,
66–67; extended, 68–71, 74–75; family
conflict over, 65; and high school curriculum, 27; higher, socioeconomic factors of, 69; as investment, 68, 69–71;
level of, and age at marriage, 57–58; in
nineteenth century, 10–13, 14, 16–20;
pilot programs in, 150–51; "real life"
situations in, 129–30; vouchers for, 148,
169–71; in work organizations, 160–63
Educational institutions. *See* Institutions,
educational
Educational vouchers. *See* Vouchers, educational
Employment (of youth), 38–41; in nineteenth century, 12, 13, 14, 21; proposed
reduction of constraints on, 148; transition from school to, 53–58, 65–66; and
vocational development, 103–8. *See also*
Labor force; Unemployment; Work
experience for youth
Environments (of youth): failure of current, 146; need for wide variety of, 6;
proposed changes in, 145–49; proposed
objectives for, 3–5; reappraisal of, 3;
schools and colleges as, 2, 156–57. *See
also* Institutions, educational; Youth
culture
Erikson, Erik, 109

Family, 2, 10, 13–14, 65–66, 116–17
Family status: changes in, 53–58
Fertility rate, 48, 58–59

Hall, G Stanley, 22, 23, 25–26, 112
High schools. *See* Institutions, educa-
tional
Higher education, distinctive features of,
87–89
Housewife, role of, 51, 54, 57

Identity, sense of, 5
Independence, economic, 3, 14–15, 53, 54,
63, 67
Industrialization: effect of on education
19–20, 21
Institutions, educational, 1–7, 76–91; age-
grading in, 9–29 passim, 81–83, 134–36;
alternation between work and, 137, 138,
157–60; (public) alternatives to, 84–87;
as certifying agency in early 1900s, 25;
changes in, from 1890 to 1920, 17–29;
as complete social cosmos, 27; comprehensive high school, 79–84; (secondary)
distinctive features of, 79–87; diminishing confidence in, 90–91; expansion of
to accommodate masses, 76–77, 78;
failure of communication in, 89; inade-
quacy of as total environment, 2; large-

scale organization in, 77–79; position
of youth in, 139–40, 142, 147; proposed
changes in, 147–57; role of youth in,
142, 156; segregation of youth from
society in, 80–81; specialization in, 78–
79; transition from to labor force, 53–
58, 65–66; and youth, research on, 173–
75. *See also* Education; Schooling
Institutions, higher educational, 87–89

Labor. *See* Child labor; Employment;
Labor force; Work experience for
youth
Labor force: impact on, of growth in
higher education, 74; and unemployment of youth, 38, 71–72; youth in,
24, 26, 38–41, 51, 52, 54–57
Legal status of youth. *See* Youth, rights
of

Mann, Horace, 18, 20
Marital status: and activity in labor force,
55, 56, 56 t, 57
Marriage, of youth, 57–63
Mass media: impact of on youth culture,
119–121
Maturation: institutional framework for,
1, 2; physical and psychological (*see*
Adolescence)
Menarche. *See* Adolescence, physical de-
velopment during
Minimum wage, 72; dual, 168, 179
Mobility of youth, 11–16, 67
Motherhood, 62–63

New Deal: and child labor, 35–36, 38–39
New Left, 114
Newman Report, 155

Organizations: work, 160–63, 177–79;
youth, 23–24, 142–43, 148, 164, 165–66

Parens patriae, 30–31, 143. *See also* Youth,
rights of
Parenthood, as definitive step into adult-
hood, 63
Peer groups, 2, 11, 12, 27–28
Piaget, Jean, 99, 100
Population: ratio of young to old in,
46–53; youth (*See* Youth population,
growth of)
Progressive Education, 129
Progressive Era, 21 n, 24, 32 n
Puberty. *See* Adolescence, physical devel-
opment during
Public service programs for youth, 108,
148–49, 171–73, 174; specific proposal
for opportunities in, 172–73

Reform, educational, 5–6, 18

Role-segmentation, 81, 140

Scholarships and subsidies, 169
Schooling: alternatives to, 67–68; economic effects of, 174; extended, 68–71, 74–75; formal, scope of, 140–43; increased, development of, 2. *See also* Education; Institutions, educational
Schools. *See* Institutions, educational
Segregation: of age groups in society (*see* Age-segregation); racial and cultural in schools, 27, 83–84, 87
Self-esteem, need for in youth, 5
Sex differences: in nineteenth-century professions, 14; in employment and enrollment pattern of youth, 50–51, 54–58
Skills, acquisition of, 3–4
Smith-Hughes Act (1917), 85
Social policy, changes in, 149–51, 177–78
Social revolution, effect of on youth, 9
Socialization (of youth), 2, 15–16, 27–28, 45–46, 48, 52–53, 63, 146
Socializing agencies, modern: compared to those of agrarian society, 10
Specialization, 21, 22, 78–79

Third World, 122
Transition to adulthood: in moving from high school to college, 68–69; in moving from school to labor force, 53–58. *See also* Environments of youth; Labor force; Socialization of youth
Tutors, youth as, 156

Unemployment (of youth): current, 71, 72–75; during the depression, 26–27, 38–41
Universities. *See* Institutions, higher educational

Vocational development of youth, 102–8
Vocational guidance, 21, 21n
Vocational schools, 85
Vouchers, educational, 148, 169–71; dissent of panel members on, 179; specific experimental proposal on, 170–71

Work and school, alternation between, 137, 138, 157–60; specific experimental proposal for, 159–60
Work experience for youth, 66, 67, 105–8, 129–30, 147–48, 168, 174

Work force. *See* Labor force
Work organizations: incorporation of youth in, 160–63, 177–79; specific experimental proposals for, 162–63

Youth: and age-segregation (*see* Age-segregation; Age-grading); alienation of, 16, 28, 29, 52 (*see also* Youth culture); concept of, 11 n, 16, 112; culture of (*see* Youth culture); demography of (*see* Demography of youth); economic problems of, 28–29, 64–76; employment of (*see* Employment); environments of, 2–6, 145–49, 156–57; increased communication among, 120, 121; and intergenerational conflict, 45; marriage during, 57–63; mobility of, 11–16, 67; organizations for, 142–43, 164; population, growth of, 46–53, 72–74; physical development of, 91–97; problems facing, 64; protection of vs. opportunity for, 166–68; psychological attachments of, 115–17, 122, 123; psychological development of, 97–111; research on, 173–75; rights of, 29–45, 143–44 (*see also* Child labor); role of in school, 142, 147, 156; socialization of, 2, 15–16, 27–28, 45–46, 48, 52–53, 63, 146; as subordinate part of society, 117–18, 123; as tutors, 156; unemployment of, 26–27, 38–41, 71, 72–75; vocational development of, 102–8. *See also* Adolescence; Youth culture
Youth culture, 112–125; as alienated culture, 118–19; and concern for underdog, 122–24; fashion revolution in, 114; impact of .mass media on, 119–21; importance of, 125; interaction of, with adult counterculture, 121–22; and interest in change, 124–25; inward-lookingness of, 113–15; and need to challenge adults, 118–19; and New Left, 114; press toward autonomy in, 117–22; result of segregation of youth from society, 28, 29, 52, 81, 114–15
Youth institutions. *See* Communities, youth; Institutions, educational; Organizations, youth
Youth population, growth of, 46–53; demographical explanation of, 47–50; difficulties caused by, 45–46; effect of on labor market, 72–74; stabilization of, 49, 53